FOLLOWING THE THREADS

PETER LANG
New York • Washington, D.C./Baltimore • Bern
Frankfurt am Main • Berlin • Brussels • Vienna • Oxford

Douglas Selwyn

FOLLOWING THE THREADS

Bringing Inquiry Research into the Classroom

PETER LANG
New York • Washington, D.C./Baltimore • Bern
Frankfurt am Main • Berlin • Brussels • Vienna • Oxford

Library of Congress Cataloging-in-Publication Data

Selwyn, Douglas.
Following the threads: bringing inquiry research into the classroom /
Douglas Selwyn.
p. cm.
Includes bibliographical references and index.
1. Social sciences—Study and teaching—United States.
2. Research—Methodology—Study and teaching—United States.
3. Active learning—United States. I. Title.
LB1584.S4438   370.71—dc22   2009018334
ISBN 978-1-4331-0607-1

Bibliographic information published by **Die Deutsche Nationalbibliothek**.
Die Deutsche Nationalbibliothek lists this publication in the "Deutsche
Nationalbibliografie"; detailed bibliographic data is available
on the Internet at http://dnb.d-nb.de/.

FSC

Mixed Sources

Product group from well-managed
forests, controlled sources and
recycled wood or fiber

Cert no. SCS-COC-002464
www.fsc.org
©1996 Forest Stewardship Council

Cover photograph by Chuck Csuri

The paper in this book meets the guidelines for permanence and durability
of the Committee on Production Guidelines for Book Longevity
of the Council of Library Resources.

© 2010 Peter Lang Publishing, Inc., New York
29 Broadway, 18th floor, New York, NY 10006
www.peterlang.com

Printed in the United States of America

To Gary and Lillian.
Thank you for the quiet, the stars,
and for welcoming my questions, large and small.

CONTENTS

ACKNOWLEDGMENTS

There are so many people to thank for helping to bring this work into being. First and foremost I want to thank those extraordinary educators, artists, authors, and historians who took time to talk with me. Thank you, Wendy Ewbank, Don Fels, Patricia Tusa Fels, Steve Goldenberg, Michael Grigsby, Georgia Heard, Judith Helfand, Jan Maher , Lorraine McConaghy, Rosalie Romano, Colleen Ryan, Roger Shimomura, Libby Sinclair, Gary Thomsen, Ted Wright, and Howard Zinn. Your work has consistently inspired me, and encouraged me to keep my focus where it belongs, on the children, and on doing what matters. I wish I could have included more of your words and your work; you have so much to offer to those of us trying to do right by our students.

In addition, Colleen Ryan read an early version of the book and offered useful feedback and encouragement.

Thank you to my former colleagues at Antioch University Seattle, especially Tina Dawson, Susie Murphy, and Don Fels, with whom I taught the research sequence to masters students. Thank you Ed Mikel for resource suggestions and for the many conversations about teaching, learning, and justice. And thank you to our education students, many of whom are now bringing inquiry research to students of their own. It was a great pleasure to learn with you.

Thank you to Dean David Hill and Associate Dean Mike Morgan at Plattsburgh State, for supporting this work, and to my colleagues at Plattsburgh State. I am grateful for the opportunity to work and learn with you. I also want to thank our students, who bring passion, curiosity, kindness, and flip flops to our classes.

I have been fortunate beyond measure to have a community of friends and colleagues who are passionate seekers, questioners, and learners. There has always been someone in my life just a little bit farther down the road than I, from whom I could learn, and others who were willing to join me on the road to find out. It makes all the difference.

Thank you to the folks at Peter Lang, for their support and trust that this book could and should happen, with a particular thank you to Shirley Steinberg and to Sophie Appel, who has been incredibly responsive, patient, and skilled in directing the production stage of the process.

Finally, thank you to Jan Maher for continuing to follow the threads with me. I am grateful beyond words for being able to make this journey with you as we continue discovering life's little mysteries.

William Stafford, "The Way It Is" from *The Way It Is: New and Selected Poems*. Copyright © 1998 by the estate of William Stafford. Reprinted with the permission of Graywolf Press, Saint Paul, Minnesota, www.graywolfpress.org.

The lesson Deep Space 3000 is lightly adapted from the Deep Space 3000 lesson that comes from the book *Engaging Students through Global Issues*, published by the organization Facing the Future, and used with their permission.

The image on the cover is a detail from the work Threads, by Chuck Csuri, used with permission.

THE WAY IT IS

There's a thread you follow. It goes among
things that change. But it doesn't change.
People wonder about what you are pursuing.
You have to explain about the thread.
But it is hard for others to see.
While you hold it you can't get lost.
Tragedies happen; people get hurt
or die; and you suffer and get old.
Nothing you do can stop time's unfolding.
You don't ever let go of the thread.

                          —*William Stafford*

INTRODUCTION

During the hijacking and hostage taking that took place off the coast of Somalia in the spring of 2009 I was reminded of Neil Postman's book *Amusing Ourselves to Death*, which came out in 1985. Postman, writing about the Iran hostage crisis of 1979–1980, noted that people in the U.S. knew nothing about the people or country of Iran, even after obsessive news coverage over a year's time. His focus was on the media, and how the daily broadcasts brought us little information about the country of Iran or its people, and virtually nothing about the historical context in which this drama was playing out. While I absolutely agree with him, I want to bring in another factor that played a role in our staying ignorant; we never asked for more. We accepted what we were told, came to the conclusions we were supposed to come to, and hoped our captured countrymen and women would somehow come out alive.

I asked my university students what they knew of the hijacking. They responded that the ship was taken by pirates, that a brave American captain from nearby Vermont was being held hostage, and that he had given himself up to save his crew. I asked what they knew of these pirates, and they really knew nothing. Their talk of pirates in general came straight out of Disney movies; robbers on the high seas, peg legs, eye patches, hooks for hands, perched parrots. And they agreed that, with luck, pirates looked like Johnny Depp.

Then I asked my students if any of them wanted to join me on an expedition to go hijack a ship. It looked like fun, I said, and we could make some good money. I said, "They're raising tuition next semester, and jobs are tight." They looked at me somewhat blankly, knowing I couldn't be serious, so I pushed some more. "C'mon, you can miss one soccer game; you can study on the drive to the coast. You can party after we've taken the ship. I've got a plan." When they still sat silently I asked them why they wouldn't come with me. They gave the expected responses; it's wrong, it's stupid, it's crazy, it's illegal, we'd get thrown in jail. So why, I wondered, would a group of Somali teenagers, who were approximately the same age as these college students, choose to give up their soccer games, their trips to the mall, their parties to hijack a huge ship and hold its crew for ransom? Does that make any sense?

The great majority of us in the U.S., like my students, knew nothing of the context in which the hijacking and hostage taking were occurring, and the mainstream media offered no help. There was no mention of Somalia's history, of the colonization and the looting of the country that had gone on for many decades, no mention of the wars and drought that had left the country in desperate straits. No mention of the dumping of nuclear waste into the waters off the Somali coast, ongoing since the Somali government virtually disappeared in the very early 1990s. No mention of the over fishing of those same waters by countries from around the world, threatening the one natural resource the Somali people had left to them. The story was reduced to pirates and the Americans who had fallen into their evil clutches, and, as was the case in the earlier hostage situation in Iran, we didn't ask why, we didn't search out the underlying reasons that Somali teenagers made choices that we could never imagine making ourselves. We simply accepted what we had been told and waited for our good, brave captain to be rescued from those bad men.

I then handed out an article that did provide some context, some background information about what was happening. The author of the article explained that the Somali teenagers were responding as a kind of coast guard, trying to protect their country from abuses taking place off of their coast, and described the nature of those abuses.

I asked the students why we didn't know this context, this background information, and they responded that it was nowhere in the news reports that they watched, and I asked them again if it made any sense that a group of teenagers would be out there hijacking ships when they themselves wouldn't dream of doing so. The students noted that the news called them pirates, not teenagers, and that they hadn't thought about it.

And that's the part that grabbed my attention and caused me to think of the Postman book. The vast majority of people in the United States seem to have been trained not to think, not to question. We as a population didn't ask why a bunch of young students in Iran took American citizens hostage in 1979 and held them for more than a year, even though it's not something we would ever think of doing; we didn't ask why the Somali teenagers were doing what they were doing in 2009. It didn't occur to us to ask. It was easy enough to repeat the stereotyped, racist rationales that were fed to us: they're different than us, they're bad, they're evil, they don't value life as we do, and so on. And because we had no idea why it was happening, our caring and attention was focused entirely on the Americans, and many cheered when the three Somali teenagers were shot and killed. Let me hasten to say that I am in no way defending what the young men did, hijacking ships and taking hostages at gun point, and neither was the author of the article I shared with the students. We were simply saying there was more to the story, and that the context, the history mattered.

This raises serious questions for me as an educator. How can I help my students to learn to approach what they read, hear, or encounter with a healthy skepticism and a critical eye so that they can ask, first, does this make sense? Am I hearing the whole story? How can I find out more? How can I work with my students so that they are able to look beyond and behind the easy headlines, to find as much of the truth as they can, and to recognize when they are being given only part of the story? How can we help our students to develop the skills, knowledge, and dispositions that will keep them from buying the next bridge, or war that some snake-oil peddler tries to sell them? And how can I help them to do the same with their future students?

Following the Threads: Bringing Inquiry Research into the Classroom is one response to those questions. I interviewed several researchers about the ways in which they carry out research, how they ask and then pursue questions until they are satisfied that they understand why things are as they are. I also interviewed a number of teachers who organize their classrooms around helping their students to become critical researchers. While my primary focus in this work is on secondary social studies classrooms, I found that those working with young children had much to offer, and their wisdom and methods speak to me as a university professor working with adults.

The book is laid out in what I hope is a simple and straightforward manner. Following this introductory chapter, I present a summary of the major themes that emerged from my interviews with the research consultants. They each go about their work in unique ways, but there was quite a bit of overlap in what they had to say, and those points of agreement are what I've brought to this work. Chapter Three focuses on the relationship between what we value and believe about children and education, and how we organize our classrooms and curriculum based on those values and beliefs. In Chapter Four I present a brief overview of the inquiry research process, offering thoughts and insights from those I interviewed. Chapter Five offers excerpts from several of my interviews with educators who are living their beliefs in the classroom. They talk about their work in ways that make clear why it is important that we help our students to learn to gain both skills and dispositions that will enable them to become responsible, life-long learners. I find their words to be encouraging and inspiring because they are actually doing the work; it's not just a pie-in-the-sky theoretical discussion. Chapter Six focuses on some ways we can support our students to look beyond the headlines, to ask questions that bring them closer to a fundamental understanding of why things are the way they are. Finally, Chapter Seven offers an array of lesson and unit ideas that will support those who want to bring more inquiry research into their classrooms and some resources to support that work.

CHAPTER ONE

Opening the Door

One year in third grade the Teenage Mutant Ninja Turtles were "in." Turtle shirts, lunchboxes, notebooks, and backpacks were everywhere. On Halloween the room was swarming with these "mean, green fighting machines." The turtles were named for four artists of some renown: Leonardo, Michelangelo, Raphael, and Donatello. I asked the students how they got those names and these eight- and nine- year olds looked at me with "that look." Their "Oh man, here he goes again" turtle sensors were tingling; they knew a "teachable moment" had arrived. It had.

We began by showing pictures of a few paintings the students might have seen: *Mona Lisa*, *The Last Supper*, some sections of the Sistine Chapel ceiling, and sculptures such as *David* (with a focus on the upper body/face). There was some recognition, some modest buzz of excitement related to those connections, but nothing major. Then we got to Leonardo's inventions. We looked at his drawings for flying machines, submarines, printing presses, cranes, robots, horseless carriages, parachutes, clocks, and various military weaponry; they were fascinated, as they looked at his inventions from five hundred years in the past. Then we began to talk about the kinds of inventions they wished a current-day Leonardo would produce, and moved into a discussion of what we might want to have in the future. They took off. They became inventors, "creating" pens that did homework assignments, machines that did chores, and manufactured unending supplies of sweets. Other inventions allowed them to fly and took them places only eight- and nine- year olds can imagine.

From there we moved into a more in-depth study of those four artists, looking at photographs of their paintings, sculptures, and prints. We then engaged in sculpture and painting, and each student painted his or her own section of the Sistine Chapel on paper taped to the underside of their desks. It was messy, uncomfortable, and when the lights went out (there was no electricity in the Sistine Chapel) we were literally in the dark (I didn't have them strap candles to their foreheads, as Michelangelo did). We also went to the art museum to look at a small exhibit of Michelangelo's prints, and as one of the students looked up, he saw artwork on the ceiling. "Look, it's just like what we did!" he exclaimed.

The students, once engaged, were unstoppable. They wanted to know every-thing they could about their turtle namesakes. They were hooked, they were ex-cited, and they were learning to learn, not because there was a grade attached, or a test to pass, but because it mattered to them.

When learning projects are built around the interests of the children, and/or when they deeply connect with material they are introduced to, they bring their full attention, hearts and minds to their work. Rosalie Romano, talking about the expeditions her students carry out in schools, says:

> In every expedition I've had, some cooperative groups absolutely soar. The kids will not stop. They're begging to continue. And that kind of intellectual engagement, that passion, that sucking up of learning and thinking and being together is highly contagious.

Artist Don Fels, talking about his experience teaching young children:

> If you go to the library at age five and the librarian shows you a picture book about something you're really fascinated by, you want to get that information. It turns out that one of the ways you get information from books is reading them. So here I was, dealing with kids, most of whom couldn't read. They had a huge incentive to learn to read when it was about something they were interested in. It is not rocket science. It's pretty straightforward. I never had to force kids to learn to read. They learned to read because they wanted to. Not because I was offering them candy, to pay them to learn to read….It was exciting to them.

Don and I found the same thing to be true working with adult students in a master's program in education. The students were required to develop and carry out a research project related to education. Many students began the process in-tent on researching what they thought they should, choosing topics like identify-ing better methods for teaching spelling to third graders. Three or four weeks into the process they would come to their advisory conferences looking de-pressed, defeated, and a bit embarrassed. With little prompting they would con-fess that while their identified question was of some interest and something that they would need for their work and their resumes, they were kind of stuck, bored, and burned out with it. They would then move into talking about what they really wanted to investigate. As they talked about their real interests, whether it was teaching math to people with math anxiety, creating a slide show of homeless kids in town, or exploring their own writing and process, these adult students began to regain their energy, their passion, their strength, and their in-terest. They were talking about what mattered to them. When we suggested that they continue in these obvious directions, they would virtually explode from the office, heading for the library, the computer, or to someone who could help them to know more. They were energized again, creative again, and engaged with the world on their terms. They were ready to practice and make use of the various research skills and strategies we were teaching them to use, because, like Don's young students and reading, they had a reason to learn and make use of them. Those skills and strategies would help them to gain information that they really wanted to have.

Politicians, business leaders, community members, family members, and educators agree in general terms about what it means to be educated, to be ready to function as responsible adults. Education Goals 2000 sums up these agreements in a fairly succinct form. The goals for student achievement, for all students include the following:

> All students will leave grades 4, 8, and 12 having demonstrated competency over challenging subject matter including English, mathematics, science, foreign languages, civics and government, economics, arts, history, and geography, and every school in America will ensure that all students learn to use their minds well, so they may be prepared for responsible citizenship, further learning, and productive employment in our Nation's modern economy.

(B) The objectives for this goal are that—

(i) the academic performance of all students at the elementary and secondary level will increase significantly in every quartile, and the distribution of minority students in each quartile will more closely reflect the student population as a whole;

(ii) the percentage of all students who demonstrate the ability to reason, solve problems, apply knowledge, and write and communicate effectively will increase substantially;

(iii) all students will be involved in activities that promote and demonstrate good citizenship, good health, community service, and personal responsibility;

(iv) all students will have access to physical education and health education to ensure they are healthy and fit;

(v) the percentage of all students who are competent in more than one language will substantially increase; and

(vi) all students will be knowledgeable about the diverse cultural heritage of this Nation and about the world community

> —http://www.ed.gov/legislation/GOALS2000/TheAct/sec102.html

Despite this apparent agreement, schools are increasingly operating in ways that guarantee they will not reach them. Students do not become competent in a wide range of subjects through a narrowing of curriculum. They do not learn to think, to solve problems, to reason, to apply knowledge, or to write and communicate effectively in classrooms dominated by scripted curricula, five paragraph essays and a test-prep curriculum that remains in place until the tests are finished, in April or May.

This book is really focused on supporting teachers to approach and organize their classrooms in ways that support the learning we say we want. The lessons and units offered here are student centered and are focused on introducing students to skills and content that will serve them throughout their lives. We make offers to the students that they won't refuse, because they are learning and using skills in service to their own interests and curiosities. In many ways this book is an example of the process I am advocating. I have chosen a topic, or more accurately a linked chain of topics that are important to me, gathered as much information as I could, from a range of sources, and am now communicating what I have found to date. I still have many questions, and certainly don't pretend to have the answers that will serve every teacher or situation, but have confidence that the wisdom of those I consulted will be of use to many readers.

I am writing *Following the Threads: Bringing Inquiry Research to the Classroom* to encourage and support educators to:

- Make connection between required course content and the lives of their students.
- Offer their students the opportunity to learn how to engage in authentic, real world research in their classrooms, and to practice these research skills on topics that are of interest and importance to them.
- Encourage students to share their findings with an authentic audience for whom the information is relevant and consequential.
- Give students and teachers permission to disconnect the automatic link that "school" often makes between research and (at least occasionally) boring, academic research papers, and to encourage students to share what they have learned through various media and modes that will best communicate what they have found with their intended audience.
- Provide examples of the ways in which history, our own stories, have been hidden from us, or lost to us, and to realize the damage that has done to our understanding of how the world has come to be the way it is.
- Offer students the opportunity to experience the joy and power that comes with learning about issues and subjects of importance to them.

Schools, Standards, and the Teaching of Social Studies

I spent very little time at school attending to my classes; my body was there, but my mind was often otherwise engaged. I do remember having intense debates in a social studies classroom leading up to the Goldwater-Johnson election of 1964; one of my classmates was strongly for Goldwater, and we would go at it on an almost daily basis for the few weeks before the election. The teacher allowed room for our fierce discussions of the candidates and issues during those few weeks, and the room was alive. After the elections we went back to the regularly scheduled programming, surveying our way through the endless laundry lists of facts and dates that made up the history curriculum, and I returned to my own internal muddle and musing.

As a high school teacher I became increasingly troubled by the overwhelming majority of students who came to me unable or unwilling to think for themselves, unable to see the connection between their lives and the history we were studying, and who were initially reluctant to carry out research that was more challenging than retrieving surface-level information from an encyclopedia. They had been "trained" by their previous schooling to approach their tasks with little interest or effort and a sense that the only reason to take on school tasks was because the teacher said so. They had no stake in the outcome of their efforts beyond a grade and assumed that there was no consequence for anyone else either. They had learned to assume the look I had mastered decades before, feigning attention, for the same or similar reasons; school didn't reach them, didn't tell them the truth, didn't offer them answers, connections or tools the students perceived as useful.

It was also clear that they behaved very differently outside of class, and outside of school. The hallways throbbed with student energy, passion, excitement, and interest, a state that lasted from the moment the bell rang, ending one class, until the next bell rang to begin another, approximately four minutes later. I remember that feeling from my own school days, the way colors and sounds sharpened, and how, for the briefest of moments, life came into focus. And then the bells rang again, and we returned to states of suspended animation.

It does not appear to have changed very much over time. I teach social studies methods classes at Plattsburgh State University, in upper upstate New York. I asked my students to read an essay about social studies and what it could be, and to respond to it. This was a first assignment and we had done very little work together at that point. Their responses told a sad tale about their experiences in social studies classrooms.

As a student you wonder why you have to take it (social studies) and what the point is of learning about stuff that has already happened. Social studies was never my topic. I never understood why I needed to take it…

For some reason I did not embrace Social Studies. As a student much younger than I am now I found the content boring and repetitive. As an adult I am wondering if perhaps my elementary teachers were as uninterested in social studies as I was…

While daydreaming in a sixth grade social studies class where my teacher was reading from the textbook verbatim, I envisioned myself in his "cushy seat" with a different approach.…I don't want to say my sixth grade teacher was unprepared or making it difficult for the class to make sense of the information, but the only thing I remember from that class is that Mexico City is built on top of a lake.

During my educational career I feel that what I got out of social studies was dates, numbers, and facts.

I do remember fifth grade social studies and I despised it. I think we did a lot with geography.…

Not one of my fifty university students, graduates and undergraduates, felt well served by their social studies classes, in general, and only one could recall an experience that was truly exciting and memorable at the secondary level. Her teacher wore a costume and incited a riot; she still remembers details of the Bolshevik Revolution. The rest recalled social studies as a blur and worry about their ability to teach it to others since they hated it themselves and remember nothing from their experience.

This is typical of the response I get from students, year after year, when they talk about their social studies experiences, and this sadly matches what I have seen in public school classrooms around the country for the past twenty-five years. The pressures of coverage, of an overwhelming list of "items" to at least mention, to borrow Walter Parker's phrase, and the tyranny of unit or year-end exams have reduced social studies and history classes to a disconnected race to a finish line that is more horizon than realistic destination. U.S. history classes rarely make it past the 1970s, or early 1980s by June, which leaves out the lives of every student in the room, and many of the teachers. And we wonder why so many students hate history.

This is not how it has to be. It is possible to engage students both intellectually and emotionally, to have them involved and energized by what happens in their classrooms, even their social studies classrooms. The kids are not fools; they would rather enjoy their time and learn about things that interest and challenge them than waste their time waiting for the bell to ring. They would love for their classrooms to be places that excite and motive them and that help them to learn about the world in ways that are useful to them. By the end of the school year many of my reluctant high school students were voluntarily staying after school to rehearse courtroom scenes, were creating extraordinary works of art illustrating key conflicts in American history, and were engaging in animated conversation about history, current events, and the questions they had about their world. On the one hand, it didn't take much; I simply opened the door and invited them in. On the other, it meant saying no to an assembly line approach, no to our textbook as the ultimate authority, and no to an unquestioning approach to US history that left the kids, their families, and communities on the outside.

There is nothing in state or national standards, nothing in the social studies canon, and nothing in the stated goals of our nation, states, or institutions that precludes teaching so that social studies matters, so why not do that? We can organize our classrooms and curriculum to help students to relate to the curriculum, to find connections to their lives and their histories.

The Joy of Teaching and Learning That Matters

What it comes to, finally, is making the decision as to what our purpose is as educators. Why are we doing what we are doing, what do we want for our children, and what do we believe is important for them to gain in their time with us? I want students to be excited about learning, and to gain skills and confidence in their ability to pose and answer their own questions. I want to create/facilitate the development of a learning community where our intention is to help each other to learn as much as possible and to share that learning. I want students who are motivated to act on what they have learned, to become engaged citizens working on their own behalf, and on behalf of their communities.

This won't happen on its own. It's up to me to organize my room, my curricula, and schedule so that it does happen. I have to invite the students in and make them an offer they won't refuse. I have to work with them to create a learning community such that we get excited together about "making meaning." This book is about taking steps to create such a classroom, centered on student interests, questions, and on connecting students to course content. It's about teaching through questions, through inquiry research, through projects and expeditions that invite students to explore topics of interest, alone and with others, and then to share what they have learned. It's about organizing a classroom to facilitate the joy of learning about the world in order to make a real difference.

And it can be done. There are teachers who have created student centered classrooms in all parts of the country, at all grade levels. They have offered their students the opportunity to learn how to learn, to pursue their own questions, ideas, and concerns, and in the process their students have experienced the joy and satisfaction that come with deep learning, from learning that matters. And once you begin to teach in this way, it is impossible to go back.

Steve Goldenberg sums it up powerfully, describing what happens in his classroom as the students begin to appreciate the possibilities attached to carrying out meaningful research:

> Once they see it they all want to do it. Once they really get that message that, in this classroom you really can find out what you're interested in, then they almost all, to a person want to do it and want to do it passionately. I really do have to pry them away from the writing table and force them to go outside or have lunch or play a game or something. It's all new and fresh for them and they see their own ideas begin to take form and shape and becoming sufficiently complex and they get excited. It's very contagious…

Following the Threads

> From the beginning I decided that I would go wherever an issue took me. The important thing to me was, "Here's a question to be solved." If there's a question to be solved you mustn't limit yourself to one particular field in trying to solve that question; you just go wherever the question leads you.
>
> —*Howard Zinn*

I have interviewed several artists, writers, and historians who also have extensive classroom experience in order to better understand how they approach and use research in their work, and to get their opinions/perspectives on how we can better teach research to our students. These researchers create extraordinary work, are passionate about teaching and learning, and have a deep interest in helping our students to become critical thinkers and deep learners about their world. They each take joy and satisfaction in following the threads of their questions to wherever they might lead, and employ a range of media and methods to share what they have found. Their voices and insights form the backbone of this work and are woven throughout the book. I've included brief biographical sketches of the consultants on page 223 of the Appendix, to provide readers with some context in which to appreciate their comments and observations.

Given the complex nature of their research, and the importance each consultant places on having individuals work in ways that are most true to them and to their particular questions, there is no recipe book, no fool-proof formula they could or would pass on about how to carry out that research. There were, however, strong points of agreement about what is important when engaging in research, or when providing a supportive environment for helping others to grow into effective and successful researchers and learners. This consensus is by no means exhaustive, and the presence of these elements does not guarantee success, but they are significant factors in supporting researchers to learn, grow, and succeed in their efforts.

Here, briefly are the strong points of agreement from the consultants; a discussion of each will follow.

- The research experience is most likely to be successful if the researcher is interested in the topic, if the research matters to him or her.

- Research takes time. It is imperative that researchers have adequate time to pursue their questions, to carry out the several steps of the research process.
- The process of pursuing a research question frequently takes researchers beyond the boundaries of any one discipline.
- Listening may be the key skill in conducting research. This means listening to oneself, first, and then being able to listen to others as the research process unfolds.
- The best research leads to an authentic consequence for the researcher and for others.
- There are many ways of communicating research findings, and the researcher can choose the most effective means of sharing what they have found, based on what they want to communicate, to whom, and for what purpose.
- There is no greater joy than learning about the world, and the process of finding out is invigorating, contagious, and rewarding.

I will discuss each point briefly through the rest of the chapter, bringing in the thoughts and observations of the consultants where relevant.

Researching What Matters

Ryan is six years old. His teacher, Steve Goldenberg, has this to say about him.

> We always have a story-writing time, and at first Ryan wanted to write a history of the whole world and the whole universe, and was having trouble finding the point for starting. I gave him a little structure, which was to have him invent fictitious characters, but have them do real things that could happen, that his characters could do.
>
> Ryan came up with three characters, Ed, Jake, and Randy, who work at Microsoft, and they take vacations together. The first vacation that he wanted them to go on was to Montana, where his (Ryan's) grandfather lives. Ryan started to research how they would get to Montana. He was most interested in their actual drive and was very happy to find maps and to find out what routes people could take to drive from Redmond, Washington to Montana. Then it became clear that he wanted them to stay in a hotel, and he was very focused on making sure to have them stay on the highest floor of the tallest hotel in Montana.
>
> I asked him, "How would Ed, Jake, and Randy know which one was the tallest hotel?" and he said he didn't know. He took a trip up to the library at our school and although our librarian is unbelievably great and we rarely stump her, this time she was stumped, so I suggested we call a travel agent. He had never heard of a travel agent, but he was fascinated by the idea of people who knew about places all over the world and might even know how many floors a hotel had.

We called one, in Billings, who at first was kind of skeptical, but then when she heard it was for a six year old student her entire affect changed. She actually didn't know which hotel was, in fact the tallest, but she made it her top priority to find it out and get back to us.

I think something happened for Ryan. This magical travel agent was very important to him. He started becoming more interested in just trying to find out about things. He wanted to know all of the museums that they could have gone to, what hours they were open, and everything they might see while visiting Montana...

Ryan went on to write a series of five books about Ed, Jake, and Randy, who always went traveling together. Ed, Jake, and Randy, in his books actually did a lot of research. They looked in travel guides and they asked people what it would be like and what people would be doing in the places they were going to travel to.

Steve's story about Ryan sums up the most important point made by every one of the researchers I interviewed; the research experience is most rewarding and successful when the researchers find value in what they are doing. Their research must matter to them and must be of appropriate and sufficient challenge for them at whatever skill and experience level they bring to it.

Ryan is an exceptional student, but the other students in Steve's class have a similar relationship to pursuing their interests. In Steve's words, "Once they understand that they can research about things they're interested in, they all want to do it, and want to do it passionately."

Don Fels, who before becoming an artist worked for fifteen years as a teacher of young children, echoes Steve's observation:

If I have an interest meter inside of me, so does every kid. And when I taught young children, it was really close to the surface. They were four, five and six, and that was part of why I so enjoyed that age, because their little interest meters were right there, right there, and right smack there. Maybe buried about one sixteenth of an inch. Most kids get very excited about things and I just let them know that I was excited that they were excited. And as soon as they were interested in something we would head off to try to look into it...

Don and Steve made their young students an incredibly powerful and elegantly simple offer; "What do you want to know about? What interests you?" There is, of course, an art to asking that question and providing appropriate support to allow students to pursue their questions on their terms, but as Don and Steve both say, once the students understand that they can research what interests them, they are off and running, whether it's researching hotels in Montana, phases of the moon, robots, or the life cycles of spiders.

What does matter is that we want to know. Poet Georgia Heard talked about her own young son's approach to learning, linking it to the speech made by the

Polish poet Wislawa Szymborska when she accepted the Nobel Prize for poetry.

> Part of Szymborkska's speech was about the phrase "I don't know," and how, she said, without that one little sentence, one little phrase "I don't know" I never would have written poetry, Isaac Newton never would have done his work, I mean, this is how we start, with "I don't know." I mean, that's the question.

Georgia goes on to say,

> So often in schools we try to cover up that we don't know. I think that's what a child's world is. I think about my son Leo. He wants to know how the world works, and his question is "I don't know," and that's where his passion for learning comes from, not from being filled up by a curriculum that someone else has just invented.

When students engage in work they value they learn that research is rewarding; it helps them to find out what they want to know, and it generates its own life and excitement. They learn that their own questions and curiosities are legitimate and matter. This is the basis for life-long learning, and for living in the world. The alternative would be for the students to learn that their questions and interests don't matter, and that the only point of an assignment is to complete it to the teacher's, or the state's satisfaction. There is no quicker way to smother curiosity and defuse creativity than to dictate to students what they will or will not investigate, and then to tell them whether they have been successful or not.

Once they have learned, practiced, and mastered the skills and processes associated with research they can bring those tools and abilities to whatever topics they encounter, for whatever purposes. It is a skill they will carry for a lifetime.

Teacher Libby Sinclair is clear that the particular subject or topic to be researched is not as crucial as having the children make the research their own.

> You can cultivate a kid interest in almost any topic, once they get truly involved in finding out about it. When they pose their questions and find answers, it becomes their own; they kind of "own" whatever it is. Just now the kids I have are not particularly knowledgeable about the natural world, but they've become passionate about the individual creatures they've learned about because their research has led them into new topics, and they are the experts; nobody else knows as much as each individual child does about whatever subject they are studying. When you have questions and find answers it's just interesting. There's something extremely satisfying about that, like digging a potato out of a hill, you know, "Whoa, found them!"

Students gain more than content when they engage in the research process, and it is this deeper learning about what it means to explore a topic deeply that may be the most important consequence of our work. And it is not only a lesson learned by the children. Libby Sinclair, again.

> I think the other thing there's not a test for is the whole idea that learning can really be a passionate experience, that you can love to learn. I don't know why, but nobody ever seems to see that as an important thing. The people who would have you assess things never include joyful reading, or "loves to learn." That is such a motivator for reluctant learners, to be interested in what you are studying and to be curious about it. It's a huge help, to help you persevere. That love of learning is really a powerful piece of it. It's really important that the kids get excited about something.
>
> When we found out about the Negro League museum we used that as a resource, and it became a service project. I didn't know there was such a thing. I guess in a way a thing that has always been a pleasure for me is that I've always felt that I was doing a research project for myself, my own learning. I learn as much as the kids every year, if not more. I think that's what's kept it interesting, to be able to learn on my own.
>
> Then I'm just like the kids, because they're excited to discover things; you're always aware of something or other that somebody's going to enjoy. You become really wrapped up in it yourself and you really care about it, to the point where looking for a map in a bookstore is not work, it's more like, I wonder what I can find, because it's fun now.
>
> I was at a parent meeting a couple of weeks ago, and one parent commented on our current class project, which is researching animals in the natural world. It is an expedition, similar in format to the Negro League project, and she said, "I just want to tell you that this is the most wonderful project because my son gets home at night and he gets on the computer, and I just want to tell you if I hear one more thing about river otters I'm going to scream...." She said, "I'm so excited that he can take this as far as he wants to." And I think that's the difference. There are a lot of projects where you have an end product where we can all look at and say, that's what it should look like, and then you have projects where a child will take it as far as that child can take it. And I guess that's my ideal project; there's a minimum for everybody and there's an open-endedness to it, so a child can go as far as he or she can, as far as his or her passion and interest takes them.

We have so many children who come from families, from communities that are not acknowledged in history books. What our children learn from this is that they are simply bit players, on stage as background, as props for the important folks, the powerful, "the deciders." We also know that the backbones of communities, of societies, are all of us "ordinary people" who run the machines, fix the roads, provide the food, clean up after others, teach, and help us to be well, and that those people tend to be invisible to history. They rightly have a place in our study of history, and we must recognize that place in our curriculum if we are to connect to the lives of our students. If we don't help students see how their stories make up the country's story, why would they care about it, and how could they not feel alienated and angry at being pushed off the page?

Michael Grigsby, a former teacher and current community college administrator spent time researching the life history of a beloved uncle, a major influence on him as he grew up in rust belt Ohio. Hiram Brooks, a successful caterer in Warren, Ohio, was a major figure in Michael's life, and served as surrogate parent, role model, and exemplar of what could be. Michael talked about Uncle Brooks and why it was important to him to research and tell the story of this man he so honors.

> I wanted to do something that gave recognition to whom I believe was an extraordinary individual, an extraordinary human being, who was my godfather. I called him Uncle Brooks. His name was Hiram Brooks. He lived in my home town of Warren, Ohio, and he was my father figure because my parents were divorced when I was very young. I never really knew my father, and Uncle Brooks kind of took that place. He was very kind, he loved me, and he and Aunt Kitty, his wife, provided guidance and support. He was a role model. He gave me my first job, washing dishes. He was a caterer, and he was very successful. I was caught by the notion of doing some sort of research into some relatively unknown aspect of American society, and I wanted to combine that with being able to see Uncle Brook's name down on paper.

Michael's journey took him into his family history, into the history of catering in the United States, with particular focus on that experience for African Americans. His interest in the story was personal and familial, but the relevance and resonance was much broader. Researching Uncle Brooks was an entry point into a deeper exploration of racism, class, and economics in the rust belt in the middle of the twentieth century, and Michael's personal interest provided the fuel for carrying through with the research. Our students find similar entry points to the nation's history through a study of their own family history, and they do the work because, like Michael, they want to know. It's personal and it matters.

Research Takes Time: Gathering and Evaluating Data

The design of the school day often makes it seem as if the things of the world belong to certain categories or disciplines, and this is true from the earliest schooling experiences on through to graduate school. The divisions are approached as if they are real; each discipline develops its own learning sequence, curricula, and assessments, and there is little attempt to integrate or coordinate with other disciplines. This is a bureaucratic, organizational decision that is not the way the real world works. We don't go out and have a "social studies" or "science" experience. We live in the world and use as many lenses and ways of understanding as we can to make sense of what we have experienced. There's a difference.

What matters are the questions: What do we want to know and what can help us to find out? How can we begin to answer our questions? Skilled researchers are masters at following the threads, wherever they lead. They pose their questions and then pursue them, via every connection and through any and all disciplines until they have fully responded to the questions, or until they have been stopped, by lack of time, resources, or access.

Poet Georgia Heard, talking about her poetry and her life says,

> I think that I definitely "follow the thread," as William Stafford named it. And that's so important. You may discover something and you think, "I didn't know that." When researching about Vietnam I found out my father was in the Tết offensive in Saigon. Then I went and researched different newspapers to learn what it was like during the Tết offensive, and I found out that Tết is a holy holiday, so then I wanted to find out about Tết, from the Vietnamese perspective, and how important it is to them. So I had all these various threads that would come up, and it was based on a passion. I wanted to know. I felt it was important, and I would follow it.

Howard Zinn put it this way:

> From the beginning I decided that I would go wherever an issue took me. The important thing to me was, "Here's a question to be solved." If there's a question to be solved you mustn't limit yourself to one particular field in trying to solve that question. If you have to go into economics, go into politics, if you have to go into genetics and geography, whatever, you just go wherever the question leads you.

Projects rarely exist within discipline boundaries. When Jan Maher was conducting research for her novel *Heaven, Indiana*, she began in several directions at once:

> I really needed to research that time and place, so I did a whole lot of research about Indiana in general. I read books about the history of Indiana, and then because I had this Underground Railroad theme I was really interested in the history of that in Indiana. And as I started to work on the material I also had this sort of theme story that included a carnival passing through so that led me to read a whole lot of books about carnivals in Indiana, and then I needed to learn about the gypsies who traveled through Indiana at the time.
>
> I went to the computer, got online on the library's catalogue and reserved twenty books at a time. I also wrote to reference librarians in towns along the route of the Underground Railroad. I gathered a humongous amount of general information from reading the books.

Rosalie Romano insists that her university students, who carry out expeditions with public school students during their junior years at university, seek out multiple sources when preparing to lead/facilitate expeditions with their public school students. She requires that those sources represent a range of ideas and viewpoints and that her students, and their students must learn to bring a critical eye to the material, and to seek out relevant and diverse sources.

> It's not enough to say one person will be my only source, because the whole point is to say it must be personal, but it can't stay there. You absolutely must learn to find different sources, preferably conflicting sources, and then you have to make decisions about what to believe, what not to believe, and on what evidence, so it's not any more just a matter of personal belief. ...The best expedition always has conflicting perspective on a specific question, so you're always having to say, "Wait a minute, if I'm looking at it from this way it's this, another way it's this. What am I going to do with that?"

Don Fels, talking about his process for carrying out research regarding the Duwamish River, said

> In the beginning one doesn't know what one is going to find. I knew the end result was that the river had been messed up, but I didn't know what had happened at this particular site. I knew nothing about it, but I guessed that there would be something interesting there, because pretty much everywhere there's something interesting if you can get a handle on it. So, I started researching, I started looking. And by looking that meant I did a lot of reading in whatever I could find that talked about the Duwamish. I looked at old newspapers, I looked at books that treated the general geographic area, I looked at old maps, and then I talked to as many people as I could find who had some memory or knowledge of the place, and they would usually turn me to somebody else.
>
> What you do, and this is true of all research, no matter what you are looking for, no matter what you are looking at, when you find one thing it sends you to another thing.

Listening Is the Fundamental Skill of Research

Each of those I interviewed placed listening at the heart of their work. They talked about listening in four main ways: First listening to oneself, to being open to one's interests, questions, curiosities, and situations; second, listening to what your sources have to say, through interview, print, video, photograph, music, or other mode; third, listening to the feedback of others, sharing comments from critical friends and others who can help you to evaluate what you have done, and to help guide you to know if there are more steps needed; and fourth, for the educators in the group, it is also paramount to listen to your students, to have a strong sense of who they are, what they are interested in, what they are saying, and how they can best carry out their work successfully.

Listening to self

This first piece is clearly the most important of all. Researchers must be able to hear themselves clearly, to identify both their true questions and their best sense of how to proceed throughout the process. Listening to yourself is often the genesis of a research project. Georgia Heard describes the beginning stages of her research into teaching poetry:

> In the beginning there really wasn't much written about teaching poetry and I guess I knew that whatever was out there didn't feel authentic to me. So I just began to do my own research and talk about my own experience, and it was amazing how the kids understood it, and I didn't have to come up with anything gimmicky. It was just my authentic experience as a writer, what I do.

Roger Shimomura was sent to concentration camps, along with more than one hundred and twenty thousand other Japanese Americans during World War II. He had his own memories of the experience, and based two series of paintings of the experience upon the diary entries of his grandmother, who was also incarcerated in the camps.

> I think that in terms of what made the work essentially function in the way it did, that that pretty much came from myself, it came from my own responses to the situation, and my own sense of working artistically in a particular way, my own degree of cynicism, what I experienced, what my grandmother experienced... which also included the way I felt towards my grandmother, the feelings I had toward her colored that, obviously.

Listening to others

Next is the need to listen clearly and deeply to others. I am using the term listening to mean being open to taking in and processing new information, from the full spectrum of sources. Skilled researchers attempt to understand, as fully as they can, what people are telling them, from their experiences and points of view, from their frames of reference. This means the researcher withholds judgment as long as possible and attempts to stay open to new information, to new ways of looking at his or her questions, and to considering the addition of additional information.

It can be a bit intimidating for students to interview others, especially adults, but they will find that most people love to talk about themselves, or to share their opinions with people who are really interested in what they have to say. Don Fels, who does extensive interviewing as a part of his research, says

> Part of the researcher's job is to make sure that the people you are talking to understand that you are genuinely interested and that it's not a trick. Once in a while people are afraid that you are going to make a fool of them somehow, so you have to disabuse them of that. In my case the most successful technique is to honestly say to them, "I'm really interested in your story." And I think every person I've ever met likes telling their story to somebody. It's very rare that people don't. Even people who feel badly about what happened, they want to talk about it. People are flattered when you say "I'm interested in what happened to you, how you grew up, or what you know about this," the fact that you are asking them for knowledge. That flatters them. And that should flatter them; it's something they know that they are giving to you. So, it's easy to get people to talk; you have to listen.

As people talk, you are listening to what they say, what they don't say, and noticing when what they say is surprising or new information to you. Howard Zinn, when he began to write his groundbreaking work, *A People's History of the United States,* was still learning the extent to which our nation's true story had been suppressed, or censored by those in power.

> I'd started out from a kind of general philosophical question that is, "What are the points of view that are omitted in any traditional telling of history?" and of course in the case of Columbus it was the point of view of the Indians. Once I decided that I was going to look for their point of view, I found that they weren't a writing society. That was one problem; there were no written records left from the Indians. And the other problem was that they'd been wiped out, which in itself was an interesting bit of information that nobody had ever told me. Nobody in elementary school had ever said that about Columbus' encounter with the Indians, so I thought "Who else was there, and who could possibly have thrown light on it?" That's when I discovered Father Bartolomé Las Casas. The writings of Las Casas gave me a wealth of information, because he was writing, he was at least looking at it as much as he could, not being an Indian, from the standpoint of the Indians, from the standpoint of the victims. So, it's a matter of asking the question, whose point of view is being left out of this story?
>
> When I was dealing with the Mexican War, the question was, there too, whose point of view is left out of the story? That led me to go to many, many, many volumes written about the Mexican War, digging and digging and trying to find out what is the point of view of the soldiers in the American army, or the leaders or soldiers in the Mexican army? That principle led me, in every situation, to look into the shadowy parts of the library.

Documentary film maker Judith Helfand recognized that any story that one enters is already in motion, and that all involved come to it with their mix of personal history, experience, biases and attitudes. When she traveled to the south to interview mill workers, and family members of mill workers while conducting research for the film *Uprising of '34*, she also recognized that, as an outsider she was not necessarily someone factory workers would trust and open up to. She knew she had to become legitimate in their eyes before they would go below the surface, and talk about the textile strikes that took place in their towns. Those strikes by textile workers were traumatic; seven workers were murdered in a small town in South Carolina, shot by their own townsmen, members of the South Carolina National Guard, who had been sent out by the governor to guard the mills against the strikers. It is still a very painful subject for residents of the town, and many who had known the story refused to talk about it until researchers came to them in the early 1990s. Judith talked about the research experience.

> Individuals do historical inquiry and they come to it with a certain kind of bias, and they come to it with a race history and a class history and a religious history...So I went to the south to research this film as a privileged, white, Jewish person from Long Island and then I wound up there talking with people about perhaps one of their greatest moments of risk taking, when they had a great deal to lose, talking about their loss, and about the impact of that loss.

Judith was just recovering from cancer that she had gotten as a consequence of unethical behavior on the part of drug companies, and she felt that her illness in a strange way helped her to connect with the workers.

> I don't think you need to have cancer and lose things to be qualified to do historical inquiry, but you have to be aware of who you are and what your experiences are so that you can figure out how you can authentically form a relationship with those people you are asking questions of, and that you really are bringing something, that you are worthy of asking about loss.
>
> You need to bring something to the table, you need to bring a level of compassion, a level of awareness that lets you honestly say, "I am lucky, and I am honored to get to talk to someone who has had such a rich set of experiences." They have to know that you know that their loss is meaningful, and their courage and their risk taking was meaningful, and it could be that my asking and my sitting and listening, if I'm able to do something with this will be the way that they know that this was worthwhile.

Listening means you are actively taking in people's stories, listening for the ways in which bias and point of view may have shaped what you are hearing. You are learning to engage in critical thinking, in analysis of what you are hearing, not as a passive "ear," but as an engaged listener. It is one of the reasons that

Wendy Ewbank has her students carry out research via interviews and oral histories.

> One of my students was investigating the Israeli-Palestinian conflict. She came to me one day and said, "I was interviewing this woman and you know, I think she's really biased. She's an Israeli woman and talked about terrorism and Palestinians." The student could see that this woman was coming from a particular perspective and she needed more interviews, because if she simply goes with what the woman said it would be clearly one sided. It was fabulous.

Wendy then talked of a second student, researching a different topic.

> There's another girl who is focusing on the lack of education in Afghanistan and Pakistan. She was trying to talk a guy who runs a restaurant in Seattle to host a night at the restaurant where the profits would go to supporting building schools in Afghanistan and Pakistan. She [the student] had been adopted from India. The restaurant owner was so happy that she was not from Pakistan; he did not trust anyone from Pakistan. So when he found out there were schools in Pakistan in this project he would say, "No, no, no, there are no real schools in Pakistan. They say there are but there aren't real schools."
>
>   She ended up going back three times to meet with this gentleman and to convince him that the money in fact was going to schools; she had the names and addresses of the schools. She in a subtle way, in a respectful way, got the man to turn around his thinking. He did not host an evening at the restaurant but he offered a hundred dollar gift certificate that she then used for a raffle. It was her persistence that made the difference. The kids realize that they can change an adult's thinking. That's powerful. Her experience with that, working with a real person, was worth a week of lessons, or more. So that's why you do it.

Listening to the feedback of others

A third level of listening has to do with soliciting the feedback and reactions of others to the work you are doing. After spending weeks, months, or even years on a project, most researchers are too close to the material to fully appreciate what they have. You need an outside eye to help with perspective and quality control. For Jan Maher, that's where the editor comes in....

> I think the parallel to having an advisor provide feedback to a graduate student writing a thesis is the editorial process. That's when, in a work of fiction, you've done what you can do, with your own obsessions and interests and yourself as an audience, and then you get this other point of view involved, and that's the person who gives you the real straight feedback about whether the work communicates to others. Or can say, "This gets through to me but I'm not sure it will get through to ninety nine per cent of the readers, so this is a place where I think you should do some tinkering."

Ted Wright talked about the process of gathering information for the re-mapping of the Sitka region using Tlingit place names, and that the process included bringing many tribal elders to a room lined with developing maps of the region.

> In Sitka's case, those maps were placed upstairs, along one wall. They had a number of meetings where people came and looked and they compared notes to determine whose memory was accurate. So there was a consensus that came to be built upon, the validity of the maps. And also, I think, for the elders it was a blast, to see what other people remembered, and how it fit in with what they knew. So, I think it was a lot of fun for these people who were involved.
>
> I think there have been disagreements on occasion, and differences of opinion, and just different memories, and that's why that process where the maps are in the room and people have the opportunity to engage in a sort of debate about that.

Those conducting the research constantly had their work on display and brought elders and other experts together to compare and challenge their memories, their accounts of the history of the Tlingit nation and the region, which allowed the researchers to both check their work and to push the conversation further.

Don Fels and I performed this role as advisors for our students in the masters program in which we taught. Our task was to reflect what we saw, to pose questions and possible pathways to our students, and to help them to think through their process so that they were operating in service to their question. Their responsibility as researchers was to listen to our feedback, to consider it in reference to their questions and process, and then to decide how to proceed. It was always their decision to make since it was their research. The touchstone was, and is always, to consider all of the information and then to listen, again, to oneself as the researcher.

Listening to the students

A fourth level of listening is specifically for educators, and that is learning to listen to your students. It is really at the heart of teaching, and most fundamental when supporting student research.

Steve Goldenberg always starts with his students.

> The most important thing is for them to know that their ideas really are important, to really make their ideas be at the top of the agenda. That's what motivates most people, if they're really going to be exceptional students it's because they're operating on their own ideas and their own thoughts and feeling that power. That doesn't hap-

pen if you have an entire, planned day, or a day when you're just not listening to the kids.

Steve has also found that when he listens carefully to his students he learns about the issues and concerns that are what are most central to them.

> I guess the most important thing is to really listen. I'm often surprised. You know, a kid starts to talk about Star Wars, really wants to learn about Star Wars, and I'm thinking, okay, he's just going to want to do the bang bang, shoot 'em up, big war thing, and then if I really listen I might find that what this kid is really interested in is concepts about home or relationships....

Steve has his mandated responsibilities as a teacher, and part of his mastery is to make sure that he is meeting those responsibilities while also listening carefully to the children. He knows that he can attend to his students, follow their lead and still guide them so that,

> We'll be sure that it touches all the basic skills that need to be touched. There'll be some words and writing in there, there will be some things that need to be counted or added up, or categorized, sorted, and classified, and there will be some relation to the natural world, either the social sciences or science, but it really can be done from their point of view.

This is no less true with older students. Rosalie Romano's university students are faced with the challenge of listening to their public school students as they lead expeditions. This is challenging for the teachers and for the university students who are interning in the classroom because they can only plan the shell or outline of the experience; the rest is being ready and able to move in the directions suggested by their middle school students. Dr. Romano talked about what it takes to teach in this way:

> That takes confidence and it also takes a mindset, an attitude that listens deeply to your kids, and responds to it, and shifts and begins making adaptations so you're always right there with the kids, able to ask the questions so that the kids keep moving, and stay engaged. They keep generating, actually not just the momentum, but the intellectual curiosity that animates the lesson, the unit, or in this case the entire expedition. When these teachers who write the lessons immediately have to adapt and change the lessons, and have to reflect on it, they begin to see that the lessons themselves are creations, nothing more, nothing less. They're not set in stone. And that they have an intellectual obligation to make sure that whatever they are teaching connects in some way with the lives of their kids, whoever those kids may be.

The Best Research Leads to an Authentic Consequence

Research in the "out-of-school world" is rarely done for its own sake. There is usually a reason, a goal in mind that is tangible, that will lead to change. It might be on a very small scale, like dealing with plotting a trip to an unfamiliar address in town, and it might be much larger, focused on helping to make significant social change, but there is a purpose to the research that is something other than a grade. Those I interviewed all engage in research related to better understanding who we are and how we came to be this way, and there is an intention to communicate that understanding to others, to make a difference through their work.

For Don Fels, his art is designed to get people to pay attention, to see the world that they most often overlook, or take for granted.

> Having art help to make people off balance is something that most artists, in one way or another believe in. I think part of the function of art is to get people to experience their world more fully and you can't do that if you just present them with what they already know. They'll look at it, say thank you and walk on. So, you have to do something that gets people to see things differently. For me, the thing is just part of the discussion, the conversation, the exchange of points of view, interest, ideas. I'm not particularly interested in the thing as a precious object. It's a vehicle.
>
> I take a long time to study a topic and then to create art. Someone comes along and maybe they only spend ten minutes, maybe five minutes, maybe three minutes. If it's working right, some part of what I've invested in this thing re-invests itself in them and they walk off with a little piece of it. I don't expect them to spend as much time on their end as I did because, hopefully, through the research and through whatever skills I have as an artist I've condensed down all that energy that I've put into it so that they can walk away with a little bit of it.

Judith Helfand talked about the relevancy and importance to her and the other filmmakers of having the making of *Uprising of '34* serve the people of the town as well as the filmmakers. There was/is a strong anti- union feeling in South Carolina, partly based on misconceptions about the role the unions played in that strike. Judith and her colleagues were, among their other goals, trying to correct some inaccuracies about the union's role in the strike and to help the town's people to a more accurate picture of their history.

> To be able to kind of reunite people, to show people this, to show them that their name was on this blacklist, for lack of a better term, and they [officers in the textile union] were actually trying to get them their job back. Well some people didn't know this, and they said, "You're kidding me, I just thought they left town." It was a really healing thing for a lot of people to get this, and I think for this process to be

healing, you're not just making a movie, but the very act of doing this kind of historical inquiry, or historical detective work, there's a restorative quality to it. I think to make it really work on both sides there needs to be a certain kind of reciprocity. If you can actually make this process really useful to the descendants of this history, then that's really, really important. If you can make somebody's risk taking, even if it's a risk they took fifty years ago, if they get the opportunity to kind of reexamine this and say, maybe that was a good thing, maybe that did mean something. ... that's something you can offer them. It was really joyous for me, and it made me personally feel like we weren't just taking something from them.

Roger Shimomura knew that most Americans were unaware of what their government had done some fifty or more years ago to Japanese Americans and he wanted to tell that story.

Having done that series (of paintings based on his family's incarceration in the camps), the Japanese looking paintings, I said that I wanted to revisit my grandmother's diary entries again. This time I wanted to do a series of paintings that were more illustrative of the actual entries. And the reason for this was because this series was meant to be an educational experience for anyone that came to see the exhibition. And the show would travel around the country to various museums and hopefully those host institutions would develop educational programming around them.

The first series that I did was based on the same diary entries as the second one. The first looked very Japanese, sort of eighteenth century wood block style, and it was easy for people to miss that point completely. The fact is that I think that most people who purchased those paintings did not want to know the story about the internment. They wanted to see those paintings as a decorative piece that they could put on their living rooms and it was fine with them if they never had to explain to their friends what inspired that work. And I knew this because out of the twenty-five paintings, all of which sold eventually, I think there were only five people that asked for the diary entries that went with the paintings, and the rest took them without ever asking for them.

The last two or three paintings in the series had barbed wire fences in them and they actually asked me to paint out the barbed wire fence, that they would buy the paintings if they didn't have the fence in there. So, that was really interesting... I can't say that it came as a surprise, but I do feel that in the end what I had done essentially was sort of plant a stink bomb in these various living rooms across the country, that sooner or later that issue was going to have to come to surface and the stench of the internment was going to win out in the end. So I was very aware of that as I was working on this new series I was going to be very direct.

There are many ways to share the results of research

Schools have traditionally favored structured research assignments resulting in structured written reports, with a vague sense that the teacher would be reading the papers. We have all written them throughout our school careers, and have read more than our share if we have taught for more than a couple of weeks. One must conclude, given the nature of the assignment, that there is no real authentic purpose to the work beyond carrying it out, handing it in, receiving a grade, and checking it off the list of requirements.

It does not have to be this way, and, if we are looking to involve students in meaningful work that has a real purpose then we would do well to encourage them to think differently about the consequences of their efforts and the impact they want to have on those who come to it. Researchers communicate what they have learned about topics through a wide range of modes that they choose for a number of reasons. They consider what they have to say, to whom they would like to say it, and the impact/response they are hoping to have on those who experience their work. The researchers also consider their own strengths, resources, and preferences for communication.

Roger Shimomura created another series of paintings, *Stereotypes and Admonitions* with an intention to communicate what he has seen and experienced, in hopes that it would move viewers.

> I really meant to establish a forum for examining racism and injustice with this other series, *Stereotypes and Admonitions*. I don't sit here and implant all of these questions or issues into the work. I just hope the work is pregnant with those possibilities, with those issues coming up between whatever group of people, whether they end up coming out as gender issues or whatever, that's great. To create this forum, for things to happen, for sparks to fly.
>
> There's a certain advantage of having something sit on the wall, and especially in a house, and to keep sending these sparks out for whoever may look at it. I've always said that, in trying to explain some of these issues to students, depending on who is standing in front of a particular painting, you have a circuitry that comes out of one end of the painting and through that viewer's head and out the other, and that circuitry just waits for a different head to come in and complete it.

Don Fels takes the responsibility of communication very seriously; it is an important aspect of his work as an installation artist. He talked about the choice he made about how to share his research findings about the destruction of the Duwamish River, in south Seattle.

> This place where the art is, is not even really a park. It's just a kind of green place where people come and have lunch. They are mostly workers around the area. They're not going to an art museum, they're not going to a history museum, they're not reading a book. They're just going to have a picnic. So my job was to snag them, to catch their attention. Maybe the fact that there's an eighty foot boat thirty feet up in the air might seem strange enough that they might be curious, so my

thinking was, if they were curious and came to stand underneath and look up, they would see at the level where they were there were these panels I made to tell the story. And I thought, if I got them this far, maybe they'll read some of it. If they read some of it, then they'll know some of the story. So I had to think through the delivery of it, and that's part of the art.

Ted Wright and his colleagues in Sitka carried out their work with the intention of both saving and revitalizing the language and culture of the Tlingit, but also of offering a cultural, as well as place-based curriculum designed to reach Tlingit students, who were often turned off or turned away by "Western" curricula in "Western" schools.

What it comes down to is that when the language is lost you lose a worldview…It means that because the Tlingit language is really a description of places and stories associated with those places, a history of interrelationships that span many generations, if those names are forgotten, then so are the stories, so are the histories of interrelations, so are the ways of understanding who the students in particular are as people within a group. What I try to do is to make it clear that it's not a western worldview, it's clearly different.

In particular, if they don't understand who their clan is, what their clan house is, how their clan is related to other clans, then they don't know anything about who they are, from a Tlingit point of view. Absent that knowledge, they are anybody; they could be the average white American citizen. That was the plan in the rest of the United States, the whole assimilation movement, Manifest Destiny, the development of the boarding schools, that whole history.

There's a generation of Tlingit speakers now who are dying off, and there are only twenty or thirty left who are fluent. There are enough programs now where it looks like the language will survive, but it will be sort of a textbook language, it will be like literacy so you know what we're passing on is sort of a superficial understanding, a textbook understanding of what it means to be Tlingit as opposed to what it really means.

It's a very logical set of connections that need to be made and the students in modern schools, in modern culture, are in a situation where you live in two worlds, and your ability to navigate both determines whether you survive.

There is no greater joy than learning about the world

There is great joy and power in learning about the world. It is most basic when we are infants, as we learn to walk, to communicate, to get what we need to live and grow, but it is no less true or real as we age. The skills and information we gather allow us more independence and the ability to become responsible for shaping our lives, for making our own choices.

We love to learn because we love to learn, and also because the learning we do opens doors. When we learn to drive we gain the freedom to travel. When we learn to read we can learn about things that interest us. Computers connect us with the larger world. There is pleasure in the learning itself, and then there is pleasure in what that learning enables us to do, and this can, and should be, at the heart of our educational process, to develop and foster the skills and dispositions that create life-long learners.

Jan Maher says the process of carrying out authentic research on a novel, a work of fiction, this way was so gratifying that she is now in the process of writing two more novels. She speaks about that pleasure and about the joy of learning:

> I'm going to answer metaphorically. It's something like when you get to the point in a jigsaw puzzle when you can see, you haven't solved it all yet but you can see that you're going to be able to. There's a kind of a thrill when you can begin to make out a comprehensible picture. The visual metaphor where you paint by numbers or on a foggy misty morning and you can't quite make out the details of the surrounding yet, when the sun comes up things become clearer. The joy of seeing the connections and patterns is a physiological thing, documented by neuroscience. The brain loves to make connections and patterns out of things. And particularly it loves to make them more than it loves to have somebody else show it, and that's where I think we sometimes miss the boat sometimes as teachers; we forget that the real thrill is in the discovery.

Finally, research is about coming to a more complete understanding about the world and how to best live in it. We ask questions, we investigate what matters to us and we try to understand as fully as we can, and to live more completely with that understanding.

Georgia Heard speaks to this as she talks about her process in researching the Vietnam War, in which her father served.

> You have to make a world, it has to be complete, it has to make sense. I need to have a full understanding of the emotional part of what am I writing about here, because otherwise I would have what Adrienne Rich called tourist poems; people would go to a Caribbean island and write a poem about the beautiful blue waters. If you don't understand the world, what kind of poem is that, really? Whatever your interest is or your passion, or I guess your obsession sometimes, you have to read about it and think about it and ask the questions until you feel that something is complete. Part of writing poetry is to help that information and that kind of sifting of information, to make it more complete and more emotional.
>
> I wanted to understand it from his [her father's] point of view, but I also wanted to understand what it was like in Vietnam, not just for him, but for the Viet-

namese. I wanted to understand what the children were doing there, what it felt like to be in a village, and to imagine a country at war like that, with my father being a tiny, tiny piece. So it was personal, but also I wanted to understand the origin of the war, so I did a lot of research on the history of Vietnam, and the whole business with the French. I also wanted to know what daily life was like, not just for my father, but for the soldiers, and also for the Vietnamese. That felt more honest. You know, my father was over there, he was fighting and I felt compassion for him, but I also felt compassion for what was being done over there, and the deceit over here in this country. I wanted to know what the culture was like that was even separate from the war and all the media we were getting in the United States. That's what I mean by a complete world.

And there has to be a personal component to it somehow. It's actually influenced how I feel about every war. I mean, with the Iraq war now, I feel like I have a better understanding and I'm more compassionate about what's going on, even though it's a very different situation, because of the work I did around the Vietnam War. So it feeds on, it makes a whole world that will last the rest of my life. And I guess it's what you want to do with kids, too, right?

CHAPTER THREE

Teaching Goals and Choices

I want the students to become absolutely aware of their own agency, of the moral obligation of what it means to be a teacher.

—*Rosalie Romano*

That's really crucial, being clear about what are you preparing them for. From my point of view, my primary motive in teaching young people is to give them the kind of material and the kind of suggestions that provoke them with ideas that would make them more active, more perceptive, more probing, more independent thinkers, and also inspire them to become active members of the society, and not simply passive recipients of whatever our political leaders decide. So to me that citizenship requirement is primary.

—*Howard Zinn*

The cliché, "To a hammer, everything looks like a nail," has relevance for educators. How we view the world, and how we value the world determines how we move through it, what we notice, and how we make choices. A teacher's values, and the intersecting values of the complex environment in which she works, have a major impact on how she organizes her room, her curriculum, and her time. If her focus is on raising test scores and socializing students to obedience, she will make choices that maximize the likelihood that her students will "learn" to sit still, follow directions, fill out forms, fill in bubbles, and to write essays that begin and end with certain key phrases. Her students may well "learn" to respond to a scripted environment in which they only respond when cued to do so. They might learn that they are only rewarded for following teacher-directed behaviors and for ignoring their own impulses; the "successful" students will adopt this behavior.

If a teacher organizes her room to build and nurture a learning community, a room in which students support each other in learning, then she is more likely to make choices that reflect those values and goals. Libby Sinclair had clear goals for her students, and for the investigation that she and her students carried out on the Negro Leagues, and she got what she was going for, and more.

I wanted the students to learn to do research that was authentic. I didn't want them to copy anything, I wanted them to read until they understood, and then write it in their own words, from their understanding. It took a long time and I think they really did that. What I didn't know and what I'm really pleased with is that the kids came these [Negro League ballplayers] as their heroes.... They came out with black heroes, which is not always the case for middle class white kids, and I think it was the historical perspective, the knowledge, and the admiration that were all really nice for them to have.

Libby also had as a goal the creation of a learning community, where students learned how to learn, and to help each other to learn as much as possible.

What I always have done with kids is to get every book I could possibly get and then have them read, read, read. Read lots of different books, putting sticky notes on the pages that had something they would want to come back to, put their names on the notes. I really talked up collaboration a lot. If I know you're studying such and such, and we talk about a community of learners, that when I find something... I love to watch the kids rush across the room to share what they've found with a classmate who has been looking for that information. That's the kind of feeling I love to have in the room and I think research promotes that. When you have your topic but you know what everybody else is doing, and then you begin to feel excited for the other person too, it's really wonderful, it feels really wonderful. I think, for me as a teacher, that's the way the room sounds best in the world is to hear that excited hum and somebody's gone over there to share with somebody else, it's what learning sounds like. So nice.

This suggests that one of the most fundamentally important acts in a teacher's preparation is to become clear about what he or she values and wants for the students. The most fundamental questions one can ask as a teacher are: Who are my students? What do I want for them? What are my goals? What is most important, what matters? With regards to research, the questions become: What do I want my students to learn about the process of research? What will a successful experience look like? What role should I play in creating the environment that will support my students to learn?

I asked Howard Zinn what his goals were when he taught his graduate students and he replied,

That's really crucial, being clear about what are you preparing them for. From my point of view, my primary motive in teaching young people is to give them the kind of material and the kind of suggestions that provoke them with ideas that would make them more active, more perceptive, more probing, more independent thinkers, and also inspire them to become active members of the society, and not simply passive recipients of whatever our political leaders decide. So to me that citizenship requirement is primary.

The clarity of a teacher's beliefs and focus lead to clarity of the work in the classroom, and shapes assignments, assessments, and curricular sequences.

Gary Thomsen, a sports marketing and events teacher at Sealth High School, in Seattle, identified a few things that make for a good project for his students, and what he wants his students to take away from their work.

> Whatever project we are taking on is one that's giving them life skills that are going to be invaluable to them, even if they don't realize that for two or three years down the road. What I want the students to cover can be transferable to any sort of project. They have to learn communication skills, they have to learn to write, they have to learn time management skills and they have to be able to learn to manage people. Sub-points to all of those are setting and meeting deadlines, producing materials and documents that contain no mistakes, and basic things that you'd take for granted in the business world. It doesn't matter if they work on a project like the Negro League's Traveling Exhibit, with a budget of about twenty five thousand dollars, or whether they do something that's more internal, say a cultural holiday celebration. Those same things get taught, regardless of the size of the project.
>
> Secondly, it's a project that has some residual benefit to the community. In the case of our barnstorming trip across country for the Negro League Museum, the greater community served is the entire country. It's a missing piece of American history and these kids filled in a lot of blanks. And I think that's good for the country, and certainly the museum.
>
> The other thing is that most of these projects have a trip element. I mean we go out on the road, and a lot of our kids have not had that experience. And I think that's a great educational experience, taking kids places that they're not familiar with and seeing other people and meeting other people in the context of what they've been researching. It gives them a whole different, and I think better perspective of this neighborhood and where they live, and it opens up their minds incredibly. I think that most of these kids will sit around and talk about the time they roller bladed across the country or rode bicycles all summer for the Negro Leagues and had to play baseball games all across Canada... it's a memory these kids will have for the rest of their life and I think it's a good one.

When you are taking on authentic research there is the chance that things won't work out. Teachers who are bringing real world experience to their students are inviting the possibility of failure or disappointment into their classroom. I asked Steve Goldenberg about that, and how he handles that with his students.

> Ideally there is no failure on the child's part. If there is failure it's on my part, in not structuring a classroom in the way this child needs. I bank on the fact that if they find their comfort level and if they are surrounded with support and nurturing, they are going to learn and it is going to satisfy everybody. When somebody tries something and it doesn't work, that's part of the learning process. A huge part of my job is to really make that okay. We talk a lot about scientists, and scientists change their guesses. The scientists who have trouble are the ones who can't change their guess.

When they try something that they think is going to happen and it doesn't happen but they still want it to happen so much that they won't try something else or think about it differently, those are the scientists who have trouble... There's a lot of opportunity to change your guess, or change your idea. That's what we thought and now we think something else and that's great. I give them a lot of praise for being willing to do that.

Steve's students are five- and six- year olds, and they can't simply go off and independently research their interests, to do something important. I asked him how he provides enough structure so that his students can succeed in their searches.

The current jargon that we use is called scaffolding. So, either way, the building is going to get built. The child is going to grow and learn and thrive. And as much as they can do on their own, fine. But sometimes there needs to be some external structure, some scaffolding, to help guide the process. I try to be conscious of and don't confuse the scaffolding with the building itself. What I am doing with the child is assisting their growth, and the majority of that is an internal process, which I can affect, but it's the child's building.

This kind of teaching also requires trust in the students. We help them to gain the skills and content knowledge that allows them to pursue their own questions and interests, and then we give them the room to do it. It is, again, a question of values and beliefs about the nature of children and the purpose of education. Don Fels spoke to this during our interview. I asked him to respond to the concern that students will be lazy and do little or nothing if we let them do what they want.

The opposite is true. If you let kids do what is essential to them they will put in enormous amounts of work, because it's generated from inside. That's completely different than requiring them to do something because you've decided. It's a question of physics. There's less friction when they are doing something they want to do.

Of course you have to help them over the hard parts, because kids come with all sorts of different skills and abilities, and some kid may want to do something with her heart that she really isn't yet able to do. So you have to help her to scale it back a bit so she isn't frustrated. Maybe she wants to learn about the Cascade Mountain Range but she doesn't have the ability to understand the geology. So, you have to pull back a bit and say, maybe we can look at the dirt or woods outside of the classroom and look at that first. So, you don't discourage her from her research, but you encourage something that has a possibility of success.

This process of making sure curriculum connects with and is built around student interest may be easier or at least seem easier in self contained, elementary classrooms, but secondary students have interests too, and many teachers, departments, and schools are finding ways to bring those interests and require-ments together. Ted Wright talks about the efforts to bring Tlingit culture, his-tory, and world view into the Western educational system.

> It wasn't until a few years ago that we realized this place and culture based study is a perfect platform upon which to build curriculum, or rather to have students build curriculum. The teacher as guide to student explorer, data collector, interviewer, and researcher is the model that we understood to be ideal in the beginning.
>
> In indigenous cultures, when you've lost touch with your ability to live on the land, then your survival is in jeopardy. For the Tlingit people it's been a matter of survival. We are working to bring the Tlingit world view and language and culture to Tlingit students in western education settings. It's a very logical set of connec-tions that need to be made and the students in modern schools, in modern culture, a situation where you live in two worlds.
>
> It's not just Alaska native kids, it's any kid in any town or city, wherever there's been a disconnect between who they are and what their parents do, and where their family is from and what the history is of the place where they live or where they grew up. And that's universal, a universal human need and priority but it's been lost. You can see the success for kids that get that, on certain reservations in this country and in others, so when it's working and if you know that it's impor-tant, than why not push it and make it part of the whole educational system.

Our goals as teachers are to focus on what is important, on what will best serve the students as they live in the world, and as they gather skills and knowl-edge and dispositions that will serve them in the years ahead. We can't predict the world our students will grow into and shape, but we can offer them a set of skills, knowledge, and dispositions that will best prepare them to live in it sus-tainably, responsibly, and with joy. If we want our students to learn skills and content that will help them to live productive and responsible lives, we have to help them to make connection between what happens in school and what hap-pens in their lives. Jan Maher speaks to this.

> The first thing that's applicable is that we don't have any business spending our time in life, which is short and precious, doing stuff that doesn't matter to us. That's a waste of a life. And way too often in classrooms we don't help students see the connections between what we hope they will learn and what matters to them.
>
> I'm not saying that we should never ask them to do things that we think matter that they don't. They're young and immature and we have some sense of where we hope they will see connections, even if they don't yet. But if we can engage them in asking authentic questions that they are really interested in knowing the answers to and help them find some of the various ways they can research those questions, they will learn that this work has real value for them. They will come to see that it is this

continually interactive process between questions and partial answers... you never get the full answers. The answers just generate more questions. That's life.

We may want our students to find what we have found, the truth that we value, but as Jan says, the discovery of their own truths, their own connections, is where the power and learning takes place. We can provide an opportunity and a structure for that search, but we have to provide emotional and curricular space for each student to make his or her own discoveries and connections. There is nothing in most required curriculums or assessments that need limit this. Students need to know how to read a map, but they can determine the particular geography, the terrain those maps will display. Georgia Heard does this when she brings poetry to students.

> I want them to realize that each person, each student in the class has, not only their stories and experiences that are absolutely valuable. I want them to know that what they've experienced, no matter what it is, that that is the material for poetry. It's not about going to some exotic place; it's about their experience. I want them to know that that's the stuff of poetry. I also want them to know that the way they speak, their own language, the words they use when they talk to their friends, that that is the language of poetry. Their own language is unique, and they need to have faith that that's going to be the language of their poems, and their experiences, that that's the stuff of real poetry.

What is true at the elementary and secondary level is also true and essential in our work at university, with teacher candidates. Rosalie Romano talked about her goals for her students in the teacher training program at Ohio University.

> I want the students to become absolutely aware of their own agency, of the moral obligation of what it means to be a teacher. They cannot ever expect to rely on a textbook, or a script, or some silver bullet to teach them how to teach.
>
> One of the things I remind my students constantly is that "Wherever you are going to teach, you are right now in a poor, working class, rural environment where these kids live in trailers, with or without running water and electricity, you are, right now the person to make a difference in their lives. And what you will do, it's not later, it's not tomorrow, it's right now."
>
> And they do come to trust their kids. I want the CARE teachers [her university students] to learn to trust themselves. Because they'll come to me and say, "Is this ok, is this ok?" And I say, "What do you think? What makes it ok to you?" They have to think for themselves.

In the larger world, research is at best a compromise, as researchers bring what resources they have to their questions. One of the most significant resources is time, and that is affected by so many different factors, including finances, other responsibilities, work situations, and so on. It is even more of a potential hurdle when one is operating in a school setting, where time and resources do not automatically expand to meet the various interests the students bring with them. But the truth is there is more time than we often acknowledge, if it's what we value as educators. Dr. Steven Covey talks in several of his books about scheduling our priorities, about making sure we design our days and organizations to enable us to spend the most time on what we value most. It is absolutely essential in our classroom work, and it is possible to organize our educational experiences to allow more research time if it is, in fact what we value most. A few of our teachers were able to respond to this question, of how do we gather the time to do this work in a classroom setting. Steve Goldenberg said:

> I feel amazingly fortunate to be in the position to have the freedom and flexibility to respond to the kids' interest in research. That's the part I can't emphasize enough that I only can do what I do because I have control of the time. I can say okay, that's what we're going to do this morning, this science experiment, and that's going to take up as many hours as it needs to take up.

Steve's administration trusts him enough to allow him to make decisions about how his time will be spent. They know that he knows what is expected, and that he has demonstrated, year after year that his students will learn what "they should," so they trust him to make the kinds of decisions that allow him to respond to the learning needs and interests of his students. He knows his students, he knows his subjects, and he is in the room, in the moment to understand what is needed.

Don Fels built time into his schedule to accommodate research, though he didn't know specifically what his young students would be researching. He was comfortable with that, though acknowledges that not everyone is.

> As soon as the kids were interested in something we would head off to try to look into it. So, my standard response in the classroom when a kid would come up to me and say "I'm really interested in this but I don't know…" I'd say, "Let's go to the library. Or, you go to the library." And the librarian would help us, or help them to find a book that would start to answer some of those questions. And just like me interviewing people about the location on the Duwamish River, one book would lead to another book, and then another. And maybe we'd find that there were three or four kids in the class who were interested in this, or five or six, or ten, and then maybe we'd read the book together. So, all we did was just follow our interests. And there is no shortage of kids' interests, so there was no shortage of material. I just planned that the kids would tell me where we were going; all I had to do was to

leave the time for it. It's not like I had to plan what it was that we were going to be looking at as much as I had to leave a certain amount of blank time in the day where we would have the opportunity to do that looking.

It comes down to a philosophical choice about what it means to educate our children, and what we want them to learn, both in terms of contact and skills. Gary Thomsen, talking about his high school sports management class, says that he organizes his class based on what he knows about his students, what he knows he wants them to learn, and on their interests.

> You have to have a clear idea of the outcome that you want to achieve, and then kind of work back and look at it in the context of what's the timeline and what are the different components that are needed to make that achievable and then you start plugging kids into it. There are some lecture days. When we move into a new area like sponsorship writing there might be a two day or three day period of me talking and them taking notes. Right after that we might break up into four or five or six groups, each doing one piece, for the betterment of the project. During an average class I'm at this table for five minutes, and then that table for five. Each table has a group leader and the leader is in charge of that group and each project has three producers and those producers are in charge of each of these little groups. You can organize the students, once you know them, so that the students are learning course content in service to carrying out a complex research and action project.
>
> Now somewhere in all of this you have to teach them how to write a project proposal. To be able to say on one, two or three sheets of paper, in a concise fashion, what the project is about, and what is required to complete it. That becomes kind of your syllabus. Then you have kids who start to get into groups that they feel comfortable with, and start working on those logistical packages that are necessary to make the project work.

Translating "real world" research to classroom settings is not simple. Classrooms usually don't have the time, budgets, expertise, and singleness of focus to dedicate significant chunks of time to a topic, and there are many students to teach. How can we take what researchers do in their professional lives and adapt that to classrooms? Judith Helfand did extensive research about an event that was both known and hidden. She researched in the various towns where the strikes/actions occurred, followed threads to the National Archives in Washington, DC, and interviewed people wherever she could find them. She is excited by this work, as a model for high school students, because it is something that can be done.

> There are lots of ways to make something authentic, but it's very important for people to know that history doesn't just get there, there's someone on either side of it. What we did in researching the film is something that other people can do. They

might not be able to make a film that gets on public television, but they can do these interviews, they can find a subject that is worthy of deep inquiry, where something happened in their community or in their town that was a decisive moment and had deep implications for them as young people even living there now that they don't really know about. And what does it mean that they don't know about it, what did that event mean? Why was it important, who got hurt, who didn't get hurt, is there a ripple effect, is there an echo, does it have deep resonance, even to this day, and if people knew about it would it change something?

It's perfect for high school kids. People love it when somebody says, something happened here but they don't want you to know about it. I mean, that's a great invitation. Something happened here and no one knows about it, or everybody knows about it, but they don't want you to know.... As soon as you tell your students, "There are things that happened in this town, and they all have to do with workers, and they all have to do with a skirmish, and they all have to do with a moment of deep unrest and civil disobedience and protest and resistance, and they don't want you to know about it. And it could be that if you knew about it, you might be able to change the inequity that still exists. Do you want to know? And guess what, they're not going to be happy that you want to look into it. You're going to ruffle some feathers and kick up some dust, people are going to hang up on you, they're probably not going to want you to do this," they are interested. Right?

There's always going to be some documents of some sort that people can use as a jumping off point. It is something that anyone can follow. I did this workshop in Minneapolis and I said, "Let's talk about hidden labor history. Everybody has hidden labor history so let's talk about it." Someone says, right here in Minneapolis we had a teachers' strike and we don't talk about that strike. And someone else raised their hand and said, "How about this? During the Hormel meat packers strike, which was ten miles from where I was teaching, I was trying to do current events with my kids. They were watching this thing go on that was completely cracking the fiber of our community and I wanted to talk about it, and my principal heard I was talking about it, and there were kids in the class whose parents were on one side of it and some on the other, and he said, 'Your ass will get fired. You can't talk about that right now.' It was like, it was current events, it wasn't hidden labor history, it was our daily life and I was not supposed to be teaching it in my class?" And that is an interesting thing.

Gary Thomsen considers his class projects carefully, based on what his students need and based on a sense of performing a service to the community. The students know that there are consequences to what they do, and that others will benefit from their efforts.

I think project based learning is great because it gives kids a chance to actually, at the end of the day, see something and to stand there and say, "I did that." I also think it's a lot easier to convey relevancy when they're doing those types of things. I don't know when or if it's going to change. Since I've been doing this I've given talks in different cities in the United States they all sort of have the same reaction, my god what a wonderful thing.

Gary's work comes at a time when many teachers are moving towards scripted curriculum, worksheets, and test preparation, under the weight of No Child Left Behind. I asked Gary to talk about his approach in this climate of testing.

I think the tests are kind of skewed in the favor of the white, two-parent kid. So what do you do with all the rest? I'm just amazed by the WASL test (the standardized test used in Washington State). I mean, I can understand why the students here get stressed out, especially in a school like this. I mean, Lakeside [a wealthy private school in Seattle] or certain parts of Garfield [a public high school that offers a program for "gifted" students], ok, they'll probably do very well and most of those kids are going on to college, but when you've got a mixed group of kids and your job is tied to how much those test scores go up it can't be good.

You have to take all of those bits and pieces of the transferable educational message and you have to reconfigure that for each of the kids. You really have to teach each kid individually, and find out where their expertise is and where their interest is, and take that curriculum and reformat it and put it to him so that he or she still gets stuff out of it so that he becomes an important piece of project.

Somebody was telling me that the educational message is being delivered the same as it was 150 years ago, and as a consequence every year we're turning out kids into society who are ill prepared. So now, starting with Gates, people look at computers as the end all to all of the problems. Kids have access to so much more information that they didn't use to have. Relevancy I think has become probably one of the most crucial things in education and yet it's hardly ever talked about. A kid is going to sit there and say to you, "Why do I need to know this, why do I need to know that?" They know they can get on a computer and they can find stuff, they that they can start their own company on a computer. It's not like it was ten, fifteen years ago even. And yet if you sit a kid down in a classroom and you don't convey the relevancy of what's going on to the real world they're going to tune you out.

Don Fels notes another advantage to working with student-centered questions and interests whenever possible, and that is the benefits that accrue for the entire community.

There's a piece we haven't mentioned that out to be mentioned. If you use this kind of process of letting the kids follow their interests, at least for a certain part of the day, beside the pleasure that it give to any individual child to follow his or her nose, you also introduce this plethora of information that the kids are bringing to each other. So, if Rebecca is interested in Ecuador and does a whole thing because her Uncle Fred once went there and brought her back a doll and it fascinated her, the kids suddenly have information about Ecuador. It wasn't on my agenda to talk about

Ecuador right now, but the kids are fascinated. Where is Ecuador? Ok, so we have to get the maps out. Oh, well, who lives there? Why do they live there and not here? How did they get there? All these, all kinds of other broad questions get dragged into the classroom because Rebecca's uncle went to Ecuador and she still remembers it. You couldn't have predicted that, and it's not like Ecuador is on a list of things we are supposed to study. But it obviously brings into the classroom a whole group of things that we are supposed to be studying about how the world works. There's a richness to the process that is quite wonderful. The only unpredictability is the actual thing, but it's very predictable that the kids will bring in way more stuff than you could ever cover in ten years.

CHAPTER FOUR

The Inquiry Process

Robert Sherrill's 1971 book *Military Justice Is to Justice as Military Music Is to Music* came to mind as I began work on this book. Sherrill was clear in that work that justice in the military shared little in common with what we recognize as justice in civilian life. The analogy holds when examining research in public school classrooms, though I might amend it slightly; school research is to authentic, real-world research as school lunch is to a home-cooked meal. Research at school is all too often an exercise in retrieval, in bringing back information that is of little or no perceived personal value, done in order to fulfill an assignment. There is no consequence to the research beyond a grade, for either the students or the teacher, and the teacher is all too often the sole audience, reading up to one hundred and fifty copies of essentially the same report in order to write a grade in a grade book.

Authentic research in the "real world," involves asking questions that the researchers truly want or need to explore, developing a plan that will help them to learn what they want or need to learn, and then carrying out that plan. It is a satisfying act to complete and serves as its own reward because it helps us to learn about something of interest. Why not use our time in school to help our students learn to master the research process in service to pursuing questions and topics of interest to them rather than having the students complete empty research tasks that mean little to them?

We can best prepare them for life after school and keep them engaged while they are in school if we are working with their interests and questions. We can work with their energy rather than working against it, forcing students to abandon their interests to follow our curriculum. A student-centered, inquiry research approach provides structure for students to learn and to practice essential research skills on high-interest topics, which improves the likelihood that they will stick with the work, even when it gets challenging or frustrating, because they really care about what they are researching and want to learn about it.

I will present an overview of the inquiry research process in this chapter, and will follow it with interviews with educators who are actually teaching through inquiry research in their own classrooms.

Real World, Authentic Research

Most of us spend a part of each day carrying out research, though few of us would think to dignify our efforts with that term. We simply ask questions, develop strategies for answering them, evaluate our results and make adjustments as needed, continuing on until we have found our answers. Sometimes the questions are small and straightforward: How do we get from Chicago to the Six Nations Museum in Onchiota, N.Y.? What's the weather going to be in the mountains tomorrow? What size washer do I need to fix the leak in the bathroom sink?

Sometimes the questions are larger and slightly more complicated: What cars in our price range are the best buy for the money? What schools are best for our children? Who should I vote for at the local, state, or national levels? What wood stove should we buy, given our house, budget, and environmental concerns?

And sometimes they are the largest and most complicated of questions: What is the most useful form of government to address the needs of an entire population? What is the relationship between democracy and capitalism? What do we do about a decreasing birth rate amid an aging society? What are the ways in which fundamentalist religions are similar, in what ways are they different, and why do so many of them seem to be so often intolerant of others? How do we balance the realities of supporting people around the planet with the realities of environmental degradation? How do we most effectively address the overwhelming economic issues we are facing as I write this in July 2009?

We use a range of resources to answer our questions, large and small, simple or complex, including friends and family, the yellow pages, local, national, or international newspapers, print media of other kinds such as journals, newsletters, books, magazines, maps, the Internet, experts in various fields, store clerks, reference librarians, neighbors, Ann Landers, and so on. We want to know something, and we find out through whatever means we have at our disposal, or can figure out to try. It doesn't occur to us to cite sources, write reports, or worry about whether someone else has asked the same question.

Learning is a process that requires and teaches patience, persistence, flexibility, problem-solving skills, pattern recognition, and an ability to negotiate various aspects of the world. We learn these dispositions and skills through modeling, through experience, and through trial and error. None of that happens if we don't have the opportunity to explore and research, and nothing sticks unless we have the motivation to stick with it.

Lenses and point of view

Don Fels gave middle school students the assignment of drawing a still life that he had arranged in the center of the room; the only catch was that they had to look through cardboard tubes (like personal telescopes) in order to view the objects. He had created a different shape across the end of each tube so that the viewer could only see what the shape allowed/determined, leading to a varied set of drawings, much to the surprise of the students who assumed that all had the same shaped lens through which to look, or more likely had not really considered what the others saw at all. It was an elegant and simple exercise that made clear to his students that the lenses through which we view the world have a significant impact on what we see and what we don't see. We each have our own set of lenses and filters, based on our particular experiences, knowledge, training, racial and ethnic background, culture, economics, gender, and history. We see and understand what we see based on who we are, where we stand, and where we have come from. Three principles arise from this lesson that are at the heart of the study of social studies and of research:

- What we see of the world is not all there is to see; it is not the whole truth, but instead is based on what we are able to see, at a particular point in time.
- What others see of the world is based on their own set of factors, and they are no more correct than we are, but also no less correct when they see the world differently than we do.
- We tend to believe the world really does look and behave the way we see it to the extent that we lose the ability to see the frames and lenses through which we are looking.

Recognizing the point of view we bring to, and the assumptions we make about the world are crucial to anyone engaging in research because they affect what questions we ask and how we ask them. The more awareness we can bring to the particular and limited view we have of our world, the more room there is for us to be open to learning from and with others, to moving beyond what we know and believe about the world. That is the essential purpose of research.

Overview of the Inquiry Process

When we think about the research-related skills and practices that we want our students to learn, to develop, and to practice they tend to fall into the following categories: identifying and refining a question (what do you want to know); stating your rationale (why do you want to know, why does the question matter, what do you already know or think you know about the topic); locating what information already exists concerning your topic or question; assessing what you now know and planning next steps; developing strategies for gaining information from additional sources; evaluating the information you find, as individual pieces and as a body of research; deciding what to communicate and to whom; creating that which is to be communicated; assessing/evaluating what has been created and making changes as needed; sharing your work with your intended audience; reflecting on the work and determining what's next.

Here is a very brief discussion of the elements of research that students need to learn and practice.

Choosing a question

This may seem the simplest and most straightforward of elements, but it turns out to be anything but that in practice. Researchers seek to formulate a question that is broad enough to offer depth and complexity and narrow enough to be meaningful and graspable. "What was the name of the scandal that rocked the Nixon White House and led to his resignation?" is too narrow a question and leaves the researcher with nothing to do. "How can we better serve the full array of students who are in our classes?" points to a general direction but is so broad and multi-faceted that it becomes almost meaningless, or paralyzing. It is often useful to begin with large questions such as the question about serving all students, knowing that early research efforts will, by necessity lead to identifying an aspect or facet of that too-large topic as a functional beginning question. Shaping a question takes both patience and practice; skilled and experienced researchers develop an ability to identify and to modify their guiding questions through practice.

It is also important that the question really matters to the researcher. Students often begin with a question they think they should ask rather than one that really interests them. It is possible to carry out research on a question that you "should" ask, but it's a much more powerful and convincing experience to conduct research on a question that really matters, and it can take some time before students trust you and the process enough to really go after what they want, but their excitement and energy is in evidence when they finally get to their passions.

Rationale

Part of identifying an appropriate question to research is identifying the reasons, or rationale for choosing that question. Ted Wright and his colleagues in Sitka have engaged in an extensive research project over the past several years:

> [To] preserve place names on a map in southeast Alaska, Tlingit place names. There are so few speakers that the names have almost disappeared, and so literally the core of the project was to get some elders to put them on paper, to identify what those places were, and in each case they identified a place and told a story associated with that place.

It has been a complex and challenging project, but the group was very clear why they took it on, and it has to do with the survival of the culture and the well-being of Tlingit children.

> There's always been a real danger that it's all too possible for the people to just die away. There's a generation of Tlingit speakers now who are dying off, and there are only twenty or thirty left who are fluent. There are enough programs now where it looks like the language will survive, but it will be sort of a textbook language, it will be like literacy so you know what we're passing on is sort of a superficial understanding, a textbook understanding of what it means to be Tlingit as opposed to what it really means.
>
> When you look at a lot of these place names, many of them have much to do with food, the harvesting of food, and food and the harvesting of food had much to do with where things were available. So the place names are in relation to those kinds of stories, those facts. If you don't know the names of the places and their histories, you don't know where and how to get the foods, and then you can't survive. So, it's a very logical set of connections that need to be made and the students in modern schools, in modern culture, a situation where you live in two worlds. You watch MTV, you play your video games, and also you're hopefully either learning Tlingit language or you're in a program where much of the culture is being passed on. You have to be able to negotiate both of the worlds; your ability to navigate both determines whether you survive.

Guided by their rationale, Ted and group have moved beyond the mapping project and are developing place- and culture-based curricula that will help Tlingit students to learn what they need to "negotiate both of the worlds." There are many directions the groups' research efforts could have gone, and their rationale has served as both an anchor and a compass, allowing them to chart a path among the many possible paths they could have chosen.

Being clear about the reasons for our choices is also important for us as teachers. We make choices about research tasks for our classes based on our knowledge of our students, of the content we are required to teach, and about what kinds of experiences we want our students to have. Colleen Ryan chose to have her students investigate the watershed in which their school is located, and in which they live. She had many reasons for bringing this research question to her math students. *Real world, & meaningful to students*

I wanted them to make connections to other content areas. I hoped the students could go out and collect data and use that also to create arguments for why we need to change habits, why we need to improve the way we deal with water. I wanted to show them how precious a resource water is, and how little potable water there is in the world, and then help them to understand how much water they really do use in a day. I hoped this would create a sense of urgency, and help them to understand why we need good quality water, and then we could progress from there.

Libby Sinclair chose to have her class carry out an expedition about the Negro Baseball Leagues because

I always liked to cover African American issues when I was working in the north end of Seattle. We've had so much more of a segregated school system in recent years so white and African American kids don't go to school with each other so much any more, and there were very few African Americans kids in my classes. It was 2000, the year the All Star Game was played in Seattle, and I happened to be a fan, and it was a year when the school had an arrangement with an artist who was coming to do some baseball related thing with every class toward the end of the year.

I didn't know much about the Negro baseball leagues but I did think that it could be an interesting topic to study. I am no expert at all in African American history and I could be mistaken on this, but my sensibility about African American history is that I don't like to teach where African American people are always the victims. I just feel that that's coming at it in a really powerless kind of way. One year we did a big focus on the Harlem Renaissance, which I think of as an enormously powerful, dignified, and wonderful era for black Americans and I thought the Negro Leagues would be interesting, especially during this year of heightened focus on baseball in Seattle. I had no idea that the history of the Negro Leagues essentially parallels *Plessy v. Ferguson* up to *Brown v. Board of Education*. It's almost the same timeline, and so it's basically a history of civil rights, or lack thereof from that same period, so it was kind of a different way to teach something.

I knew the kids would like baseball and I just felt like it would be a different window, something we hadn't done before but would cultivate some respect for people who had to do something that was difficult at the time they had to do it.

The clearer we are about the reasons we have chosen the particular direction for our expeditions or research tasks, the more able we are to focus the experience so that our students learn and experience what we have intended for them. We can shape the projects to include the content and skills we want our students to meet and master.

Strategies for gathering information

Researchers take their next step by locating information that has already been gathered and reported on by others, to see what those who have already walked that road have to say. Many questions posed by naïve researchers (naïve as in new to a field rather than unskilled or somehow lacking) have already been asked by others, and the researcher must first establish what is currently "known" about her question. As she locates existing information she may confirm her question as a valid and legitimate subject for further research, but she also might find that, through the work of others she now knows what she wants to know. At this point the researcher may well decide to shift to another topic, or to approach her initial topic from a new angle.

Once they have reviewed the current research on their topic and confirmed that they are moving forward, researchers now must identify where they might find information, and then strategize how to approach each potential source of information. How might they find articles or documents? How will they make contact with individuals who might know something of their topic, and how will they approach those individuals to make the best use of their time and gain as much information as possible? How will the researcher budget her time to get as much information as possible, given realistic constraints of time, resources, skills, equipment, and the size of the task? And what will she do with the growing pile of data she has gathered?

Evaluating the research, inch by inch and row by row

Researchers have to evaluate the research they gather, to determine whether it is reliable, whether it is useful, and whether it supports, contradicts, or offers new insights on the other research that has been gathered. There is usually more than one account or way of understanding any topic or issue, and it is the task of the researcher to develop a strategy for evaluating the data from each source on its own, and then to evaluate what has been found in total, from all sources, in order to make meaning from it.

The researcher's task is to evaluate each article he is reading, the interview he has just completed, the video clip he has just watched. He has to determine if it is accurate, if it is supported by evidence, if the writer/speaker knew enough to say what he or she has said, and whether there are significant viewpoints or data that have been omitted. The researcher must also understand what he is reading or hearing within the larger context of his question.

He then reminds himself of his original question and asks "What do I now know? What do I need to know? Are there voices that are dominating or absent? Are there things about which I still know nothing? Are there things that don't make sense? Are there contradictions, or pieces that don't yet fit? How can I find out what I still need to know?" The researcher then adjusts his research strategy, if needed, and continues.

I asked our experts to share some thoughts about how they make sense of what they have found. Many of the researchers talked about making meaning of conflicting data. Howard Zinn, noting first that his early discoveries of omissions in his own education led him to bring a "healthy" skepticism to what he was encountering, talked about how he approached making sense from multiple perspectives.

> It made me look even more carefully for information and for points of view that I did not know, and made me ask the question, "If I didn't know this about Columbus, what else don't I know about these incidents that I have learned about?" It just makes you dig deeper and farther afield, and to question why I hadn't been taught a more honest version of US history in school. That is a very important question, because it creates a suspicion, that certain things have been withheld, for ideological reasons, and makes you even more concerned about finding out the truth about a particular incident.

This initial caution also encouraged Dr. Zinn to think about whose voices he was not hearing, and to notice which voices were dominating, were over represented in the telling of US history. He then developed an approach to evaluating what he was and was not hearing.

> I think it's understanding that the accounts you get of any particular event are going to be told through a very subjective lens, and that you'll get different accounts. I think the best you can do is multiply the number of points of view, get as many different points of view as possible and sort of cross check and see where they corroborate one another. If you suspect Las Casas is developing an animus against Columbus, you know he might exaggerate what he is seeing, then you have to check him against other accounts. In fact, the best kind of check is against an account by somebody who has a different point of view, but which actually corroborates what

Las Casas is saying. Las Casas was saying, you know these Indians were not war-like, they were very gentle and they were very generous you might think, oh he's romanticizing, and then you read Columbus' diary and it says the same thing.

Understanding that, you try your best to understand, not simply accept blindly, any one account or any one point of view, but get enough information from enough different sources so you can sort through them and see where they either corroborate one another or contradict one another, and you have to make your own judgment.

And then I think it's important to be honest about what you find out. That is, when you are not sure of something to say you're not sure of something. You may not discard the information, like CBS wanted Dan Rather to discard the information about Bush and his record of service as a member of the national guard because it wasn't fully corroborated, but what would have made more sense was for Dan Rather to say, "This is what we found out about Bush but we're not absolutely sure about this piece of evidence or that piece of evidence..." And I think this point about honesty in disclosing your own bias and honesty in disclosing the inadequacy of what you have found is very important.

Lorraine McConaghy, historian at Seattle's Museum of History and Indus-try, notes that responsible historians begin their real interpretive work once their data has been collected, and they are very cautious about putting too much weight on any one source.

As you evaluate the data you've gathered you're beginning to look for meaning... to figure out what's really important, what's significant and what stories, what mean-ings can be pulled from it. That is the first act of doing history. It's interpretive. It has to tell us why it's important, what's significant about it.

Dr. McConaghy continues:

Historians make their arguments based on the preponderance of the best evidence. Preponderance means to me the heaviest weight of the best evidence. How do we qualify our evidence? This goes to the heart of being critical. If I have an oral his-tory interview, it may or may not be less reliable than a letter, than a piece of corre-spondence. It depends to a degree on the intent, the audience, and the bias of the primary source.

This is where you begin to get very cautious about erecting this huge edifice on a piece of evidence that may be in conflict with others. Where we'd like to believe this but there's this conflict. How are we to resolve that?

Historians have what they call the rule of three. And it's a very powerful and important rule when doing research. It holds that no argument can be successfully defended unless you have three separate pieces of primary material to support it... It keeps you from erecting this huge interpretation on a slender, perhaps flawed, bit of evidence. However, for under-studied, under-documented groups, people, neighbor-hoods, we might not be able to find three independent primary sources. I would en-courage teachers and researchers, even if they end up having to pitch it out the window, that there's reason why there's a rule and that when you bend it or break it you take a tremendous risk.

I understand about the limited time and perhaps needing a more limited goal when you're setting out. I would just suggest that it's important for kids to realize from the start that they need to learn to be skeptical in their approach. Not cynical, but skeptical. Skepticism is a healthy social studies attitude.

Jan Maher also worked with an immense array of data by weighing one against another. She did an extraordinary amount of reading about central Indiana in the middle of the twentieth century, interviewed family members who lived there and then, to match or compare their stories with what she was reading, and was able to take a trip through the Indiana region as the twentieth century became the twenty-first, which served as an additional check as to the accuracy of what she was building and creating in her novel.

I didn't want to get anything wrong in terms of historical research on the Klan, for example, but I also had memories of members of my family who told stories of watching Klan parades down the street that we lived on in Marion, Indiana, and being aware that the target of their hatred, in addition to black people in the 20s and early 30s in Indiana, was Catholics. My father's family was Catholic so I had family stories to check the emotional truth of the response to the Klan on the part of somebody who wasn't in it. My mother had similar memories that I heard directly from her.

So, one kind of cross-checking was against family stories, which of course are subjective, but then if what those family stories reveal is corroborated by scholarly research stories, when many families are talked to and many anecdotes are collected, then it becomes a sense that my family's experiences are somewhat representative, something I can bank on.

Ted Wright, talking about the process of bringing together various stories of the land and culture of the Tlingit in Southeast Alaska says:

Different people claim to be experts, and some people are more expert than others. I think it's the same way everywhere; whoever is putting it together kind of decides. And later they might be called to task for their interpretation or their views. One of the advantages to having this be a community process is that if you do too much of that, having it be your own view, how you interpret the various ethnographies or whatever, then you get in trouble, or somebody will call you on it or you'll be obviously too biased.

Some of it is self-evident; you cross check between what the European observers found, and what the elders remember, and what the stories and place names actually represent, so there's a lot of cross checking that goes on just by virtue of those comparative realities, both in the oral records and later in the written records.

The guiding mechanism for evaluating and compiling the data is, once again, your research question and your reasons for doing the work. Why have you done this research, what do you want to know, and what understanding can you come to based on what you have found? How does what you have found respond to your original question, what do you now know, and where does that leave you in response to your question? Is it still your question, or do you now have a different question that claims your attention?

Revising

It is most often useful for researchers to share their work in draft form with others, to get feedback and to determine that the message that they intend to communicate is actually communicated effectively. This step allows for reflection and for mid-course adjustments. It is important that the people approached for feedback have enough knowledge, caring, honesty, and tact to provide useful feedback that leaves the researcher both confident and wiser about the effectiveness of her work.

Some researchers/artists prefer not to share their work in mid-process, but most find it useful to employ an outside editor, to step back and view their work in a detached way in order to clearly see if it is functioning as they have intended.

Communicating

Researchers then must decide what to communicate about what has been found, the purpose for the communication, and the best way to do that. This may look like a traditional article or research report, but it also might take the form of a short story, a children's picture book, a play, painting, poem, documentary, musical composition, novel, movie or sculpture. It might become a photography exhibit, or a new wing on a house, or perhaps show up as a menu item at a restaurant. The key features in this area are the topic, the impact they wish to have on their intended audience, the researchers' own interests and skills, the resources they have at their disposal (time, money, skills, equipment, friends, etc.), and the message they want to convey. The writers, visual artists, film makers, historians, and educators I interviewed for this book offer us models of choices made by researchers to share the results of their research through diverse means. Roger Shimomura has the impact he wants to make in mind as he is creating his paintings.

Every time I started a new painting it was strictly an issue of how I was going to trigger those various sets of responses that I felt that I wanted in the work, to have different people respond in different ways, to paint under the knowledge that a lot of kinds of people are going to look at this work and have different experiences, and I wanted something there for all of them.

He talked more specifically about his intention to communicate content as well as compelling art with his second camp series.

I received a twenty-five thousand dollar award to do a series of paintings, and revisited my grandmother's diaries about her time in the internment camps during World War II. Having done that first series in 1980, the Japanese-looking paintings, I said that I wanted to revisit those diary entries again. This time I wanted to do a series of paintings that were more illustrative of the actual entries. And the reason for this was because this series was meant to be an educational experience for anyone that came to see the exhibition.

I knew that I was walking a sort of artistic tightrope, and that in some ways I was risking a sort of credibility that I think I had gained up to that point. Because the series that I did, the first diary series looked very Japanese, sort of eighteenth century wood block style, and it was easy for people to miss that point completely. The fact is that I think that most people who purchased those paintings did not want to know the story about the internment. They wanted to see those paintings as a decorative piece that they could put on their living rooms and it was fine with them if they never had to explain to their friends what inspired that work. And I knew this because out of the twenty- five paintings, I think there were only five people that asked for the diary entries that went with the paintings, and the rest took them without ever asking for them.

The last two or three paintings in the series had barbed wire fences in them and they actually asked me to paint out the barbed wire fence, that they would buy the paintings if they didn't have the fence in there. So, that was really interesting...

I can't say that it came as a surprise, but I do feel that in the end what I had done essentially was sort of plant a stink bomb in these various living rooms across the country, that sooner or later that issue was going to have to come to surface and the stench of the internment was going to win out in the end. So I was very aware of that as I was working on this new series I was going to be very direct,

There's a certain advantage of having something sit on the wall, and especially in a house, and to keep sending these sparks out for whoever may look at it. I've always said that, in trying to explain some of these issues to students, depending on who is standing in front of a particular painting, you have a circuitry that comes out of one end of the painting and through that viewer's head and out the other, and that circuitry just waits for a different head to come in and complete it.

Don Fels talks about his work as an artist, and his intention to share what he has discovered in provocative ways: For him, the art is not an end point, but a means to cause people to understand their world differently, or at least a means for having them consider that possibility.

> For me, the thing is just part of the conversation, the exchange of points of view, interest, ideas. I'm not particularly interested in the thing as a precious object. It's a vehicle....

The product

The researcher presents his product, in whatever format is appropriate and hopefully has the opportunity to both reflect on and gather data on its effectiveness. For several of the researchers featured in this book, their research product is not an end, but more often a means to stimulate further conversation, or to provoke others to re-examine what they thought they knew. The true products of extensive research are often additional questions and possible paths for their next exploration.

Some Notes and Cautions Related to Authentic Research

Inquiry, student-centered research is authentic in that it is carried out in pursuit of a real question and is carried out in a manner that approximates how it is done in the world. Ideally, it is also authentic because there is a real-world consequence to the research that is of importance to the researcher, and hopefully to others. Students ideally have the opportunity to share what they have learned with a "real" audience, be it another class, the PTA, the city council, family members, or their classmates. This public sharing both raises the stakes and provides a focus for the communication.

Managing time for this research journey is not simple. The best research experiences are as open-ended as possible and understood to be somewhat unpredictable since the researcher truly doesn't know what he or she will find. There may be dead ends and unexpected roadblocks or discoveries, which makes the process harder to fit into a predefined schedule, and this can be a challenge in a school setting. It's one of the reasons that some teachers choose safer, more predictable tasks for their students to take on, though it cheats students out of the learning that comes from engaging in the more complex experience. If a teacher decides to structure assignments to allow students to engage in authentic, open-ended research there are a few things to keep in mind:

- The student may or may not find the information he is looking for, or may require more time and additional strategies for finding that information. The teacher may need to play a larger role in supporting particular students or groups of students in organizing their research, or may need to step in and help students to define what would be a reasonable project for them to carry out, considering time, resources, and skill levels.

- The original questions may give way to other, more relevant, compelling, or realistic questions as the research continues. It gets better when students land on a question that matters to them, and they need support and "permission" to recognize and act on their changing appreciation for the questions they are asking.

- The researcher will begin with assumptions and whatever background knowledge he possesses, but his research must be focused on learning all that he can about his question, rather than to simply find evidence to support what he already "knows."

- There is no one, complete source for information, and a thorough search requires consulting several different kinds of sources.

- The most effective manner of reporting or sharing findings may only become evident after the research has been done. What the researcher decides to communicate about his or her research, and to whom, will have a strong bearing on the ways in which they chose to communicate.

- This kind of research takes patience, trial and error, and the ability to make connections and to see patterns. It takes practice, and paying attention.

- The results of her study may be disappointing to the student researcher, or seemingly complex and contradictory, with some data supporting one conclusion, other data another. This is actually a more realistic finding than the reductive, simplistic, black and white world many school texts and curricula present to students. The student may, because of the limits of time and resources, fall short of a full and complete understanding of their topic, again a realistic result for most of us. She will report honestly on what she has and has not found and come to realize that it is a topic she can continue to research for as long as she is compelled to do so.

Experts and Novices

It is useful to remember that there is a significant difference between experts and novices. Experts are practiced at their work, tend to see patterns and whole pictures quickly, and have the ability to make effective decisions relatively efficiently, based on their expertise, their experience, and their ability to chunk information according to significant ideas or concepts.

Our students are relative novices, which means they lack experience, subject matter expertise, and are more likely to get overwhelmed with information because they lack the knowledge and skills to organize it effectively. What this means is that we must support our students, offer them guidance and structure, and make sure the assignments are realistic for students learning both content and skills. The fact that our students are novices is not a reason to avoid inquiry research projects; it is the reason to introduce them to the research process. How can they become experts if they don't leave the novice starting line? We can be kind to them and to ourselves by offering appropriate tasks that are engaging, realistic, and of appropriate consequence. Students have to feel safe enough to take some risks, to make an effort to learn new skills, new behaviors, and that's best done in a supportive environment.

Sherrill, Robert. 1970. *Military Justice is to Justice as Military Music is to Music*. Harper and Row: New York

CHAPTER 5

Interviews with Teachers

The voices of those I interviewed are heard throughout this book and form its backbone. Their individual and collective wisdom inspire me, and I'm excited to share their thoughts with others. I have gathered significant excerpts from their interviews into this chapter. Their voices come from classrooms ranging from kindergarten through university, and their orientations are unique. It may seem odd to include the perspectives of those who work with young children in a book focused on secondary and university education, but their approaches to research and to children have much to offer educators at any level.

Steve Goldenberg: Kindergarten/First Grade

Steve Goldenberg, the first voice you will hear, works with five- and six- year olds in a private school outside of Seattle. He has taught there for close to thirty years and is a master at centering his curriculum around the students' interests, questions, and needs while also teaching the material he is required to teach. Steve gives his students periods of time during the week when their assignment is to "do something important." He has been a mentor and inspiration to me throughout my teaching career, and I'm still trying to do something important in my classroom.

Steve is talking about Ryan, one of his students:

Ryan, it very soon became clear, was an exceptionally bright kid, able to figure out lots of stuff about the world that most five- and six- year olds don't have a clue about. We always have a story writing time, a journal writing time, and at first he wanted to write a history of the whole world and the whole universe, and was having trouble finding the point for starting, so I gave him a little structure, which was to invent fictitious characters, but have them do real things that could happen, that his characters could do.

Ryan came up with three characters, Ed, Jake, and Randy who work at Microsoft, and they take vacations together. The first vacation that he wanted them to go on was in Montana. Ryan has a grandfather who lives in Montana, who he had visited and enjoyed visiting and he thought that Ed, Jake, and Randy would certainly enjoy that. Actually Ryan was more interested in the drive to Montana than he was in what they would do once they got there. He was very happy to find maps and find out what routes people could take to drive from Redmond to Montana. And then it became very clear that he wanted them to stay in a hotel. And he was very focused on making sure to have them stay on the highest floor of the tallest hotel in Montana.

So I asked him, 'How would Ed, Jake, and Randy know which hotel was the tallest?' and he said he didn't know, so we talked a bit about how people would find out those things. He took a trip up to the library at our school, which is often a place that we start these kinds of research projects, and, although our librarian is unbelievably great and we rarely stump her, this one we did stump her on. She called a librarian in Montana who did not get back to us right away, so we explored some other possibilities. He had never heard of a travel agent, he didn't really know about them, but he was fascinated by the idea of people who knew about places all over the world and might even know how many floors a hotel had.

We called one, in Billings, who at first was kind of skeptical, but then when she heard it was for a six- year old kid her entire affect changed. She actually didn't know which hotel was, in fact, the tallest but she made it her top priority to find it out and get back to us.

I think something happened for Ryan. This magical travel agent was very important to him. So then he started becoming more interested in just trying to find out obscure facts about things. He wanted to know all of the museums that they could have gone to, what hours they were open...

He went on to write a series of five books about Ed, Jake, and Randy, who always went together to different places. Ed, Jake, and Randy, in his books actually did a lot of research. In one book they decided to go to Mardi Gras. They looked in travel guides, and they asked people what it would be like and what people would be doing. And finally Ed, Jake, and Randy decided that they would make their own hats, and go to Mardi Gras, just to show off their hats, and then come back home.

D: Ryan is clearly an exceptional child.... But I know that a lot of what happens in your room is focused on what I would call research, about kids finding out about the world, dealing with their own questions. Could you talk a bit about what you are going for and how you set things up so that the kids can do their own research.

S: Once they really get that message that 'yes, in this classroom you really can pick anything you really want to learn about,' they all really want to do it. And even at that age, some kids are used to people saying that but not really doing it. So if you let them really do that then they almost all, to a person want to do it and want to do it passionately. I really do have to pry them away from the writing table and force them to go outside or have lunch or play a game or something. It's all new and fresh for them and they see their own ideas begin to take form and shape and becoming sufficiently complex and they get excited. It's very contagious...

D: What is it you want for them when you are setting your room up?

S: The most important thing is for them to know that their ideas really are important, and that I really do make their ideas be at the top of the agenda. Of course there are some things that need to be filled in that they might not encompass, but we'll be sure that it touches all the basic skills that need to be touched. There'll be some words and writing in there, there will be some things that need to be counted or added up, or categorized, sorted, and classified, and there will be some relation to the natural world, either the social sciences or science, but it really can be done from their point of view, and that should be a joyous, exciting thing to them.

D: What does it mean to back up the approach that truly values their interests and ideas? What does it mean to truly act in that way? What do you do?

S: I guess the most important thing is to really listen. I'm often surprised. You know, a kid starts to talk about *Star Wars*, really wants to learn about *Star Wars*, and I'm thinking, ok, he's just going to want to do the bang bang, shoot 'em up, big war thing, and then if I really listen I might find that what this kid is really interested in is concepts about home or relationships....

D: So your listening is to bring out what they are really interested in, and to support their looking at what interests them in the way they want to encounter it....

S: I really believe that's what motivates most people. If they're really going to be exceptional students it's because they're operating on their own ideas and their own thoughts and feeling that power.

D: You say you do have your own agenda. What kinds of things are on your list when you think about your agenda?

S: It's pretty much pro-social, meaning the use of feelings. It's not just a world of inanimate objects. Some of what they are studying really does relate to humans and to the experience of being human, and it's not just walled off into material. It's my personal value that that's a good thing for us humans to be doing...

D: You want them to learn more about relating to other people...

S: And about relating to themselves, knowing what their own feelings are. And sometimes that's a little difficult for kids, a little scary, and they might not come to that on their own, so some of those I tend to push up a little higher than they might tend to be in their natural place.

I try to incorporate diversity. I use every opportunity I can to get them to research things that are out of their known world and to learn about new things, about other people, other cultures. And I have a social justice, peace agenda that I somewhat shamelessly make sure emerges every year... it doesn't take much to get these kids excited about something so when someone mentions it I'll give it a little extra feedback and make sure it gets some play.

D: I remember from my time in your room, and still use it as my guiding light the idea that kids should have time to do something important.

S: Right.

D: But it's not enough to say, go do something important. These are five- and six- year olds. You have to provide the structure and support that allows them to do that successfully. So how do you provide that structure and support?

S: The current jargon that we use is called scaffolding. So, either way, the building is going to get built. The child is going to grow and learn and thrive. And as much as they can do on their own, fine. But sometimes there needs to be some external structure, some scaffolding, to help guide the process, and again, it's one of the things I try to be conscious of and don't confuse the scaffolding with the building itself. What I am doing with the child is assisting their growth, and the majority of that is an internal process, which I can affect.... I know for sure how to stop it, to stop their growth, to stop them from taking risks, to get them to be fearful and to close down.

D: How would you do that?

S: One way is you teach them dishonesty. You tell them that you really care about what they want to learn about and then you don't let them do it, and two, then you do it in a way that you as the teacher always hold the power and you judge them right, wrong, good, bad; there're hundreds of ways, they're so sensitive at that age. All that you really need to do is tell someone else in their earshot what a great job they did on something and that will belittle the child you didn't tell what a great job they did. I'm sure everyone can construct their own model of what poor teaching is.

D: How do you begin a unit of study?

S: I've been trained by the students over the years. Say we're going to learn about salmon. We'll have a meeting and I will say, 'Tell me what you know about salmon.'

And I will make sure that everybody, no matter what they say, feels good about their contributing to the group's knowledge. Really moving the focus from what do I know, meaning each individual child, to what do we know as a group? And always modeling something I don't know. Saying, 'Do the salmon always go to the same stream? I thought they did but I'm not sure. And I'm going to try and find out about that.' And hope they take the bait and can identify things they want to find out.

D: Do you actually do your own research while they are doing theirs?

S: Yes, I'll take a book or, more likely, I'll ask them if they would like to help me find out. And they live for a job. If I ask if anyone would like to go to the library and get a book on salmon they'll all want to go. The hard part is choosing one or two and making it clear that they'll get a turn later, not right now but they'll get a turn too. They live and die by the politics of scarcity...

That's mostly what the dance is. If they don't come up with the interesting question or idea then I will, but I try to give them enough space first, and I find that it happens over and over and over again if you leave enough space. For example, and this is a physical plane of leaving space, but in my room I have a science table. We call it the science table, but I purposely don't fill it up with stuff. I almost always leave some room on it so a kid can bring in something that they found, or are interested in, and put it on the science table. Once they start to do that with physical things, like they'll bring in a bird's nest or a shell and we'll see how we can learn about that, but then they start bringing in their thoughts. That's it in a nutshell; listen to the kids, find out what they really want to do, and help them to do it.

D: You have certain attitudes about who kids are and what education is about that have led you to the choices you have made. Can you talk about them at all? In order to operate in the way you do, you have to have some level of faith and trust in them.

S: Absolutely, I bank on the fact that every child, even the ones who are struggling, even the ones who are deeply suspicious, or the ones who have strong learning issues, that all of them have a passionate interest in something, and if I can only help them find it and give them the forum for them to play with it in the way it needs to be played, that it is going to be their play. It's going to be a skill they can take with them their whole lives.

D: You've been doing this a long time. Do you have a sense of what you are more confident at and skilled at? What have you learned to do better? You made a clear point that the kids have taught you a lot of what you know.

S: That's it, to really let myself be trained, and to do it a lot of times overtly, to do it with the kids. And to be really clear with them, you know, to say 'I'd really like to support what you're doing, and I'm not sure how best to do it.' I say, 'I'm going to try this.' I invite them to test things with me. 'What would happen if I tried this, how would that feel to you? Or, what would happen if you tried this?' And then they might ask me, 'Well, Steve, what would happen if you tried this?' So, being willing to be led as well as to lead is something that has taken me a long time to get comfortable with. The more you do it, the more you need to do it...for me it's the only thing that really works.

D: What do you want your students to carry with them when they leave your room?

S: More of themselves. I want them to have more of a sense of knowing what they know, and perhaps knowing what they might want to know, and try to go with at least some strategies that at least worked in this one particular class, in this one way, to have a reliable strength.

D: There are lots of tools around, and they can learn to use those tools to help them find out what they want to know.

S: Exactly. And really to focus on the process, to get genuine enjoyment from it, and success, to feel that you're good at something, so that it becomes a reliable strength, even when the chips are down. They can say to themselves, 'Even when I'm not feeling so great I can do this, I can decide what I'm interested in, and not just in an academic way, but can decide emotionally and socially what I'm interested in and have successful strategies.' And to get them to be aware that they're actually picking some of those strategies, which for most kids that age is headline news; they don't really experience the world that way, it's coming at them pretty darn fast.

D: For someone teaching research at middle and high school, how different is it to teach in this way?

S: Hopefully not that different at all. I think it's a harder job. The older the kids get, the more scars they have, the more demands they have. It's different when they're worried about what college they're going to get into, or what score they may get on a test. Following your bliss in eleventh grade is not something that many parents and teachers have an easy time doing. I would really hope that that same feeling is there, that feeling of excitement. I think it happens in fits and starts in high school, still, it happens perhaps in the drama club, in the arts studio, maybe even in the science class where there's a real recognition of intellectual thought and it gets really recognized and celebrated. I worry now that since we can't leave any child behind we can't give them any time to think about it.

I would love to see people who do it well on that level. It would teach me a lot. Which is, by the way how I learned to do most of this. By watching other people who do this and stealing as many of their ideas as I could.

D: So you were carrying out research yourself.

S: All the time. Absolutely.

D: What does it mean for you to be doing research? How do you approach research, and that includes in your own classroom?

S: I really believe, and this is probably one of my better delusions, I really believe that the children are training me at least as much as I am training them. They are experimenting with me, but as I mentioned before, in the ideal sense we go back and forth.

I can't help but always be on the lookout. It doesn't have to be a classroom. When I see a kid and I watch what they're doing I'm hoping to pick up some clue, something in their body language or in their eyes that tells me something that their words aren't saying, or if they are going to be articulate about it, listen to what they're saying. I certainly love watching other teachers in classrooms that know how to do the dance.

Often what I learn a tremendous amount about is what not to do. When I subbed for a year, when I was starting out, I think I learned a lot about what definitely not to do. You know how we had that discussion before about how we could stop kids from learning and shut them down and all that. That's how I really learned that there are some very serious rules in that regard. No matter how much you smile, no matter how many bright and shiny objects you offer to reward them, once you have crossed their little boundary they will never forgive you for it because you have broken their hearts. And their will.

D: The idea of leaving space... what does it take to leave space?

S: It takes some explaining... people might come in my room and it might not be set up like other rooms are, and those who are open to at least talking about it, I say to them come back in twenty minutes and see what the room looks like then, because that's what I'm really after.

D: And what will it look like? What will they see when they come back?

S: The kids will have begun to rearrange things the way they need them to be, and take the supplies they need and focus on the areas they need. I will certainly be adding to them but I will wait for them to make the move if they are willing to make that first move.

I would listen. They're going to come in; half of them will come in talking a mile a minute about the latest thing that's on their minds and the other half will come in absolutely stony silent and not wanting to talk to anybody or to do anything because no one actually asked them if they wanted to go to school today. They got dragged here against their will and they are deeply offended. They want to find some comfort thing, perhaps a friend, or me, or maybe their favorite color crayon to just go lose their grief in until they're ready. And the other half will be babbling almost incoherently in parallel, talking to each other about the thing that they've been dying to just say. So I will wait to see what's growing up out of there, and ideally it will sort itself out and weave its own little fabric and kids will start being attracted to something that calls to them at that moment. And I do set some things out....

D: But there are things you're supposed to teach!!!!

S: Words will be said, and some of those words will be so interesting that people will want to write them down. Pictures will be drawn and other people will want to know what they are so we'll have to think about what words to put on those pictures. Games will be played, and they'll have to figure out if you want to play by the rules, and if so, then what are those rules, and there will be games that involve counting things, things will be noticed, a bird will be flying past the window, a tree will be growing outside, the universe will be happening and we'll just have to investigate it. That will happen every day. I bank on the universe being there and it always provides.

D: Can you talk about the possibility of failure. One of the risks in allowing things to go where they go is that it won't work. It will not get to where you want it to go.

S: Ideally there is no failure on the child's part. If there is failure it's on my part, in not structuring a classroom in the way this child needs, or understanding that this classroom cannot fit the needs of this child. So, it might mean the child needs some support in something, or the family might need some support, but more often than not, it will be a failure on the classroom's part to really try everything that should be tried to really find that place where the kid can have that comfort level. I mean I bank on the fact that if they find their comfort level and if they are surrounded with support and nurturing, they are going to learn and it is going to satisfy everybody.

D: But when somebody tries something and it doesn't work, that's part of the learning process.

S: Absolutely. That's a happy accident, and a huge part of my job is to really make that ok. We talk a lot about scientists, and scientists change their guesses. The scientists who have trouble are the ones who can't change their guess. When they try something that they think is going to happen and it doesn't happen but they still want it to happen so much that they won't try something else or think about it a differently, those are the scientists who have trouble...

And there's a lot of opportunity to change your guess, or change your idea. That's what we thought and now we think something else and that's great. I give them a lot of praise for being willing to do that. I tell them overtly that a lot of times little kids can't do that because they always have to be right from the start, but you guys are old enough to know that when you come to that point of changing your mind so that you really are right, rather than telling someone you're right when you're wrong, because people are going to know.

D: How do you help them to evaluate what they find?

S: What I really do is help manage the dialogue around it. Some of it gets back to not doing the overt praise thing so they don't come to expect me to say 'You did a great job on that, good boy,' and then feel deprived when they don't get it. Also, in this classroom, people are encouraged to express their feelings and sometimes those feelings are critical of other people and what they're doing, so what we're doing is teaching everyone how to manage that in a way that works for everyone's feelings. That's hard because we all have our insecurities and sometimes we want our stuff to be better than someone else's, and sometimes it is and sometimes it's not. How we transact that is huge and it has to start as early as possible so they know it's safe. Otherwise, they're just not going to risk, and none of this works if they don't risk.

D: And risk means...

S: Try something even if you're not sure what you're doing and be willing to change your guess, or to do it over, or to learn something more.

D: It's certainly one of the hardest sells we have at the masters level is to say to students, 'Ask a real question, one you don't already know the answer to, and find out what you can. And it may not work, or lead to something useful, and that's ok.'

S: And to be absolutely honest, I like to stack the deck the first few times they make guesses so they're at least somewhat close to what they're going to find out when they do the experiment.

D: That's the structure, the scaffolding that leads them toward success.

S: It's manipulation; it's making them think that they thought about changing their guess when maybe I suggested it.

D: You're sneaky....

S: Absolutely. You have to be. And they're sneaky too. And that's why it works so well. We have a lot of mutual respect for each other because to be sneaky you have to be smart.

Don Fels: Artist and Early Childhood Teacher

Don Fels is an artist who spends a great deal of time researching our complex and interactive world and rendering it meaningful through installations, paintings, and other forms and formats. He talks about the research that he does in service to the art he creates, with particular reference to a public art installation he created along the banks of the Duwamish River, a river that was turned into an industrial waterway as it serviced the growth of Seattle.

Don Fels was also a teacher of young children for fifteen years before becoming a full-time artist, and he and I have co-taught masters classes in education. We also talked about the role that research plays in the lives of children, within and without the classroom.

DS: What is an artist? How do you describe yourself?

DF: My editor says that she tells people that I am intellectual. The trouble with that word is that it's way too pompous sounding, but I like that term because, in the real sense of it, an intellectual would be someone who works with ideas, and that's what I do. It's true that I do make art, and I do physically like to make things, but most of the work I do is not the physical making part. Most of it is the thinking up and researching and editing part.

DS: What does it mean to work with ideas? When you work with an idea, what are you doing? What are you looking for?

DF: I'm interested in what things mean. I'm interested in how things change in relation to each other and to people, and how people change in relationship to things. The word idea, the root word comes from the word "to see" in Greek. We look at the world and from it I think we get ideas. I'm really interested in looking at things. Whether it's looking at the physical world and rendering it into an art object or looking at something abstractly and trying to understand.

DS: So, to make it more concrete, to relate it to the Duwamish project, what were you looking at? What was the question?

DF: I had a commission to make art about a kind of dis-used portion of what was called an industrial waterway, whatever that means. Essentially it was a river that had been messed up by industrial use. Not by accident. They straightened it, they dredged it, they threw a lot of very bad stuff in it… and "they" was "us," of course. I don't want to make this sound like we're good guys and they're bad guys. These were the very companies that defined Seattle's success; Boeing, for example. Boeing was a prime abuser of this piece of water, with everyone's buy-in. Folks said "Fine, go for it, do what you need to do. Make airplanes, and move 'em down the river and get them out of here and sell them, for millions of dollars."

DS: And if the river actually has its own life, its shape and curves and current…

DF: Forget about it. Doesn't matter. What's important is industry. So then the city says to me, can you make art about this place? And originally the city's intention was to memorialize the good founders of Seattle. My interest was not to talk about good guys and bad guys, or to debunk the founders, but to say, 'Oh no, it's much more complicated than that.'

Ok, here's what's interesting. I was dealing with abstract ideas but I wanted them not to be abstract in their presentation. So, in order to get to that place one must do a lot of research, synthesize the research and present it in such a way that to the viewer or the visitor it seems concrete, even though what you start with is a very abstract notion.

In this case my abstract notion was that this river, which can stand for the environment in general, had been abused by the process of accruing wealth in a city. It goes on in every city all around the world. This was just a particular way that I could show this in action. So, I was sort of given this one section of the river to research and I set about to find out all the information I could, which involves all kinds of different ways.

DS: This is typical of the kinds of art projects you take on, where there is something in the physical world you are investigating, and you are investigating through the physical world to get at something much more abstract, or layered.

DF: In the beginning one doesn't know what one is going to find. I knew the end result was that the river had been messed up, but I didn't know what had happened at this particular site. I knew nothing about it, but I guessed that there would be something interesting there, because pretty much everywhere there's something interesting if you can get a handle on it. So, I started researching….

DS: When you research something, what are you doing? I don't assume everyone means the same thing when they use that term.

DF: I started looking. And by looking that meant I did a lot of reading in whatever I could find that talked about that particular place in a particular time. I looked at old newspapers, I looked at books that treated the general geographic area, and old maps, and then I talked to as many people as I could find who had some memory or knowledge of the place, and they would usually turn me to somebody else.

What you do, and this is true of all research, no matter what you are looking for, no matter what you are looking at, when you find one thing it sends you to another thing. So, if you find the name of a man, Mr. Thornburg, whose father used to live there, he will say to you, invariably, 'You should meet my friend Mr. Smith, because Mr. Smith grew up here and he would love to talk to you.' So, you make an appointment and talk with Mr. Smith and along with Mr. Smith comes Ms. Jones who also grew up here… it's always like that.

Part of the researcher's job is to make sure that the people you are talking to understand that you are genuinely interested and that it's not a trick. Once in a while people are afraid that you are going to make a fool of them somehow, so you have to disabuse them of that. You say, 'No, no, no, I'm just gathering information.'

DS: What is it you do that convinces somebody that you are really interested?

DF: In my case the most successful technique is to honestly say to them, 'I'm really interested in your story.' And I think every person I've ever met likes telling their story to somebody. Even people who feel badly about what happened want to talk about it. People are flattered that you are asking them for knowledge. And that should flatter them; it's something they know that they are giving to you. So, it's easy to get people to talk, you have to listen.

DS: But you come in prepared.

DF: Yes, you have to listen. As you do more research you start to realize there are certain questions that you want to have answered, or to get as close as you can. To use this place as an example, I found they made boats there. Well, what kind of boats, who made them, where did they go? What were they made out of, what did they look like? Those were things I wanted to know. I didn't start out having any interest in these boats. I didn't know there were any. I never saw them. They aren't there now, the place is empty.

Once I found there were boats there, I thought, 'Oh, they made wooden workboats here, nobody makes wooden workboats any more, that's kind of interesting, and a boat is a fairly interesting physical object, so maybe I could make art out of it.' Because since the city was commissioning me to make art, I had also to be thinking, 'Where can I get an end product out of this that will work in this situation?' Part of my job, my self defined job, was to find something that I could symbolically use that was concrete, real. So, I settled in my mind on using a boat, made big. We made it 5/8th scale; it's eighty feet long, and it's thirty feet up in the air. That's just sort of what ended up of evolving.

What I think is important to realize is that I didn't start out to build a boat on this site. I was looking for some way to re-present the site, to represent it. The boat seemed a good way to do that, because it was made there, because as it turns out, it was an amalgam in terms of its design among the immigrant people who settled in this area. There were groups of fisherpersons from the Scandinavian countries, mostly Norway, and there were fisherpersons from the southern Mediterranean countries like Italy, Greece, and Spain, and they all ended up on this site living because it was cheap and accessible to them and it was on the water.

No one had plans or anything for building boats that would work in this location; it was all in their heads. But they evolved a style of boat making that is shaped by where each group came from and the environment here. And presto, they had a new style. Some of the wooden boats that they built eighty years ago are still being used in the Bering Sea, in Alaska, one of the worst, environmentally difficult places to do anything, and they're still operating because they were so perfectly made for that environment. I found that interesting.

What was doubly interesting for me, and why I thought this was a good symbol, is the port of Seattle, which was paying me to do this work, threw all these people out. They knocked all their houses down, knocked all their boat-building places down, because they had development ideas of how they were going to do stuff, and in the end they couldn't do any of them.

And the story that I found fascinating was that you had this group of immigrant people, with no power but a lot of knowledge, creating something that was useful in the new world, which everybody applauded, which made money for a large number of people. It all seemed to be working so well, and then it was just knocked down because a larger entity had no interest in it. That's a subtext in what I was interested in displaying. And the boats were never used in the Duwamish because the river was already fished out, which is still another story.

So, conveniently to me, the boat was a way of telling several stories, interlocked together, that had a physical place, in Seattle, and a kind of intellectual and emotional place in a larger, broader discussion.

DS: I know that when we've talked before, part of your notion of what art is or does is that it causes people to be off balance...

DF: Having art help to make people off balance is something that most artists, in one way or another believe in. I think part of the function of art is to get people to experience their world more fully and you can't do that if you just present them with what they already know. They'll look at it, say thank you and walk on. So, you have to do something that gets people to see things differently. That is, if I'm looking intently at something I want to use my intent looking and thinking about it to cause someone else the possibility of looking at it in new ways. It's some kind of equation ... I put in x amount of hours, hundreds of hours, thousands of hours, looking and thinking about this situation, then I create something, make it, and then along comes someone else, and maybe they only spend ten minutes, maybe five minutes, maybe three minutes, but if it's working right, some part of what I've invested in this thing re-invests itself in them and they walk off with a little piece of it. I don't expect them to spend as much time on their end as I did, because hopefully, through the research and through whatever skills I have as an artist, I've condensed down all that energy that I've put into it, trying to decipher this equation so that they can walk away with a little bit of it.

DS: So the art is not the end point in a sense, it's really a part of a conversation.

DF: Exactly. For me, the thing is just part of the conversation, the exchange of points of view, interest, ideas. I'm not particularly interested in the thing as a precious object. It's a vehicle.

DS: You are, through your art, frequently presenting viewpoints that most people are not familiar with. You are actually giving voice to a lot of information. It's one of the things that I think about in relation to the students in our classrooms; it's one of the things I want our students to be doing. These school projects frequently involve their families, or places their families may have lived at one time, and often explore aspects of their communities and cultures. It often means finding out about things that are not well documented, not well represented in literature, not easily accessible. Can you talk a little bit about that?

DF: When you're telling me a story, I can hear the part where I go 'Huh, that's pretty interesting,' because, usually for me there is something that has more than one reading to it. It starts to open doors to other issues, other questions, other concerns. Once that's happened enough times, you start trusting your instinct for finding those things, like hunting in the woods, you know, you're taking a trail and you don't take this trail, you take that trail. Why? Because you've learned something about following a trail. So that's one thing that I've learned to do.

DS: So the goal of your research is to find something that gets your "huh" going?

DF: Right, because there is no thing out there. There's everything out there. I mean, it's important to say again, this site was not given to me because it was especially valuable for information; it's just a place on a deserted river. The fact that it turns out to have all this interesting information is the same as if you went anywhere else, but if you look there is information that is interesting everywhere. You just have to look, and you have to find a way to make it visible.

The other part of the art is distilling from what are probably complicated, long-winded stories the part of it that you can do something with. Because most people have their own stories like that, they might not find it very interesting. But there might be a nugget in there, one part of it that might be useful, and so you have to learn to squeeze it down, and that's something kids can learn to do. It involves a lot of editing. Editing becomes a big important issue here, where you chop away at the stuff that isn't the essential stuff.

DS: Then you have to offer your viewers or listeners enough clues to understand the story you are telling. When you strip away the context they may not be able to "hear" what you are saying.

DF: For example, this place where the art is, is not even really a park. It's just a kind of green place where people come and have lunch. They are mostly workers around the area. They're not going to an art museum, they're not going to a history museum, they're not reading a book. They're just going to have a picnic. So my job was to snag them. How can I get them interested enough? So, maybe the fact that there's an eighty-foot boat thirty feet up in the air might seem strange enough that they might be curious. My thinking was, if they were curious and came to stand underneath and look up, they would notice there were these panels I made to tell the story. And, if I got them this far, maybe they'll read some of it. If they read some of it, then they'll know some of the story. So I had to think through the delivery of it, and that's part of the art. And kids have to do the same thing. If they do research they find out information, then they have to figure out what they're going to do with it. I mean just typing it into a report and handing it to a teacher is kind of boring. But if they can make something out of it that might engage people in a way they didn't expect, that could be the opposite of boring.

DS: You didn't know what you would find, or when you would find it. And you didn't know how you would communicate what you found. That's a challenge in a school setting.

DF: The end point is where you decide it is. And that's a big problem with schools and kids. They've been told over and over again that there is an answer, and what there really is, is a question. There are lots of questions. There isn't an answer, or not necessarily the one you were looking for.

DS: So there has to be room in the structure of the assignment for whatever happens to happen, and for that to be ok.

DF: That's a big issue for some teachers. Some teachers do not like the expandability of that. No one really knows what they are going to find. There's always something there. There's no shortage of information. There's a shortage of interesting questions, but there's no shortage of information.

DS: You taught a long time with little kids, and have taught with all ages up through adults. When you are helping somebody learn how to do this work, what is most useful in helping them? It's not so easy, because frequently you are asking kids to behave in ways that they have been taught away from behaving in this way.

DF: I guess I have some kind of internal interest meter. As long as it keeps moving then I know I'm on the right track. When I start to lose interest in it, then I know I've strayed. And it's not that I'm everyman, it's not that I say if it interests me it'll interest everybody. But it's a lot of work to do research, and if it isn't interesting to you, you won't keep it up.

If I have an interest meter inside of me, so does every kid. And when I taught young children, it was really close to the surface. They were four, five and six. And that was part of why I so enjoyed that age. Because their little interest meter was right there, right there, and right smack there. Maybe buried about one sixteenth of an inch. I just let them know that I was excited that they were excited. And as soon as they were interested in something we would head off to try to look into it. Now when I taught with the young kids, we used the library a lot. The school had a library, and as I have learned many times since, the librarian was thrilled that people wanted to use the library. So, my standard thing in the classroom when a kid would come up to me and say, I'm really interested in this but I don't know... they'd ask me a question, and I'd say, let's go to the library, or, you go to the library. And the librarian would help us, or help them to find a book that would start to answer some of those questions. And just like me interviewing people about the river place, one book would lead to another book, and then another book. And maybe we'd find that there were three or four kids in the class who were interested in this, or five or six, or ten, and then maybe we'd read the book together. So, all we did was just follow our interests. And there is no shortage of kids' interests, so there was no shortage of material...

For teachers who are thinking about planning for this...I just planned that the kids would tell me where we were going. All I had to do was to leave a certain amount of blank time in the day where we would have the opportunity to do that looking. I would try to augment it by bringing in some stuff that seemed like it would carry our discussion forward. But usually when we were doing this there wasn't any endpoint, we weren't going anywhere particularly, nor were we even necessarily going to make something. We were just exploring. If the interest kept up, and if there were enough kids with some kind of related interest, we might all do a project together. Maybe we'd build something. Maybe we'd make a play about it. Maybe we'd go to the dress-up area and pretend something. There were all kinds of things we could do. There was never a shortage of possibilities.

DS: The goal was to be interested in things and to follow the interests.

DF: Yeah, a fun goal. And some people say I could do that because I was working with young kids and didn't have to meet learning goals. Well, that's baloney. It has nothing to do with age. We were learning to read, and write, to do number stuff, develop social relations, but we did all those things around these escapades of ours, these explorations.

DS: That seems to me such a crucial point. When we taught our masters students [Don and I taught a research sequence for several years in a master's in education program] it wasn't any different. Our approach was to ask, what are you interested in? There are some things you need to learn about the process of research; why not practice them on something you really want to know about?

DF: It seems so obvious I'm really baffled by why everyone fights it so much. If students are learning to carry out research, what difference does it make?

DS: And the line we used often in the class was, if you know where you are going, it's not really research.

DF: And it's not that interesting. If the kids already know the answers, they don't ask the questions.

DS: One of the issues for teachers is that individual interests take different amounts of time and it is a logistics challenge. How do you manage kids going in 28, or 128 different directions?

DF: That's a skill that teachers can learn. There are all kinds of tricks; some kids can help other kids, kids who have already finished the research part can start making something, or they can do class work, or read a book, or another task. I mean, there are ways to manage that; it doesn't take a lot of experience to learn how to do that. It's true that it's different than saying, now boys and girls, everybody turn to page seven. Certainly you are in complete control then. But, how many people are really paying attention to page seven? Two of the thirty kids in the class?

DS: Which comes back to the question, what are you doing as a teacher? What is your intention? If it is to be in control, that leads to one set of choices or decisions. If it is to stimulate kids to learn how to learn, to follow their interests and excitements and to learn to gain the skills to be lifelong learners, that leads to other choices. Learning the skills to learn about the world, and following your interests are obviously not mutually exclusive.

DF: No, in fact, the opposite is true. It's all so logical it's almost embarrassing to have to lay it out, but of course if you go to the library at age five and the librarian shows you a picture book about something you're really fascinated by, you want to get that information. It turns out that one of the ways you get information from books is reading them. So here I was, dealing with kids, most of whom couldn't read. They had a huge incentive to learn to read when it was about something they were interested in. It is not rocket science. It's pretty straightforward. They wanted to read because they wanted to decode that information because it was important to them.

I never had to force kids to learn to read. They learned to read because they wanted to. Not because I was offering them candy, to pay them to learn to read; it was exciting to them. I think this is basically genetic. I think there is a need and a desire to learn that is programmed into our brain, because if you don't learn you die. It's a survival technique. And it's incredibly strong in kids.

All you have to do with kids is to offer them a chance to learn and they naturally thrive because they are programmed to naturally thrive. That's how the human species has advanced. They want to learn. It's just that they may not want to learn what somebody else thinks is what they need to learn.

DS: This is important. One argument against letting students do what they want is that if it is up to them they will be lazy and do nothing. And that's so wrong. Kids don't want to be bored. They want to be involved and challenged and interested.

DF: If you let children do what is essential to them they will put in enormous amounts of work, because it's generated from inside. That's completely different than requiring them to do something because you've decided. It's a question of physics. There's less friction when they are doing something they want to do.

Of course you have to help them over the hard parts, because kids, as you said earlier, come with all sorts of different skills and abilities, and some kid may want to do something with her heart that she really isn't yet able to do. So you have to help her to scale it back a bit so she isn't frustrated. Maybe she wants to learn about the Cascade Mountain Range but she doesn't have the ability to understand the geology. So, you have to pull back a bit and say, maybe we can look at the dirt or the woods outside of the classroom and look at that first. So, you don't discourage her from her research, but you encourage something that has a possibility of success.

DF: There's a piece we haven't mentioned that out to be mentioned. If you use this kind of process of letting the kids follow their interests, at least for a certain part of the day, beside the pleasure that it gives to any individual child to follow his or her nose, you also introduce this plethora of information that the kids are bringing to each other. So, if Rebecca is interested in Ecuador and does a whole thing because her Uncle Fred once went there and brought her back a doll and it fascinated her, the kids suddenly have information about Ecuador. It wasn't on my agenda to talk about Ecuador right now, but the kids are fascinated. Where is Ecuador? Ok, so we have to get the maps out. Oh, well, who lives there? Why do they live there and not here? How did they get there? All kinds of other broad questions get dragged into the classroom because Rebecca's uncle went to Ecuador and she still remembers it. You couldn't have predicted that, and it's not like Ecuador is on a list of things we are supposed to study. But it obviously brings into the classroom a whole group of things that we are supposed to be studying about how the world works. There's just a richness to the process that is quite wonderful. The only unpredictability is the actual thing, but it's very predictable that the kids will bring in way more stuff than you could ever cover in ten years.

DS: If students are following their interests in various ways, how can you assess their work?

DF: You have to use all kinds of skills in order to find, and notate, and present this information. They're either doing it or they're not. And if they are having trouble with a particular part of that, that's a clue to you that they're having a particular problem. If Rebecca wants to read about Ecuador and she's in the fourth grade and can't read a book about Ecuador at that grade level, you know she has a reading problem, because she really wants to know about Ecuador. The motivation is there, one hundred percent. She wants to read this book, and it's a book that should be readable by a student her age, so you know something's wrong. So you have the ability there to start seeing that she has a bit of a reading lag, and you can begin to work on that. And you can say that to Rebecca. I know that you want to read that book and it seems like it's a little difficult. Let's see what we can learn to fix some of that problem. Rebecca is going to want to do that because she wants to get on with reading the book.

Whereas some of the other stuff that happens in regular school, motivation becomes an issue. Does she struggle with reading it because she is struggling, or is it because she doesn't really want to read it? Sometimes that's not totally known.

I miss teaching. I don't teach now because I don't have time, but I miss the interplay with the kids, I really enjoyed that. It was really stimulating to me. That's something else I should say. When you are following the true interests of kids, it's a net physical, intellectual, and emotional gain for the teacher. I went home tired, because I was concentrating a lot, but never depleted. I always got more from them than I gave them, because there was always so much going on, there was so much raw enthusiasm that they would generate. It would buoy me. It was tiring sometimes.

DS: Well, teaching is tiring no matter what. I would often think about how tired I was when things were going well, and think, how draining would this be if it weren't going well, or if I didn't love this?

DF: Watching the clock, waiting for it to get to three. But I know I got enormously more from the experience than I ever gave them.....

Libby Sinclair: 4th /5th Grade Teacher

Libby Sinclair has taught fourth and fifth grade in the Seattle School District for fifteen years. She worked in an alternative program in North Seattle for most of that time, and this interview primarily focuses on a project she did in that school. Libby has recently moved to work in a much more racially and economically diverse school in South Seattle.

D: Why is it important to have students research in depth and to take time to get to know their topics well?

L: First, I would say that once the kids get truly involved in working, once they have questions and search out answers, it becomes their own. The students I am working with this year are not particularly knowledgeable about the natural world, but they've become passionate about the individual creatures they've learned about, because their research has led them into new topics, and they are the experts. Nobody else knows as much as each individual child does about whatever subject they are studying. The whole idea of students becoming experts is part of it, and when you have questions and wonder about something, and then seek an answer and find it there's something extremely satisfying about that. It's like digging a potato out of a hill, you know, 'Whoa, found them!'

D: Can you talk about the Negro League Project you did with your fourth/fifth graders. How did it come to be and how did you go about doing it?

L: I chose to study the Negro Baseball League because I always liked to cover African American issues when I was working in the north end of Seattle. We've had so much more of a segregated school system in recent years so white and African American kids don't go to school with each other so much any more, and there were very few African Americans kids in my classes. It was 2000, the year the All Star Game was played in Seattle, and I happened to be a fan, and it was a year when the school had an arrangement with an artist, who was coming to do some baseball-related thing with every class toward the end of the year.

I didn't know much about the Negro baseball leagues but I did think that it could be an interesting topic to study. I am no expert at all in African American history and I could be mistaken on this, but my sensibility about African American history is that I don't like to teach where African American people are always the victims. I just feel that that's coming at it in a really powerless kind of way. One year we did a big focus on the Harlem Renaissance, which I think of as an enormously powerful, dignified, and wonderful era for black Americans and I thought the Negro Leagues would be interesting, especially during this year of heightened focus on baseball in Seattle. I had no idea that the history of the Negro Leagues essentially parallels *Plessy v. Ferguson* up to *Brown v. Board of Education*. It's almost the same timeline, and so it's basically a history of civil rights, or lack thereof from that same period, so it was kind of a different way to teach something.

I knew the kids would like baseball and I just felt like it would be a different window, something we hadn't done before but would cultivate some respect for people who had to do something that was difficult at the time they had to do it.

D: What did you want the kids to get, to experience, to learn?

L: Well, there's the content itself and then there was the process. I think the process is important no matter what the content. I start with generating questions about the topic, to see what we know, what we think we know, and what we want to know. I asked, 'Has anyone ever heard of the Negro Baseball League?' No, nobody. So we started listing every question they could think of. We distilled the our list down to about five or six main guiding questions, with all those little questions on the side, going every which way, and we left room on that same piece of paper to add questions that might come up, and we talked about how we might begin to learn about this.

I actually did a little assessment, I asked, 'What do you know about the Civil War, what do you know about slavery, about Reconstruction?' They were fourth and fifth graders and students this age typically don't know a lot about history, but they literally did not know anything about slavery. I was appalled by that, so I decided that before we got too far into it, perhaps we needed to go back a little bit to provide some historical context, so we literally did a survey course, really fast, just like blip, blip, blip, nothing big. Then I read them a couple of novels that deal with race relations, slavery, and African American history, which I think is a better way for them to get into it, to get a feel for the times and the attitudes and discrimination. I had to show the prejudice of the times because if they didn't understand the prejudice I don't see how they could have understood why there was a separate baseball league. I read the novels while we did some other setup activities, in the beginning.

Then they started doing their research, but by this time they knew something about slavery, they knew something about how white people felt about black people during that period. We looked at Reconstruction, at the Klan and other hate groups, just enough so that they knew that things were tough.

I also got in touch with Gary Thomsen, a fabulous high school teacher at Chief Sealth [please see his interview in this chapter, starting on page 99]. He's wonderful, and he had his kids do the most fabulous project and research on players and really important issues. I called him and said we really need to see what you and your students are doing. We took our kids over there and had the high school kids present their work to the fourth graders and it was so exciting, it got them very jazzed about it. That's how we started the actual research.

D: What happened when you visited with Gary and his students at Sealth?

L: Gary told them the story of how he and his students had actually traveled across country on bicycles, simulating a barnstorming trip. They'd gone to all the same places the Negro League players had gone, washed their uniforms by hand, experienced some of the same racism because little towns thought these were black players coming though the students were actually white, but people were prepared for black players and had all sorts of negative expectations. So now that we'd listened to their story of how they had done that we were really impressed. We had also listened to what these neat high school students were telling about the men who played these games, and they had to ride buses, and couldn't eat in the same restaurants and had to sleep in the buses all night. The kids' reaction was huge; they had never heard these stories. And just kind of getting a taste of what the older kids had done was inspiring.

I don't think they had caught any particular names, but when we came back I had put twenty or thirty players' names up on the wall and I said, pick somebody, like Cool Papa Bell, who became one of our favorites, and start doing research. I had hit every library in town and brought a lot of books so the kids had plenty of material.

D: Was the Ken Burns series out yet?

L: Yes, and we used that a lot. *Shadow Ball* is the fifth inning, or episode, and there's another video called something like, *The Sun Never Sets on the Negro Leagues*, from the Negro League Baseball Museum, and there's a commercial film called *Bingo Long's Traveling All Stars*, and it's only slightly inappropriate. It was really a good one to show how clever the African American ballplayers had to be. They would clown around, and sometimes have to decide to lose a game on purpose so they wouldn't get shot. Or they'd win and get out of Dodge real fast. The movie was good at clearly showing the danger involved for the players.

Once they had done reading, and reading and reading and reading and began to know something about their guys, then I would show some of these things.

And they were just thrilled, because they had read that Satchel Paige had a huge foot, and when he pitched he would put his shoe up really high, and throw people off. When they could see actual footage of the real person they were really excited. And what I always have done with kids is to get every book I could possibly get and then have them read, read, read. The kids would put sticky notes on the pages that had something they would want to come back to, put their names on the notes. They kept track of what was most useful, and shared with each other. I really talked up collaboration a lot. We talk about a community of learners, and I bet that's true right now with the animal research my current students are doing, that if they know a classmate is studying such and such, they'll make sure to share anything they find about that topic with her. I love to watch the kids rush across the room to share something with a classmate. That's the kind of feeling I love to have in the room and I think research promotes that. When you have your topic but you know what everybody else is doing, and then you begin to feel excited for the other person too, it's really wonderful. I think, for me as a teacher, that's the way the room sounds best in the world is to hear that excited hum and somebody's gone over there to share with somebody else. It's what learning sounds like, and the pleasure of learning something.

They read and then I provided them with scaffolding, basically headings. Fifth grade is sort of where paragraphs make sense; paragraphs don't always make sense in fourth grade so I've used headings. They gathered information and wrote about early childhood, their baseball history, their personal adult lives, and interesting facts. They had a whole book of baseball nicknames that were just hysterical. Funny stories. The way we set it up, the kids did a lot of popup books and artwork. We did the research, got it all edited, got it all finished and then I created folding panel books made out of this stiff paper, and they transferred their research onto these books. We had fun making things fold and move and turn. They were really works of art when they got done; they were quite beautiful. Then they did oral presentations to the rest of the class and by the time we were done everybody knew about all the baseball players, and even though they each only did one, they all knew about all of them.

We had this correspondence with Buck O'Neill, at the Negro League Baseball Museum, who just recently passed away. The kids had been so enthusiastic about these tee shirts, because the Sealth kids in Gary Thomsen's class had made tee shirts to help fund their trip, so my kids had to make tee shirts too. They researched all the different team names, and they did art work. Each drew a really cool image from a team, and then we transferred those images onto shirts. They sold these tee shirts, as a service; we raised five hundred dollars, and we made a gift of that, plus four tee shirts to the gentleman we've been corresponding with at the museum, and that was a pretty exciting, really exciting thing. Buck O'Neill sent us a poster, signed. It was very special.

You asked me what I wanted the kids to get out of the expedition. I wanted them to learn to do research that was very authentic; I didn't want them to copy anything. I wanted them to read until they understood, and then write it in their own words from their understanding. It took a long time and I think they really did that. You know the synthesizing of information is really hard for young kids. I think that until you've read the same fact over and over again in several different sources everything's new, but then you can say I already know that, and then you can take it and turn it around. I think it works like that.

But what I didn't know and what I'm really pleased with is that the kids came out with is these ball players are their heroes. These ball players are the heroes for a whole generation of African American young people and families, and I never knew that my students would come out of this experience with these men as their heroes as well. They just thought the players were the most wonderful guys, and they particularly appreciated the hardships they experienced. They admired them for having suffered, really, but they more admired them for somehow having stuck it out and playing that game in spite of everything They came out with some black heroes, which is not always the case for middle-class white kids, and I think it was the historical perspective, the knowledge, and the admiration that were all really nice for them to have.

We had a couple of gentlemen who came in to class who had actually attended Negro League ball games. One was the principal of another school in Seattle, and he remembered growing up in Meridian, Mississippi, and how important the Negro Leagues were. We had learned "Lift Every Voice and Sing" before he came in, but then we found out from our guest that it was sung before all the Negro League games, so they knew the song but they didn't know it had that role as well.

There was another novel I read to the kids, about a custodian who had been a Negro League player too. *Searching for Buck McHenry*. That was a cool story. Reading all those gave the kids a background, and when the principal came in and talked about having been at the games they were on the edge of their chairs. 'You were there?!!!!'

D: What did you want them to get, and also how did you think through both content and process?

L: Respect for the African American experience. I think for white kids, I just think that we are so unaware as white people of what the black experience has been. So, to me it's just a different window. But when you admire someone and then you see someone you admire be treated with disrespect, I think when you can feel it then that whole understanding of racism is easier to understand because there is some pain in it for you. You can "know" the dates, or the "names," but you don't care unless you feel it.

We really did have a wonderful year. It seems to me we did something with the whole notion of *Plessy v. Ferguson*, the whole thing right up to the fifties. In the fifties, when the Negro Leagues still existed and then they didn't. The whole question of whether it was a good thing or a bad thing that the Negro Leagues basically came to an end was a hard one. The kids thought they were so wonderful and they weren't quite in touch with the fact that they only existed because of discrimination. So, something that they'd come to respect and be excited about, they had their teams they loved and their guys they loved. All "their" guys couldn't go in the majors, and didn't go in the majors and the whole thing fell apart, but it was because doors were opening. So there was a little sadness on their part but it was a great conversation to have.

The other thing it led us to was the question "What do you do when you know something is not right?" There was a book out called *Great African American History*, and it was one of the many books I had for the kids to use for their information, and there was nothing on the Negro Leagues at all. And the kids were just speechless. How could this be a book about *Great African American History* without anything about the Negro Leagues? I said, I wonder if the author didn't understand how important this particular part of African American history was, or perhaps he had some stereotype about athletes, or who knows what. We decided that perhaps the author didn't get it, so we did a huge persuasive letter writing deal. We found the name of the author's agent at the publishing house and they did all their writing practice, first draft, second draft, third draft, and all that, and wrote very eloquent letters explaining why the Negro Leagues should be in the book, using details from their own work. We wrote letters and sent them off to the publisher. The sad thing was the letters came back. I re-contacted the publisher and sent them again, didn't get an answer for the longest time. We finally got some sort of letter saying "the author's unavailable...." It sounded like the author was not in such good shape, maybe ill. So I had to unfortunately say to the kids, you know you did what you could, and that's what we could do. I said, you made the effort, and maybe this time it won't work but the next time it will. So, there was kind of a lesson in that too. And the letter writing practice was excellent; the kids were quite passionate because they knew something, and it could have had the possible effect of influencing another version of that book. This time maybe it didn't, but another time maybe it would. I like that it had the potential for them to make a real impact on a real subject in the world.

D: How long did project take?

L: You know it lasted a while, but there were lots of other things happening. I reserved time; reading the novels out loud were sort of pre-project. We started the reading for research probably in October, and they spent about three weeks just reading. We would take an hour plus every day, browse the books, because they are looking at the pictures, too, but they were sharing with each other. Then we worked on the tee shirts and all that by the end of fall. So I think we did the majority of the research in the fall. The letter writing we did in the winter. Bits and pieces of it lasted most of the first half of the year. We shifted gears towards the end and looked at modern baseball. We ended the year doing Macbeth, a play in nine innings. It was so great. Did you know that the Macbeths have been beating the McDuffs for four hundred years? We had a ball with it. We had broadcasters calling the play, we had fun with it. It had all these baseball elements that were, by then just pure fun. It started out in this more serious vein, and I'd say that it lasted till February.

D: The kinds of concerns that people raise with this kind of teaching.... Some of the concerns have to do with time, and how much we are supposed to cover, and some have to do with the notion of integrating a curriculum around themes. Can you talk a little bit about how that works for you?

L: Actually, you know I'd have to say that, particularly in my current teaching situation, I'm aware that one of the things that people might be used to that I did not have to get used to at my former school is the constant assessment, constant assessment, constant assessment of small, really focused skills. So that when you do a project like this, one of the difficult things is to prove to people that there are skills being developed. I just don't always have the sheet of paper that I can hand to someone that shows how that is assessed. The assessments are every two weeks where I am now; it's just constant assessment.

D: Could you just talk about the kinds of skills and kinds of learning that your students are doing in this kind of project...

L: Reading through the material on somebody in a number of sources and figuring out what's important that you want to come back to is a reading skill. What meets the criteria for our paper? We're looking for this category, and that category, and that category. Reading skills for nonfiction, really learning how to read nonfiction and learning how to find out what it is that's actually useful and important. That's a big one in terms of our reading goals, for example.

To be able to write coherently, and to learn the skills of crafting your writing so that it's interesting, so that it's edited and so that it's complete. I think research writing is really interesting for kids because it's concrete. This is one of the things I've found; research is much more interesting for boys than a lot of the writing we do, like narrative writing and personal writing and things like that. Almost all the kids, but I notice particularly the boys who are the reluctant writers, it really gets kids writing, and they learn to write coherent paragraphs with topic sentences, and they develop the ability to organize their writing so that things that go together, those are writing skills that are easy to see in research.

When we do these service projects, I don't know if there's an assessment for any of that, but I would say, developing character qualities, thinking about the kind of people we hope we're producing, thinking not only about what they know but who they are, really being able to have kids write about what a stereotype is and how they know. Most kids have experienced it, because they're kids. People don't wait on them first, they wait on the adult behind them, and I would ask them, what is the stereotype there and they say, they think kids don't have any money. Or they think kids aren't really important, or they think kids aren't really shoppers, or whatever. Kids are pretty easily able to identify stereotypes, and to write about them. Something like that is also valuable I think to really develop sensitivities that they can also write cogently about their own experiences. The social action piece, seeing something that isn't right and asking, 'What can I do as a concerned citizen?' One thing I can do is write a compelling letter and try to persuade someone that their point of view can be changed over to mine. And how do you do that? You have to use tact, you have to use courtesy, up to a point, and you have to use facts. Those are such valuable life skills. We used to have to do persuasive writing in the fourth and fifth grade, but apparently that's for older grades now, but persuasive writing is really exciting kind of writing.

We did a lot of money management when the kids managed the tee shirts. They made them, they sold them, they did a lot of art work, they designed them, and they did a lot of research on those teams, on what those teams' names were and what their logos should look like. They didn't look like the traditional ones; they made up their own. They helped advertise and sell the shirts, kept track of the funds; it was complicated.

Those would be the main things. I think we did what we were supposed to doing, and more. We did the things we would need to do in any writing activity, all the writing, the editing, all the conventions and everything else, it was all in there.

D: And the development of a learning community that you talked about before.

L: Yes, that was pretty special. I think the other thing there's not a test for is the whole idea that learning can really be a passionate experience; that you can love to learn. I don't know why, but many of the people who would have you assess things never would include joyful reading or "loves" to learn. I think that that is such a motivator for reluctant learners, to be interested in what you are studying and to be curious about it. It's a huge help, to help you persevere with something. That love of learning is really a powerful piece of it.

And you know the social studies stuff that we rarely seem to have time to teach any more, it's built into something like this. The research is a study of our culture, and our society, and our history. We made a timeline, we did pull out a timeline of some of these things as the kids read about them, when slavery started, and when some of the things we read about happened, we put them on a timeline just to put it all in place. They were really looking at how our culture evolved historically and socially.

D: Learning in context is definitely part of what students are supposed to be learning.

L: Here's another thing, I know that there are a lot of attitudes that are shaped by the end of fifth grade and sixth grade, and I think the reason I like teaching this grade level is you can still help shape kids' attitudes around things like race, and around things that are value laden. So this kind of a study seems as important as some of the other things they could be doing because it helps shape their attitudes a little bit, toward African American people and toward our history.

And I think it's really important that the kids get excited about something. Emergent curriculum can get really messy, but the kids came back from Gary Thomsen's class saying, we've got to do tee shirts. And then we found out about the Negro League Museum and used that as a resource, and used that as a service project. I didn't know there was such a thing. We discovered it. So I guess in a way a thing that has always been a pleasure for me is that I've always felt that I was doing a research project for myself, my own learning. I learn as much as the kids every year if not more. And I think that's what's kept it interesting, to be able to learn on your own.

D: It has to have an impact on teachers.

L: And then I'm just like the kids, because they're excited to discover things, you're always aware of something or other that somebody's going to enjoy. And you might see it somewhere along the way, or discover it. You become really wrapped up in it yourself and you really care about it, to the point where looking for a map in a bookstore is not work, it's more like, ooh, I wonder what I can find, because it's fun now.

L: I was at a parent meeting a couple of weeks ago, and one parent commented on the current research project, which is somewhat similar to the Negro League project. She said, 'You know, I just want to tell you that this is the most wonderful project because my son gets home at night and he gets on the computer, and I just want to tell you if I hear one more thing about river otters I'm going to scream....' But she said, 'I'm so excited that he can take this as far as he wants to.' And I think that's the difference. There are a lot of projects where you have an end product where we can all look at and say, that's what it should look like, and then you have projects where a child will take it as far as that child can take it. My ideal project requires a minimum for every body and then there's an open-endedness to it, so a child like this can go as far as he or she is able to go.

What's so fun is I think that every body in our group generally has a decent piece of work, and some kids can just go as high as the sky.

D: I remember hearing or reading, and I don't remember who said or wrote it, that kids rarely get to experience excellence, to experience what excellence looks like, in school. The whole idea of knowing what it means to do something incredibly well, to know what it means to do that, is rarely part of the school experience.

L: You're so right. That's such a good point. You see these pieces on the wall that all look the same. Kids ask that 'How many paragraphs do I have to write?' kind of thing. And when I hear that I always say, well, you know that you have to have a beginning, a middle, and an end, and I hope you'll make it the best you can make it. So, I agree, it is exciting when they can run with it. I think that it's the engagement that provides the motivation that allows you to put in the extra time because you're interested, and you persevere because you're interested, and it's that perseverance that often takes you over the hump, to keep going when it gets challenging. That excitement leads to excellence because they are proud of their work and they want it to be good.

Wendy Ewbank: Middle School Teacher

Wendy Ewbank teaches social studies at Seattle Girls School in Seattle, after years teaching in the Edmonds school district. She is an extraordinary teacher with high expectations for what her students can do, and they consistently rise to meet her expectations. Her classroom is filled with the voices of her students, and with ideas and questions. They are always working with big ideas, with important ideas, and driven by a desire to gain skills and content knowledge, and to understand how the world works.

DS: To start, I know you have students engaged in projects and research much of the time. Why? What are your goals in teaching in this way?

W: I want what we do to matter. It will matter more to them if they help shape where we go, how we go. If they have a choice in the topic, or at least in some aspect of the topic they have a personal stake in it. Doing this "go fetch a bone and bring it back," worksheet approach, or textbook questions-at-the-end-of- chapters approach, doesn't really give us citizens who can meaningfully participate because they're critical thinkers. They won't come up with anything new, they wouldn't challenge anyone else's claims and assumptions. If there's anything that underlies the way I like to teach social studies it's that notion of multiple perspectives on anything, so that as often as we can, students are weighing evidence and then deciding what to believe, whether it's me, or books, guest speakers, or anything else. I don't use textbooks, and I've never been required to use them, thank goodness.

One of the Washington State history books comes to the conclusion that Native Americans "lost control of their land," in quotes, lost control of their lands, "to the expansion of a country." Darn them, they just stopped watching it and lost it.

You mentioned that research takes time and you have to go where it takes you. One of the biggest learning experiences for me and for kids was to start with this textbook summary and then to say, 'You're part of a group called 'truth in textbooks,' and you've been hired to rewrite the chapter.' I gave them a list of events that happened and said, 'In small groups pick what events you think were most critical in the loss of Native American territory and come up with your own thesis, which hopefully is not that the Native Americans 'lost control,' and then you write the chapter summary based on your research.' I don't think any of those kids will pick up a textbook unquestionably ever again. And I think they learned that content a whole lot more than if I'd just presented it to them.

D: How do you get the students to care about the projects you come up with, assuming it has not come from them?

W: A lot of it is your own passion. A justice angle is particularly important to middle school kids. For example, after we worked with Jan Maher, performing her reader's theater piece *Most Dangerous Women*, we researched and created other document-based plays. The students worked in small groups to make document-based plays dealing with social movements in American history. Women's movement, the labor movement, the Civil Rights movement, the farm workers movement. They feel it matters. I didn't really have to sell them on that. These things matter. There were injustices and people overcame them somehow.

They do a lot of research during their third term concerning an issue they care about. We call it our "pay it forward" project, and the first thing they have to do, before they decide on the personal action they are going to take in a service way, they have to write an essay on the root causes of the problem, and then hopefully the action plans they come up with will address root causes so they can work to eliminate the problem.

D: What would be an example of this kind of project?

W: For example, lack of girls education. We had one girl focus on India, one girl focused on Afghanistan, and one on Rwanda. So, different root causes in each, whether it's conflict, loss of parents, poverty, and/or intolerance. Poverty is the answer wherever you go. Cultural bias. They do things like read *Three Cups of Tea*, Greg Mortenson's book about setting up schools for girls in Pakistan and Afghanistan, getting back to what you're saying about modeling somebody who's actually doing it. How do the adults deal with this same issue? They are required to interview at least one person, hopefully two, who is/are working for nonprofits on that issue so they can get an idea of what people are doing to address some of these systemic, root causes. It's not like, as seventh graders, they have to come up with it all on their own. They are given a lot of support and guidance as they carry out their investigations.

The girl who focused on India is herself adopted from India, and she came up with the idea of fundraising. She raised enough money for a scholarship for one girl to attend school through secondary. In her name. One kid at a time. That's profound, to think that she, here in seventh grade, has impacted a life forever. And she really did it.

D: And she knows that it is possible for an individual to make a difference, to take an action that makes things better.

D: I assume during the course of these assignments you are presenting and practicing relevant skills dealing with how you conduct research, how you interview, how you evaluate information....

W: Right, and it starts before they are at the point of actually interviewing all these community members. They first worked in groups on a documentary on the history of Seattle through the lens of a particular group. Each group of students researched the history and experiences of particular populations in Seattle: Chinese, Latinos, women, Japanese, African Americans, religious minorities.

D: The history of that group in Seattle?

W: Right, and they had some choice in that. So, as a group they are going out to collect interviews from members of that group, or with people who have worked extensively with that group, and they're doing background research, for text and photographs and things like that. Then they produced a video documentary, a ten-minute documentary and we had a little film festival, where we showed their documentaries to each other, to their parents and family members. They got up on panels so they could be questioned by the audience. It comes back to your point that there should be a purpose and an audience. Their work matters not just because the mainstream story of Seattle is told all the time, but there are all these untold or under-told stories. Here's a way for them to learn through each other's work, and to practice research, because we're going to use this later. By the time we get to their independent projects, because they each do their "pay it forward" projects on their own, they have had supportive groups doing interviews in threes, where one would videotape, one would question and one would be keeping the log. Then it's not so scary to go out and do it on your own. We teach things like doing preliminary research before speaking with someone, asking open ended questions, really listening so that you use a person's answer and not just go with your scripted questions, no matter what the person says. We encourage them to think on their feet, and to frame questions as they go along.

D: What's hardest for them, what's most challenging?

W: One of them is what I've just mentioned, where they go in with a preconceived notion and if the interview goes outside that they're not sure, and they freeze. They kind of keep asking their questions, anyway, and that is an abstract thinking thing that, some of the seventh-grade kids are just not there yet.

D: The Girl's School starts at fifth grade. Do they do any of this kind of work before they get to you? Is there a coordinated approach to research that goes up the grade levels?

W: That's a really good question. There's a lot of involvement with community members but it's less open-ended research, and not so much a social studies focus. There's much more of a math and science focus in fifth and sixth grade. They're dealing with community members at places like the Aquarium. There is definitely a focus on public speaking. Things like that begin on day one. They are really ingrained in what we do. Most of their research in sixth grade is from books and websites, and not people. We introduce that.

D: And the reason you emphasize research with people is?

W: Especially when it comes to the present day, a wealth of information is to be had from individual people and it can be much more tailored to what you're actually looking for. Also, increasingly you have to be a "cop" when it comes to kids lifting things from Internet sources. The more tailor-made you can make your assignments the less likely it is that they can find what they are looking for on the Web. It requires a nuanced approach to questioning people to get what you need. I think it's a way to protect the integrity of the work the kids are doing, to make it not so easy to find in a text format. That's not why I do it, but it's a nice byproduct that makes it truly original.

D: You're asking them to do hard work.

W: Yes, and it's so worthwhile. I'll give you two instances as examples of why this is worthwhile.

One involves the girl who is focusing on the lack of education in Afghanistan and Pakistan. She read Greg Mortenson's book *Three Cups of Tea*. She was trying to talk a guy who runs a restaurant on 45th to host a night at the restaurant where the profits would go to supporting building schools in Afghanistan and Pakistan. She's another girl who was adopted from India. He was so happy that she was not from Pakistan; he did not trust anyone from Pakistan. When he found out there were schools in Pakistan in this project he would say 'No, no, no, there are no real schools in Pakistan. They say there are but there aren't real schools.'

She ended up going back three times to meet with this gentlemen, and to convince him that the money in fact was going to schools, she had the names and addresses of the schools. She in a subtle way, in a respectful way, got the man to turn around his thinking. He did not host an evening at the restaurant but he offered a hundred dollar gift certificate that she then used for a raffle. It was her persistence, and she and the other kids realized that they can change an adult's thinking. That's powerful.

Another girl, her issue was the Israeli-Palestinian conflict. Ok, a seventh-grade girl is taking that on. She came to me one day and said, 'I was interviewing this woman and you know, I think she's really biased. She's an Israeli woman and talked about terrorism and Palestinians.' The student could see that this woman was coming from a particular perspective and she needed more interviews, because if she simply goes with what the woman said it would be clearly one sided. It was fabulous.

And her experience with that, working with a real person, was worth a week of lessons, or more. So that's why you do it.

D: Do the students share their projects with each other?

W: Yes, they share along the way and then we have a culminating night for this project and there's a wide range of what kids choose to do about their issue. They have presentation boards, and they make public service announcements about their issue and what they want the public to do about the issue.

At the night event we have a simulated activity where they sit in a group of about thirteen; we break them up into three groups, and we give them the opportunity to "apply" for a million dollar grant. They have to come up with a proposal that addresses the root causes of multiple issues. What will they do with that money if they get it? The audience watches. The task is given to them that night; they don't know it's coming.

Prior to this evening I do some activities in class where they have to facilitate a policy-making exercise. We use immigration policy and then the Seattle School District assignment plan based on integration, the one that flunked the Supreme Court test. We did a town meeting on that and said, well if the Supreme Court says we can't then what should we do? So, I offer them some practice facilitating their own discussion about a controversial topic, where they're trying to come up with a solution. So they've done a little work with this kind of thing, so that night we just put them together, and they had to maybe be willing to abandon their own cause if these other causes were more compelling. It was great; they were thinking on their feet, and having this great conversation. The parents all said, 'Oh my gosh, if we could be that civil with the people we work with.' And to hear them use the language; 'Well, the root cause is.... Or we could solve this and this if we did this and this....' Or talking about cycles of things. Just amazing higher order thinking, and it's because of all the independent learning they had done that now they were sharing. It really worked.

D: You were thinking about the projects you have done that are examples of those points of agreement about good research. Can you name a few others?

W: Back to the idea that it matters, one of the research projects that really worked well is that I gave them the criteria based on what I learned at the US Institute of Peace, and from reading Jared Diamond's *Collapse*. Students investigated what causes societies to collapse? That would be from Diamond's work. They researched what causes societies to be at risk for conflict, inspired by the Institute of Peace. Based on research I gave them, their task was to come up with recommendations for the United Nations. They worked individually and then together to decide on the countries most at risk, and then to make recommendations to the UN about what could be done in those countries to make a difference.

I gave them a ton of websites, things like, number of unemployed men, environmental degradation, scarcity, high fertility rate, declining GDP. They were looking for overlapping factors. It was a real world example, and I didn't have to say, we're doing this because it matters. I said on day one, 'You know that in most conflicts in the world today, ninety percent of the people being killed are civilians.' And it's in the news and they care about people being hurt. And this goes back to that justice core. People are being hurt; how might we be able to prevent this? So, in a way it's a class pay-it-forward project, at the same time they are doing their independent things. All of this is happening third term.

I separate the list of websites by subject, so for example if the topic is large numbers of unemployed men, these websites might give you information about that, high fertility rates at these websites. It was pretty easy for the kids, so then they're looking for intersecting countries, and identifying which countries have lots of these things going on? They share these in a small group, and try to convince each other of the three most in need. Once they decide on the three countries they work together exclusively on those and do more research. Then they offer recommendations based on their research, focusing on root causes. They were fabulous. It worked really well. [Wendy's plan for this project is included in Chapter 7, beginning on page 199.]

D: One of the questions that comes up when you teach this way is how can you teach this way given what the state says or what the standards say?

W: I'm in a unique situation being in a private school, but I did this work in a public school too. It still works, you can fit it in. One of the state standards deals with foreign policy, skill standards around doing research, around different kinds of writing, around making presentations and sharing information. It's there. It's just a matter of being creative about it, and about doing the homework. That was a lot of work for me to put it all together. And I love that stuff. It makes my job more interesting, to read those cool books and visit these amazing websites and come up with something that I know is going to work with them.

D: This is one of the things that has emerged in a nice way from all of the people I've talked with about teaching. What really makes this work possible is that this approach also applies to them; they get to learn and research and grow as they prepare for and work with the students, so they keep growing and learning.

W: Absolutely. It's a way to use our professional development. To think about what you can do with our students, when we're in the midst of our professional development opportunities, to come up with those chunky assignments while you're in that intentional mode. That's when I come up with some of my best ideas. Maybe it's emphasizing the search in research, as you said, it's a verb.

D: It's not that you just walk out and do it. And, like Don Fels said, I make the thing, but that's not the point of it. It's to communicate, to cause people to look again, to see the world differently. Take the familiar and help people to see it again, and to see it in context.

W: Context is a big part of it. I was just thinking, as I'm writing this curriculum for Kennewick Man, and seeing the privileging of scientific research over people's story, over the Native American idea that we know what we know because of oral history; those stories are dismissed, discarded by Western science. I want kids to know that there are multiple ways of knowing things and multiple kinds of knowledge. I think research can also do that, the more perspectives they get.

This type of research doesn't fit in the AP curriculum, that says coverage, coverage, coverage. It should.

D: So what do you do when the kids run into frustration? Brick walls, dead ends, the road is windier than anticipated?

W: You've got to have a lot of tricks in your bag, and one of them is in a lot of cases they need research words for the search they are doing. Some of it is finding the basic websites they need, or the books they'll need, or helping them to locate the people they can talk to. I do a lot of that. And sometimes it might mean saying, 'This question doesn't seem to be working for you. So let's not go down that road if it's really getting frustrating. It's ok to do that, it's not time wasted. You've learned some stuff, or you narrowed down. It's just like a person said at a workshop, you wouldn't marry the first person you meet; don't settle down with the first site or topic you come across. You're narrowing down your choices, you're narrowing down where you're going to go. There's no such thing as a dead end. It's rerouting, it's all a part of the journey.'

I think that regular check-ins are really important when you do this kind of research so that you can catch those things before they've gone too far down the path. You can troubleshoot and check in every few days to find out how they are doing.

D: And you don't start with complicated stuff at the start of the year.

W: Exactly. We start with paired assignments, rather than individual or group work because they are both likely to be engaged, and one can model better research approaches for the other.

D: So those I interviewed had this list of "lessons learned." Do they seem on target to you? Do they match your experience? Are there other wisdoms to add to the list?

W: They really resonate. And you've got listening to fellow students in there. And really listening to the current batch of students to see where they are, rather than remembering what happened last year and going with that. Sometimes you change criteria for the rubric based on what's happening, or even eliminate a part of the assignment. You really need to be flexible yourself and be willing to make change based on what you are hearing from kids.

D: What happens if it doesn't work? If it doesn't go where you hope it will go?

W: I think it depends on how wed you are to a particular outcome. Could it be that other outcomes you hadn't anticipated are actually occurring, and they're not bad, they're just different? I think you have to ask yourself, is this worthwhile? If it's not worthwhile, be honest with yourself and your students, maybe problem solve with them and say, 'This isn't working the way I had intended. Can we work together to figure out how to make the best of the situation, or should we just go on to some other thing? You must have learned something? Whether you've learned about working, or about the topic, there has to be something salvageable.' Engaging students in figuring out what to do with it can be very useful, very productive.

D: One of the things that Howard Zinn said was that you have to be honest about what you found, which can include being left with questions, or doubts about certain aspects of the research. You are not responsible for inventing things, you are responsible for reporting what you have found.

W: I think it's great to use the word reporting, because if kids can think of themselves as investigative journalists, or that they're interrogating evidence, like lawyers, they recognize that they are not in control of the information there is to find, but need to be responsible to it.

Gary Thomsen: High School Teacher

Gary Thomsen teaches Sports and Events Marketing at Chief Sealth High School, in Seattle, Washington. Sealth is a school with a very diverse student population, many of whom are low income and/or second-language learners. Mr. Thomsen has become well known over the years for carrying out ambitious, creative, and challenging projects that involve students in research and actions that take them out of the classroom and into the community. And sometimes further. The project for which he and his students are best known involved first researching the history of baseball barnstorming in the western US and Canada by African American ballplayers and then taking an actual barnstorming tour themselves, riding bicycles and playing baseball across the country, from Seattle to the Negro Leagues Museum in Kansas City. Gary's students carried out the research (first learning how to do so), documented and sorted the data, planned their own barnstorming trip, raised funds, kept track of the budget and spending as they traveled, documented the trip, and donated the research they collected to the museum. Four years later, another of Gary's classes took up the Negro Leagues topic again and hosted a traveling exhibit from the Negro Leagues Museum, raising the funds and managing the exhibit at school while also producing a twelve-session seminar series on race and social justice issues. It is certainly not a typical high school marketing class, and needless to say it is not a typical experience for the students, but it is representative of the approach that Gary Thomsen brings to teaching. I spoke with him about his work and his approach during the visit of the Negro Leagues exhibit.

G: My background's in business, not education, so I'm an out-of-the-box kind of teacher, largely due to my ignorance of proper teaching methods. I learned early on that if the kids had input into what we did they would be more interested in it. And my life would be a lot easier. So we don't use books, we're a project-based class, or experiential learning I think they call it now. The goal is to get the kids competent in fundamental skills, skills they'll need in the real world like communication, time management, people management, record keeping, etc.

D: Can you talk a bit about the Negro Leagues project and how that came to be?

G: The original idea for the Legends of the Road project came about when a friend and I were at a baseball tournament in Canada. We were looking out at this stretch of highway heading east and I said, 'Wouldn't it be great if we could wake up every morning and go to another town and play ball, just like the barnstormers?' That was really the inception of it; the funny thing was, the idea wouldn't go away. I started thinking this could be a pretty cool project, so I started doing some research on the Negro Leagues and the black barnstormers and realized the potential legitimacy of my little scheme.

That September, in what would prove to be one of life's little quirks of fate, I got a call from Bob Kendrick, marketing director of the Negro Leagues Baseball Museum, who had seen a piece that *Nightline* had done on [former Seattle Schools Superintendent] John Stanford. A portion of the *Nightline* story focused on a bicycle ride we had taken to the Field of Dreams in Iowa, to raise money for the John Stanford Book Fund. In talking with Bob, he mentioned that one of their biggest concerns was the fact there were only two hundred and seven still living players from the Negro Leagues and surprisingly little was known about their playing days and almost nothing on their barnstorming travels, so, we began exploring ideas about what we might do for the Museum and collectively agreed that researching black player movements in the western US, and interviewing as many of the still- living players as we could, would have the most impact.

So, I had the idea in mind before I broached it to the class and, one day, I walked in and said 'What do you guys think about this?' Now, you can usually tell right away if the kids are interested in something by how much discussion ensues, and since I was getting more than the usual amount of questions I said, 'Let's do some research on these black baseball barnstormers.'

After a couple of weeks the kids were actually starting to dig up some interesting information and so I rather off handedly said; 'You know, if we get some good stuff on these guys, maybe we could re-trace one of their routes.' Then, I just sort of let it sit for the better part of the year to see what kind of research the kids would turn up and what kind of sustained interest they'd have. My hope was, from the beginning, that there might be some kind of trip involved, but as far as the class was concerned, starting out, it was just going to be a research project.

D: So initially were you thinking this would be a project for the entire school year?

G: Initially, yes but it quickly became apparent that I'd bitten off more than I thought. So as it turned out, this became a two-year project, with the first year focusing strictly on the research.

D: Given the project's size and scope, how did you organize your students?

G: I divided the kids up into groups and gave each group 2 to 3 states and /or provinces. During class, they got on any un-used phone we could find and did nothing but call people. Given the lack of available information on the topic, the first calls were usually to the local newspaper and the kids had to explain what they were doing and somehow try and get the person on the other end to go through old newspapers to see if there were any stories on barnstormers in their area. After several calls they started to become more comfortable and after a couple weeks they really started to dig up some fascinating information. What was even more rewarding was that they were really getting into it. There started to be a competition as to who could get the most information in a class period, who could uncover the most interesting fact, who could make the most calls. So once that barrier of communication had been crossed, then we started to move forward very quickly.

The other critical issue was the storage and documentation of the information they were uncovering. Since at least a few of the kids were familiar with the Excel program, we used that to create the data base template. I began by having the kids create a data base on Excel, listing the locations of where the player had played. Once they found where he played, then they had to find the phone number and contact name for the mayor, local librarian, the chamber of commerce and of course the local newspaper in those towns. Then they'd have to call them and explain what they were doing. The kids would ask if they knew of anybody who might have seen the barnstormers come through their town, or if they recalled any newspaper articles written about it, or did they know of anybody who had played against them. And that's how it started, teaching them how to use the phone and how to convey what it was they were doing, and then keeping track of it.

D: How would you describe the skill level of your students, as it pertained to research?

G: The vast majority of students involved did not begin with very good research skills. Some had the rudimentary skills necessary to complete high school papers, but most fell short of even that. Consequently, I spent a good three weeks going over tips on how to un-cover the information we needed and we actually put a camera in the classroom to document and critique their efforts. I typically get a lot of kids whose first language is not English, and it was a real challenge for them to get on a phone and try to explain what we were doing.

Fairly early on, based on the documentation that was being uncovered, one of the kids concluded that 2000 would be the hundredth anniversary of barnstorming. So, since we couldn't find any records of barnstorming prior to 1900, we talked with the Museum and suggested doing some sort of a Centennial event in recognition. The kids came up with the idea of recreating a barnstorming trip and riding bikes to draw attention to it. Their rationale, which was perfectly logical, was that since it was so tough finding people who had either played on those barnstorming clubs, or had seen them play, a little publicity might get them to contact us. And it worked. By the end of the first year the kids had identified over six hundred US and Canadian towns where these men had played. So, that summer we decided to take a preliminary trip to meet with the folks they had talked to, and hopefully expand the data base, while scouting out locations for the following summer's barnstorming re-creation. It was during this "scouting trip" that we garnered over 150 historical items related to the black barnstormers, ranging from old photographs to supposedly non-existent baseball cards that the black players of the early 1900s used as business cards. And, perhaps our best find was the forty plus hours of interviews we got from former barnstormers and local players who had actually played against them.

During the project's second year the majority of class time was spent putting the actual logistics of the barnstorming trip together. They continued on with the research as well and by the end of year two they had compiled more documented information on black player movements in the western US and Canada than the Baseball Hall of Fame and the Negro Leagues Baseball Museum had, combined.

D: What did you hope the kids would get out of this?

G: A lot of kids that I see have two issues. Number one, they don't tend to think big. When I ask them what they want to do, they can't tell me. And two, most of them haven't had much success in their lives, so consequently they don't really think these projects are going to happen, they don't believe that they can collectively pull it off. So, in general, the goal of these projects is to give the kids a sense of confidence and self-fulfillment, while teaching them transferable skills that will help them throughout their lives. On a more specific basis, the trips provide a chance for them to see and experience things they may never have the opportunity to see, or do again. And of course in the process, they're doing something valuable for, in this case, the Negro Leagues Museum.

D: What did a typical class day look like?

G: Our daily regimen was to get on the phone and get information. The whole focus of the class became, "How do you get research?" We did plenty of role playing— having the kids practice making calls and answering questions, and then after a few days they'd get on the phone and try again. For this type of research it's imperative to ask enough of the right questions to get the information you need, or, to get a name and number of another person who can provide additional information. In a sense we taught them how to create a research phone tree and by the end of the project they had talked with over 2,300 people.

It was also critical for us to update our data base on a daily basis so that we could either follow up on it when we were on the trip or at some later date when we had money. And so updating the database was also a daily exercise.

D: Were you surprised at the information your students uncovered?

G: One of the really great things about the research was the number of people who had memorabilia or documentation they wanted to share with us and so that forced us to deal with another question: How to get access to the documentation and how do we insure its safety /integrity? Ultimately we had some folks mail us documents or memorabilia, and others we scheduled to meet when we went through their town. At the end of the day it was this prospect of getting a lot of documentation and memorabilia that justified going on the road and so by the end of that first year we started to look seriously at actually doing the bicycle trip. That first summer we took a couple of kids to research a possible route and to meet with the contacts they had uncovered. Since we wanted to pick towns where the barnstormers actually stopped and played, our goal was to find not only thirty-five towns where they frequented, but also towns where there was a wealth of historical information that we could pick up during the trip. We spent nearly five weeks that summer traveling through the country conducting interviews and collecting more research.

D: The summer after that, after spending the year planning and fund raising and preparing, you actually took a bunch of high school students on a bicycle and baseball barnstorming tour. Can you talk a bit about the barnstorming you and the kids did?

G: The project, "Legends of the Road" had two components, and one underlying goal; what can we do to draw attention to the Negro League barnstormers and to the Negro Leagues Baseball Museum. The first piece was riding bicycles and playing baseball games, which is what generated the media attention. That was the hook.

The second piece was collecting research and doing interviews on the road, over a period of 71 days, and making sure that everything was compartmentalized so that it made sense when we got done. Ideas are one thing, turning them into reality is like pushing wet spaghetti. In addition to the on-going research, now the kids had to figure out the logistics of all of this. I mean, how do you move twenty people five thousand plus miles down the road, connecting 35 cities, riding bicycles for up to 200 miles a day and then playing a ball game that night? What they did was nothing short of amazing, I don't know of any professional production companies that could have achieved that— not on the budget we had.

During the trip itself the kids were comprised of two groups. There were the ballplayer-bike riders and there were the production kids who had gone through the class. On a typical day the production kids would get in a van at around 4 a.m. and drive to the next town on our schedule. They would conduct interviews along the way, both on camera and tape recorder, and collect any sort of research documentation they could locate. When they got into the town we were staying, they would also have to: negotiate hotel rates, if that had not already been done, look for places that we could possibly get free or discounted food, coordinate media and press conferences, which happened in every town, confirm and coordinate all of the ceremonial activities that were planned around the team arrival, make sure we got copies of all of the press coverage and then go to the library and get on the microfiche and go through years and years of newspaper articles, which was a key supplement to the research.

Meanwhile, the bicycle-baseball kids just had to worry about riding anywhere from one to two hundred miles a day and playing a baseball game, sometimes on the same day.

So, we had these two separate, yet very much connected, groups moving across the country in different locations, one group by van, one group by bike, both of which had to be at a predetermined place at a pre-determined time.

D: What happened at the end? What did you do with the information you collected?

G: We had these huge plastic buckets and all of the documentation, ranging from baseball cards from 1905 to old newspaper articles, everything went into those buckets, and when we got to Kansas City it was all given to the Museum. All of the information that we acquired over the two years was deposited in Kansas City and is waiting for the time that they get enough staffing to actually go through it. As I understand it, eventually it will be put into the research section of the Museum where people will be able to get a sense of what the barnstorming movement was like, while gaining an appreciation of how far these guys traveled, just to play ball. The only thing we retained was the sixty hours of video the kids shot during the project, which we intend to use for a documentary. We're just now getting to that point.

D: A lot of your projects are very big, but are there certain steps that need to be taken that would also be used for smaller projects as well ?

G: All of our projects, big or small, involve a set of steps, from creating the idea to actually producing the event. We start off brainstorming ideas and gradually whittle them down based on a preset base of criteria, which for us are:

➢   Is the project relevant and can it be clearly defined?
➢   Does it have the potential to benefit the students after they leave high school/college?
➢   Does it benefit the community, local or national?
➢   Does it benefit the school /district?

No matter what project we work on, we go through all six steps.

Steps	Skill Set / Curricula
Brainstorming: What's the idea?	• Creative thinking skills • group work • conceptualization • visualization
Planning: How's it going to get done?	• Critical thinking skills • group work • logic • linear thinking
Research: What do we need to know?	• Verbal and written communication skills • group work • research techniques: • Computer usage / keywords • Source options • Source locations • Collection /organization
Logistics: What needs to be done?	• Critical thinking skills • Verbal and written communications • group work • research • accuracy /organization

Funding: What's it cost? How are we going to get it?	• verbal and written communication skills • marketing • inventory identification • event positioning • sponsorship packaging • sales • accounting
Production:	• Do it.

The first step is, "Ok, you've come up with this idea, now, what has to happen in order for this idea to get done? How do you do it? You want to ride a bike across country, what are the things you need to know in order to do that?" And so you have to teach them to start looking at things analytically.

The next step, regardless of the project's size, involves research. They're going to have to find specific information. If we are biking across country, what roads will we take? How many hotel rooms will we need? What will that cost? How will we contact the people we want to interview, and so on. This segues into the next step, which is logistics, because with any project there are myriad details that need to be identified and resolved. The kids have to work together. They have to be able to work in groups, and the groups have to learn how to communicate with each other. That combination of research and logistics is the biggest component of the project, being able to get kids to communicate and to work in groups.

So, depending on the size and scope of the project, and assuming they've successfully completed their research and logistics package, they then get into the fund-raising step. They've done all their due diligence. They've got the idea, they know how it's supposed to be done, they know the logistics, so they've got a road map. Now they've got to go out and get the money for it, which is really like a final if you will. If they've done a good job researching, completed a thorough logistics package, and, if they've learned how to communicate, they should be able to sit in front of a board or panel and make a presentation that will get the money to fund their event or project.

The last step is actually doing it. At that point we get into things like: How do you learn to get along with people in stressful situations? How do you maintain your focus to accomplish your piece of the project? How are you going to develop a budget and manage the money when we go out on the road? Communication during this execution phase is extremely critical. And again these are all transferable skills

At the end of these steps my goal, my hope, is to give them some life skills that they can use, regardless of what they choose. Project-based learning forces kids to look at things in totality. Even if their part in a project is very small, we make sure they understand their role and their importance in the overall project.

One of the most important aspects of projects, from my perspective, is that from the very beginning we challenge them to be creative. I mean, a lot of people a whole lot smarter than us have done some research on barnstorming and re-created local events to celebrate it.

But we wanted the kids to think bigger, to find a way to unearth more information and to create an event that would draw national and international attention to the Negro Leagues. So, I approached it as learning the two-step. First, look at a situation and be able to understand it, and secondly, be creative enough to look at doing it in a different way, essentially trying to get them to look at alternatives, to embrace Robert Kennedy's quote, Some people look at things the way they are, and ask why... I dream of things that never were, and ask why not?

D: How do you assess the students' work?

G: I'm a proponent of portfolios, and one of my beliefs is that if a kid can fill out a grant application and get funding for a project, in my estimation they're showing proficiency in language arts and writing. It displays their proficiency in the real world. Why are you making this kid take the WASL [Washington Assessment of Student Learning, the state wide standardized test that all students must take and pass to graduate from high school]?

Likewise, if you can sit down and organize your thoughts so that somebody says, 'Yes, we'll give you some money for that,' then in my class you're going to get an A in the communication piece because you were able to pull together and present the information necessary to get someone to give you the money. So in my case, the project is the final.

D: One of the reasons for the book is the assumption that having an authentic reason for doing something gives you a whole lot more juice for learning what you need to learn in order to do the thing you want to do. You work for a real consequence.

G: We do. I've found it's easier for kids to embrace foreign concepts if they're striving for something tangible. It adds reality to the situation instead of just dealing with it in theory. You can talk about the importance of communication for weeks on end, and they still don't really get it. But put them in a situation where they have to present their project to a prospective sponsor, and it's a completely different ball game. They get it.

D: This is a new experience for many of the students you work with. They've never worked this way before. How do you help them learn how to carry out real research in pursuit of a project that has interest or meaning for them, that takes multiple steps and requires them to work together? What do you do?

G: First of all you have to decide on a project, and that can be a challenge since most kids have never done anything like that before. The key is to throw out examples of things that might be of interest to them. With my students I can guarantee you that if I throw out an idea that has something to do with basketball almost every hand will go up. Now, if you don't have experience in the field doing projects, then you need to start looking at what's going on in the world that your students are interested in, whether it's basketball, skateboarding or anything else. And then you need to figure out what you can do, project wise, related to that interest that will hook the kids, that will grab them so that you can then tie it into their interests.

Over the first couple weeks I keep asking them for their ideas, and I write all the ideas down on the board. I always have to say, and this is a key point, that 'the only bad idea is an idea that you don't throw out, that you don't share' and I continually remind the students of that.

Once we have a good list of ideas then we'll start discussing the merits and challenges of each one until we get down to a workable list of possible projects to work on. At that point I'll explain that we need to base the project on three things: What's the relevancy to the kids; what's the relevancy and value to the school; and what's the relevancy and value to the community. The community can be the school, the neighborhood, or the country. We use these three criteria to review the ideas and collectively discuss each one's merits until we gradually cull them down to the final list. Generally we come down to, depending on the number of ideas, up to five projects that the kids want to do, and then we go on from there.

Depending on the class size, I might divide them into smaller groups and have each group look at the possible choices, analyze each of them and report to the rest of us why they would or would not be good projects for us to work on. I'll tell them to talk among themselves, make a list of pros and cons for each and come back in fifteen minutes, or half an hour and tell us why they like them, why they don't, and what their choice is.

Working in smaller groups gives them the courage to express themselves more openly, but it can still take a couple of days for them to come back with their choice(s) because they're still working through the group dynamics. Eventually you get a consensus of what they want to do, and they also buy into it because it was their decision, and so they're motivated to follow through.

After the projects are selected I go in and break down some of the obstacles they'll encounter and try to give them a realistic overview of what they can expect. For instance, a lot of kids know how to use computers, but I spend quite a bit of time giving them insights on how to use key words to find the information they're looking for, and getting them to write down specifically what they're looking for, and why. That's the first step. During class I'll type in some key words and give them some examples of how to get started. Then, we start brainstorming possible sources we can use to find information, and we put them on the board. Obviously there's the computer, but there's also librarians. And, we've got some pretty good universities in town, and several museums, like the Museum of History and Industry. And for the Negro Leagues project there's the Negro Leagues Baseball Museum.

So, we start by listing all the possible sources that we know of, that might help us get the information we need, and then I continually reinforce using those sources. You have to say to the kids, 'These people are basically going to help you do your assignment, to get your A. Again, kids are used to reading a book, memorizing it and being on their own to get an A on a test or paper. But I try and get them to use people as sources, as helpers in getting them to accomplish their goal. I say to them 'If you want to do that on your own that' s fine, but why not just call this guy at the University of Washington, why not call the Negro Leagues Museum and just write down what they tell you? Think about all the hours you're going to save.'

Using the Negro Leagues as an example, I had this student who was reading a book called *Only the Ball Was White*, and I really wanted her to keep reading it, but she was looking for little bits of research material that would take forever. I gave her the phone number of a guy at the Negro Leagues Museum and urged her to call him. I told her, 'If you like the book keep reading it, but this book is going to take you probably a week to finish, and you could get more in ten minutes with the phone call than you could from the book.' She called, and she got all of the information she was looking for plus ten or twelve more sources just from her twenty-minute conversation with the guy at the museum. Needless to say she was really excited when she got off the phone. And she still continued reading the book because she really liked it. So once you get them over that hump, when they look at these people as resources they can use, then it's a lot easier.

Timeliness is another big issue. Often times, kids will spend a week or more looking for information that can and should be gotten in one class period. That leads into the first of many mini lessons on asking for help. Getting the kids to ask adults for help is a huge challenge. So we spend a lot of time making sure they have a clear understanding of what it is they need to get, and getting them comfortable going to a librarian or teacher, and saying, 'I've got this research assignment and I'm having trouble with it, can you help me?'

From there I'll pose the following scenario, 'What are you going to do if they say—I don't know anything about that? Are you going to just thank them and hang up? No, you need to ask them if they have any ideas of people you might call to get that information.'

So, here again I'm trying to get them over a hurdle, this one being what do you do when somebody says 'No, I don't have any information.' I'll try and get them to ask the person, in five different ways, if there's any help they can provide. For instance:

'Can you think of anybody who might know something, who might have some information?'

'Do you think somebody at the newspaper would know anything?'

'Do you know of anyone who was around during that time?'

D: I assume there are a range of skills and comfort levels among any group of students.

How do you handle that?

G: Depending on the size of the project, there are certain kids who are just so shy that they are very limited as to what they can work on and be productive, so we start them out in jobs that offer a more protected environment. Having said that, nobody escapes the communication piece of the curriculum. The communication piece, in large part, is getting on the phone and either delivering or acquiring information. They all have to do it and even the kids who aren't going to get on the phone to collect research still have to go through it. They're still going to have to make phone calls, they're still going to have to know how to convey information and they'll still need to know how to handle "nos."

D: You are offering a unique and extraordinary experience for your students but it's certainly not the easiest way to teach. What is it you want the kids to experience? Why go this way, why put this kind of project front and center of what you are doing?

G: Number one is teaching transferable skills that are going to benefit them down the road, even if they don't realize that until years later. Plus, personally, I think experiential learning is where you can have the most impact on the kids, and in turn, where they reap the most benefit. Communication skills in particular are hugely critical if you want to achieve success, in any field, and these types of projects require tremendous amounts of written and verbal communication. Since the kids produce the trip, and subsequently lay out the day's events, being able to communicate clearly takes on a whole different level when you have kids spread out over say, 20 miles, in one-hundred-and-ten-degree heat. Having the necessary support, and meeting points, becomes very critical.

Secondly, this type of project-based learning has, I think, some residual benefit to the "community." In the case of the barnstorming trip, I think the kids' work is of benefit to the "greater community" of the country, in that they've provided a missing piece of African American history in particular, and American history in general, that fills in a lot of blanks. And I think that's good.

The other thing is that a lot of these projects have a trip element, we go out on the road and a lot of our kids have not had that experience. And I think that's a great educational experience. Taking kids places they're not familiar with, where there's a different way of life and meeting other people in the context of what they've been researching gives them a whole different, and I think better, perspective of their own neighborhood and where they live. It opens up their minds tremendously. Thirty years down the road I think most of these kids will sit around and talk about the time they roller bladed across the country or rode bicycles all summer for the Negro Leagues and had to play a baseball game. It's a memory these kids will have for the rest of their lives and I think it's a good one.

D: What do you want your students to learn from these projects?

G: What I want them to learn are skills that can be transferable to any sort of career they choose. They have to learn communication skills, they have to learn to write clearly and effectively, they have to learn time-management skills and they have to learn how to work in groups and manage people. Sub-points to all of those are meeting deadlines, turning out work that contains no mistakes, being able to think critically, to overcome obstacles, and to be passionate about what it is you're doing. Basic things that you'd take for granted in the business world. So it doesn't matter if they work on a project like the Negro League's Traveling

Exhibit, with a budget of about twenty-five thousand dollars, or whether they do something that's more internal, say a cultural holiday celebration. Those same skill sets get taught, regardless of the size of the project. Obviously they're more in depth and covered in a wider range on a bigger project.

D: What's key to making these projects work?

G: I think one thing would be learning how to manage the kids in a business sense— putting the kid in a job where you can maximize their skills. The beauty of doing projects, even small ones, is that they have a number of components that allows a kid to do something they like, while working on something they don't. For example, you might need publicity, which could include posters, fly-ers, press packets, etc., which are primarily art based. Now the kid who maybe can't write very well may be artistically creative. So, that kid becomes part of your creative team and guess what, even though they may not like writing they do like art and those posters require creative writing, which they'll learn because it's part and parcel of doing what they like — that poster. The trick is to put the kids with the appropriate skill set in a job they like, and then it becomes a lot easier to improve the skills they're deficient in. I see it as having to take all of those bits and pieces of your educational message and reconfiguring that message for each of the kids. I think you really have to teach each kid individually. To find out where their expertise is and where their interest is, and then take that curriculum piece, reformat it, and put it to them so they'll get the most out of it. And in the process they feel like they're an important piece of the project.

D: So really getting to know the kids is a pretty essential piece of this.

G: Sure, and being able to motivate them. We do projects that can cost up to seventy thousand dollars and when you pitch businesses on supporting some-thing at that level they expect things to be done when you say and how you say. Starting the event a month late because you couldn't get it done on time doesn't fly. Nor should it. So you really have to know and understand the kids you've got working on the project. Each kid is different. Each one is in it for a different reason; some just want the grade, some really want the experience and some might be interested in doing something related after they get out of school, so you have to be aware of each of those interests. The better you know the kids the better you're able to address and successfully deal with those kinds of issues. You also have to have a clear idea of the outcomes you want to achieve. Once you have those then you can work backwards, look at the timeline and the dif-ferent components needed to create the project and then start plugging kids into a specific area based on their skills and abilities.

When we take on a project I teach the students how to write a project proposal. To be able to say in a concise fashion, on two or three sheets of paper, depending on the complexity of the project, what the project is, why it should be done, what are the objectives and what are the components. And that becomes our syllabus, our plan. Generally that process takes three to four weeks and by going through that exercise, the kids have a much better understanding of what it is they're trying to do, and by extension, it gives them a better perspective into the planning needed. Of course, then you have to go back and look at each of those components and put together logistical packages for each one and at that point you start to have the kids migrate into groups they feel comfortable with.

D: I can't imagine many teachers being able to do all of that research and organize a trip across country at the same time. Are there ways for them to incorporate research and the other components in smaller projects?

G: Sure. I was thinking of that earlier. You can certainly do smaller projects. You could do a living history project of your classroom, or of your school. At the end of the semester students could make a presentation on who are their classmates, where do they come from, why are they like they are? And in the process you could certainly employ most of the project components, although you probably wouldn't need to go out and get funding for it. You could even take it a step further and ask, "Who's in our neighborhood and how did they get here?" That becomes a living history of the neighborhood. Or do a project on the architecture of a small town. How did it get to look like this? At the end they could give a presentation based on those questions.

D: Two related questions, because this is a school context and we are swamped with standards, are you working with those in mind? And do you ever connect to other classes?

G: I'm very aware of the standards and generally agree with them. Mine is a Vocational Education class, and my interpretation of the Voc Ed philosophy is to take the skills kids are learning in, say, Language Arts and get them to use those skills in a real world situation. At our school kids do a fair amount of writing in Language Arts. I teach them how to use that skill in a business context, in the form of writing a grant or sponsorship proposal. Consequently the standards in here, in my class, are essentially business standards and those are very high.

I'd love to work with teachers in other disciplines. I would have loved it if the Social Studies department had done the historical research on the Negro Leagues and Barnstorming. I'd have loved it if the Language Arts department had written the grants and sponsorship proposals. Or, just the correspondence to the various people we were trying to interview, develop the interview questions and done the interviews. I think that would have been a wonderful LA project, and I think that's a great Social Studies project. I think it would have been great if the Science and Math departments had gotten involved in figuring out how many calories the kids were burning as they rode, what the nutritional requirements were, calculating the distances, etc. But it didn't happen because everyone was too busy teaching to the WASL, too busy getting kids ready to pass a test instead of letting them put their LA or Social Studies or Math or Science education to practical use, which just might help them down the road.

D: You clearly value teaching through projects, and by having the students function as active researchers and learners. What is the benefit of doing that?

G: I attended a seminar when I first started teaching and a professor from Stanford was talking about how our "educational delivery," the way we teach, is essentially the same as it was 150 years ago. And, as a consequence, every year we're turning out kids that are ill prepared for the workplace. I found that horrifically fascinating, and yet true.

Kids today have access to so much more information than their predecessors did a generation ago that traditional teaching methods often times fall on deaf ears. Making education relevant, I think, has probably become one of the most crucial things in education and yet it's hardly ever talked about. A lot of kids sit there and say to you, 'Why do I need to know this?' They know they can get on a computer and communicate with people all over the world, they can create things, they can even start their own company, so if you don't make a lesson relevant to the real world, they'll tune you out. The reason I like project-based, or experiential learning, is because it makes education relevant. It gives kids a chance to actually use their education to create and produce something, which, at the end of the day, allows them to stand there and say, 'I did that.' Plus, as I've said, it also gives them a chance to learn valuable interpersonal skills, skills that are largely absent when sitting on a computer.

D: I think so too. One of the reasons I'm doing this book is to encourage more active, involving, relevant, student-centered learning experiences. That flies in the face of a lot of people's experience of what you need to do to deal with the testing requirements, with No Child Left Behind. No Child is driving people to do worksheet type activities, to make sure the kids can deal with the tests, rather than to focus on what will serve the students so that they can live well in world. Those are really different events.

G: True, and a lot of kids don't learn that way. So what do you do with all of them?

D: What you're doing, hopefully.

G: A good example of that is, I have a kid [we'll call "A"] who's taking my class four periods a day. Seems he had this tendency of getting thrown out of his other classes so he'd end up coming into mine and finally the administration figured they might as well put him into my classes to keep him out of the halls. Now, this kid has had some gang experiences, he's done a little marketing on the street, but he's really a good kid, a bright kid. But, needless to say, he's also not shy about letting a teacher know if he thinks an assignment is "bs," which does tend to derail a few lesson plans. His goal, after high school, is to open an under-age club so kids can have a safe place to go, so that's a project he and I are working on. He's learning how to write a business plan and at the end of the se-mester he'll meet with some local bankers to see about getting a loan. He shows up every day, always on time, works his tail off, and is doing a remarkably good job of putting together this business plan. He's using extensive writing, math and finance skills and is on the phone daily getting information for his project.

In the meantime he's running the merchandise store we've set up as part of the Negro Leagues Museum exhibit that we brought here to school. Now, we've got about twenty thousand dollars of merchandise in that store, which isn't ours. But we haven't lost an item, and every night the books balance to the penny, and this kid is overseeing the whole store. He came up with the inventory sheet on his own, inventories everything daily and hasn't lost a receipt. He also came up with the system on how we track sales and re-ordering. He's great with the peo-ple who come in and is a damn fine salesman to boot, and I've never heard him say any of this was "bs."

Now this kid is learning language arts, math, finance, computer applications, marketing and even social studies, but he's learning them in a way that's rele-vant to him, and these skills are going to help him when he gets out of school. [A side note: after graduation A did meet with three local banks. The first two turned him down due to lack of collateral. The third, however, did approve a loan and he opened the club four months later.] He likes it because it's some-thing that he can use in the future. It's not reading a book. And he's a kid that, if you just shove a book in his face he won't read it. So again, these are the kids you kind of wonder about and say, well, ok, what are we doing for them?

Howard Zinn: University Professor Emeritus

Howard Zinn has written dozens of books, hundreds, if not thousands of essays, columns, articles, and editorials, and his work A People's History of the United States changed the way many people have approached and taught history. Professor Zinn's focus on including the voices of those who have been left out of history has helped us to revisit what we thought we knew about our own story, and to understand it more fully. Howard Zinn is still active in his eighties, writing columns, giving speeches, and offering support to people working for social justice all over the world.

We talked about history, and about the way he approaches a research task by focusing on making sure all relevant voices are heard. We refer in this conversation to an essay Professor Zinn wrote on former New York City mayor, and New York Congressman Fiorello LaGuardia called "LaGuardia in the Jazz Age." The essay, which appeared in The Zinn Reader (Seven Stories Press, 1997), caught my attention because I knew something about LaGuardia and am fascinated by him, but also because so many people fly into and out of LaGuardia Airport without having any knowledge of where the name came from, which ties into the "hidden history" theme I address in Chapter Six.

D: You're officially a historian… so what is one of those?

H: It's always the case that people who confront somebody whose knowledge of something is very impressive, really don't know very much about the effort that went into that, and so they give it some sort of magical quality. I assume a historian is just a mediator between an awful lot of information that resides in various forms about the past, a mediator between all of that information and a public which doesn't have access to that information, or doesn't know how to get access to that information, but which might benefit from it. That's as close as I come to describing what a historian does in the abstract.

D: How did you find your way to that?

H: I was a shipyard worker for three years, then went into the air force and came out and knocked around various jobs and actually didn't go to college until I was twenty-seven years old. I wasn't sure what I would do with my college education. I was politically sort of a radical, as a result of my shipyard experience and as result of reading on my own, and I went into the academic world with only one intention, and that was to make use of whatever I would learn for bringing about social change. I could have accomplished that, I thought, in a number of different ways, and at one point I narrowed it down to two possibilities. One was that I would become a lawyer, become a kind of Clarence Darrow, about whom I had read; I felt that it was a glamorous and important way of entering the world. The other possibility was to become a teacher and have an effect on young people. I actually made the decision about becoming a teacher rather than a lawyer because it was the fifties, and McCarthyism was at its height, and several of my friends who had gone to law school found that they were not getting past the bar examiners because of their political records and their political beliefs. I decided I'd have more freedom as a teacher. I know that during the McCarthy period teachers were also subject to political scrutiny, but still I thought there was more leeway in a classroom than in a courtroom.

Once I decided to become a teacher I wasn't sure what field I would go into that would be socially useful. I went back and forth between economics, philosophy and political science, and I decided on history because I thought, that's fundamental, that whatever you do, whatever field you go into, history is basic. I decided to concentrate on history, which is then what I set out to do, first at NYU and then at Columbia.

D: It becomes very clear from your writing as well that you certainly haven't left economics and the other fields behind.

H: No, and I never felt that I was in a discipline that I must stick to, that I mustn't cross over into other disciplines. It's very interesting that word discipline; it suggests that you'll be punished if you step outside the boundaries of your field....

D: Isn't that often how it works?

H: It's true, it's absolutely true. And so from the beginning I decided that I would go wherever an issue took me. The important thing to me was, 'Here's a question to be solved.' If there's a question to be solved you mustn't limit yourself to one particular field in trying to solve that question. If you have to go into economics, go into politics, if you have to go into genetics and geography, whatever, you just go wherever the question leads you.

D: I wonder if we might talk about your essay "LaGuardia in the Jazz Age." One of the reasons I want to talk about this piece on LaGuardia is because millions fly into and out of LaGuardia Airport and have no idea that there was actually somebody connected to it, that he played a role in the airport existing at all, and had a significant life beyond that.

When I was growing up my parents listened to a recording of the musical *Fiorello*, presumably based on his time as mayor of N.Y., and their memories of him were that he was a nice guy who read the comics on the radio during the Depression. Why did you choose to write a book about him?

H: I actually sort of stumbled on LaGuardia. I had been interested in other kinds of topics and was planning to write about Big Bill Haywood (of the I.W.W.) until I found that the department of justice had burned most of his papers. I was just walking through downtown Manhattan and came across this building, the municipal archives. There was a woman sitting at this desk and I said, 'What do you have here?'

And she said, 'Mrs. LaGuardia has just deposited the LaGuardia papers here.' Well, I was sort of mildly interested, and said 'These are the papers from when he was mayor?'

And she said, 'Yes, ninety percent of this is papers from when he was mayor, and then in this little corner we have papers from when he was a congressman.' So that was a new bit of information, that he'd been a congressman. I went over to those filing cabinets and pulled out a few of those folders, and immediately my interest perked up. He was no longer just a colorful mayor of New York; he obviously was a politically radical congressman.

D: The work that you do is often taking material that has been presented in an almost formulaic way over the years and looking at it differently, which means you have had to basically blaze your own trail. How do you organize yourself to go about doing that?

H: When you look at a different aspect of somebody's life, asking questions that others may not have asked, you're often led to a different set of information. You know, all of the research about Columbus, so much of it so repetitive about his actual voyages, his financing, and his motives, and his actual navigational skill, and...

D: We know how to maintain a myth...

H: Yes, and how many people paid any attention to the Indians, to the people he encountered, and what about them, and what was their life like before he came? Somebody's recently written a book called *1491*, in which that person asks, 'What was Indian society like before Columbus arrived?'

In my case, I started out from a kind of general philosophical question that is, 'What are the points of view that are omitted in any traditional telling of history?' In the case of Columbus it was the point of view of the Indians. And once I decided that I was going to look for their point of view I found that they weren't a writing society. That was one problem, there were no written records left from the Indians. And the other problem was that they'd been wiped out, which in itself was an interesting bit of information that nobody had ever told me. Nobody in school had ever said that about Columbus's encounter with the Indians, so I thought 'Who else was there, and who could possibly have thrown light on it?' That's when I discovered Bartolomé Las Casas. The writings of Las Casas gave me a wealth of information, because he was at least looking at it as much as he could, not being an Indian, from the standpoint of the Indians, from the standpoint of the victims. So, it's a matter of asking the question, whose point of view is being left out of this story? When I was dealing with the Mexican War, the question was, there too, whose point of view is left out of the story? That led me to go to many, many, many volumes written about the Mexican War, digging and digging and trying to find out what were the points of view of the soldiers in the American army?

D: Much less the Mexican army.

H: That's right, or even Mexican leaders, or any Mexican point of view about the Mexican War. So that sort of principle led me, in every situation, to look into the shadowy parts of the library.

So, with LaGuardia I researched his time in Congress because that was something that had not been written about, and it was interesting to me.

D: One of the fascinating things to me about the writing you did with LaGuardia is that the point of view that's been missing all these years, is LaGuardia's.

H: Yes, that's true, that's absolutely true.

D: So, you have that kind of organizing question and intention to surface or investigate what hasn't been said. So, you have a clear bias or point of view in a sense...

H: Absolutely.

D: How do you then evaluate what you're finding? You know, everybody writes the particular history they want to remember, or want others to remember. How do you sort through the disparate accounts of things, or know how much weight to give things, knowing that people shape the world according to their own understanding, beliefs, and biases?

H: I think it's understanding that the accounts you get of any particular event are going to be through a very subjective lens. And that you'll get different accounts. I think the best you can do is multiply the number of points of view, get as many different points of view as possible, and cross check and see where they corroborate one another. If you suspect Las Casas is developing an animus against Columbus, you know he might exaggerate what he is seeing, then you have to check him against other accounts. In fact, the best kind of check is against an account by somebody who has a very different point of view, but which actually corroborates what, in this case Las Casas is saying. Las Casas was saying, these Indians were not warlike, they were very gentle and they were very generous, and you might think that he's romanticizing, and then you read Columbus's diary, and it says the same thing.

So, understanding that you try your best to understand, not simply accept blindly, any one account, any one point of view, but to get enough information from enough different sources, so you can sort through them and see where they either corroborate one another or contradict one another, and then you have to make your own judgment. And then I think it's important to be honest about what you find out. That is, when you're not sure of something, to say you're not sure. You may not discard the information, like CBS wanted Dan Rather to discard the information about Bush and his record of service as a member of the national guard because it wasn't fully corroborated, but what would have made more sense was for Dan Rather to say, 'This is what we found out about Bush, but we're not absolutely sure about this piece of evidence or that piece of evidence.' I think this point about honesty in disclosing your own bias and honesty in disclosing the inadequacy of what you have found is very important.

D: You've written that when you started to do this history of the US, starting with the Columbus story that a lot of what you were finding was news to you, it was totally surprising.

H: That's right.

D: Did that change how you approached the rest of your research?

H: It made me look even more carefully for information and for points of view that I did not know, and made me ask the question, 'If I didn't know this about Columbus, what else don't I know about these incidents with which historians are quite familiar, and that I have learned about?' It just makes you dig deeper and farther afield.

D: And to also ask the question, 'Why don't I know?'

H: That is a very important question to ask, because it creates a suspicion that certain things have been withheld, for ideological reasons, and makes you even more concerned about finding out the truth about a particular incident.

D: Why is it important for people to know about LaGuardia and his time as a congressman?

H: Because he was unique as a congressman, because he was not your run of the mill Democrat or Republican. He ran as a Republican, although once he ran as both a Socialist as well as a Republican, a strange combination. He was beholding to neither party, he was remarkably independent and his views were quite radical compared to his colleagues in the Congress, especially in his class consciousness, his concern for the poor, his criticism of our policy in Nicaragua, his feel for immigrants. All of these were more radical than the views of his colleagues and so I think it is important, you might say, as a role model, to see that it is possible to be in politics and not to follow the orthodoxy of the two major parties. It is both encouraging to see that, and you might say inspiring to see that kind of independence. It also sets off in dramatic contrast, the orthodoxy of the major parties and the extent to which the Democratic and Republican parties are not that far apart. For those reasons I thought it was useful to do something about LaGuardia's congressional career.

D: I assume it was to some extent a very welcome finding, an inspiration for you as well.

H: Yes, it was. It certainly was for me because I wanted this biography to be about somebody I admired.

D: Why don't people know about LaGuardia?

H: They didn't burn LaGuardia's congressional papers, but there didn't seem to be a lot of interest in LaGuardia as a congressperson. Maybe it's because his years as a mayor overshadowed that, and maybe also because his independence as a congressman, and his political views as a congressman were not as pleasing to most orthodox historians, or orthodox publishers. And then the additional factor simply that part of his life was really not well known. It was sort of gone, and until his papers appeared in the municipal archives, there was really no body of information about his congressional career which was obvious and evident, and which would have led people to explore it further.

D: I think from this distance it's hard to understand how little information was out there. We take for granted CNN, or CSPAN, or the Internet, and the twenty-four hour news cycle. If LaGuardia were around today he'd be on television constantly because he was such a fiery and compelling figure.

H: That's true. In the pre-television days the record was either a written record or an oral record, and if you didn't have access to the written record and you didn't make contact with those people who could give you an oral history, that history became lost.

D: A couple of questions related to the classroom.... What is it that, when you think about kids coming up into the world, through schools, how can we best prepare them to deal with the world, perhaps as historians, but as able citizens?

H: Yes, that's really crucial, that is, what are you preparing them for? And you have to make a decision as to whether your first concern is to prepare them as professionals, to prepare them to be successful in their professional field, or whether your first concern is whether you want them to be active and engaged citizens in society. Now the two are not mutually exclusive, and it isn't a matter of one or the other, but it is a matter of emphasis. And from my point of view, my primary motive in teaching young people is to provoke them with ideas that would make them more active, more perceptive, more probing, more independent thinkers, and also inspire them to become active members of the society, and not simply passive recipients of whatever our political leaders decide. So to me that citizenship requirement is primary.

D: And I assume that you've met many times that experience of shaking people's very tightly held faith, and the art of doing that in a way that does not leave them discouraged or paralyzed or despondent.

H: Yes, that part of it is a real challenge. It's relatively easy to give students the kind of information about the existing society that sobers them, but then the challenge is to not sober them to the point of passivity.

For instance, I taught this course for years called Law and Justice in America. The basic idea was to really change their view, which has been imbibed for so long by so many generations, that the law is sacrosanct. I wanted to persuade them to look critically at the law, to look critically at the justice system, not to believe that because the justices of the Supreme Court wear black robes and sit on high, that they are necessarily infallible, or necessarily moral in their judgments. I wanted them, in other words, to develop a very, very critical, skeptical view of law and the judicial system and the idea of imprisonment, and then of course there's that second part which is difficult. And that is, at the same time, while in a certain sense disillusioning them about the way things are, to hold out the possibility of changing things by pointing historically to the way that people in the past, who were critics of the system did not themselves simply become cynical and retire from the field of engagement, but set out to change the system.

D: So, there has to be models.

H: There has to be historical models, and there are historical models if you look for them. And there too, you have to be careful not to exaggerate the successes, to point out the difficulties, to point out how many times movements of social change fail, but at the same time bring out those instances in which people and organizations and movements have succeeded in bringing about some very important, fundamental change.

D: Two related questions: Who served as mentors or models for you? And who are other people that you would suggest that students read, or encounter now, as both inspirations and models?

H: As to my own models and mentors, I suppose I admired Charles Beard as a historian because he was clearly not following the orthodox path. He dared to write a book critical of the founding fathers, or at least pointing out that the founding fathers were not simply concerned with everybody's welfare and had interests of their own. More recently I suppose Richard Hofstadter was a model for me. Another thing I should say about Beard, he wrote in clear and lucid prose, he wrote books that people could understand. He was a model for me in that kind of independence.

D: Which in itself is amazing. The whole idea that you are writing for so-called "ordinary" people rather than "the academy."

H: Yes, and to me that was always important. And, therefore some of my models were people who were not academics, but who wrote popular books about serious subjects. Upton Sinclair, for instance, and Jack London, and John Steinbeck. My models were often people who wrote fiction, but who wrote the kind of fiction that had a social impact, and was sometimes more descriptive of a historical period, even though it was fiction, than any non fiction account of that period. *The Grapes of Wrath*, to me gave a more vivid and accurate picture of the 30s, and a more arresting and provocative and stimulating picture than you would get from simply reading a nonfiction account by a historian of the thirties.

D: That whole question of what do you want to communicate about a time and a place becomes crucial.

H: The really important things about a period can be lost in a welter of information which leads nowhere. The information must lead the reader somewhere, must point to something, must have a sharpness to it. Very often writers of fiction accomplish that and popular writers accomplish that. Today when I think of historians who I would recommend to be read today, I suppose I'd recommend different people for different things. I would recommend that people as far as possible go to primary sources and documents and oral histories. For instances, the history of the civil rights movement is better known if you read the oral history that was put together by Henry Hampton, that came out of his series, *Eyes on the Prize*. Or the oral history of Howell Raines called *My Soul is Rested*, and of course all of Studs Terkel's oral histories. To convey World War II through Studs Terkel's book *The Good War* is, to me much more valuable than reading a history of World War II. And similarly with his book *Hard Times*, on the Depression, so I certainly would recommend those oral histories.

And for provocative analysis I certainly would recommend that people read Noam Chomsky, warning them that…

D: It's not easy reading.

H: It's not easy reading, but suggesting that they might find it provocative even though it's not easy reading. I would suggest that rather than reading his real books that they read interviews with him. There have been several books of interviews with him. When people are interviewed, and it's true with Noam Chomsky, his language is more informal, more easy going, you don't have to deal with footnotes.

And I'd urge people to read people like Barbara Ehrenreich, I'd urge them to read fiction like Barbara Kingsolver's book, *The Poisonwood Bible*, a remarkable history of the Congo, and to read that alongside *King Leopold's Ghost*. It's often a good approach to read fictional account of a period alongside a non fiction account of a period.

I mean there are historians I recommend for certain periods of American history. I recommend that people read Eric Foner to get a good picture of reconstruction. But I'd also urge them to read WB Dubois's *Black Reconstruction* to get his point of view about reconstruction. These are just a few suggestions.

D: Are there writers who are more conservative, who have viewpoints unlike yours who you nonetheless admire and or recommend that students read?

H: There are writers I admire for their literary ability, like Saul Bellow, John Updike, Nabokov, but whose political views are very different from mine. As for historians, Eugene Genovese, a one-time radical turned conservative, has done admirable scholarship on slavery. I admire the style of historian David Fischer though his work doesn't fit my ideal of engaged historiography.

D: And the bottom line is read.

H: Exactly. Go to the library. You've probably encountered this too, where people come up to you and ask 'Where can I get information?' I tell them, 'Go the library, go into the stacks. Just look around, see what grabs your interest, your attention.'

Rosalie Romano: University Professor, Teacher Education

Rosalie Romano is an assistant professor of education at Western Washington University. She was, for many years a professor at Ohio University where she ran the CARE program with undergraduate teachers-to-be. Dr. Romano has a passion for learning, for democratic education, and for making sure that her students are prepared to truly serve all the students with whom they will be working. She designed and supervised expeditions that her university students carried out in the public schools during their junior years, and talks about that process in this excerpt from our interview.

D: In a large nutshell, what is it you want your students to experience, to come away with from their time with you so that they are ready to do their good work?

R: I want our university students to become absolutely aware of their own agency, of the moral obligation of what it means to be a teacher. They cannot ever expect to rely on a textbook, or a script, or some silver bullet to teach them how to teach. The students are juniors when they are expected to carry out their expeditions. They are at that point in their program where they are going to be student teaching in a year, they've gotten the NCATE template lesson plan shtick that we have to do, but have they ever understood the power, the intellectual power of creating curriculum? That takes confidence and it also takes a mindset, an attitude that causes them to listen deeply to the kids, and respond to what they hear.

D: You have mentioned that you have your students teach through expeditionary learning during their junior years. Could you talk about what expeditionary learning is and lay out how it works? Where does the question for an expedition come from? Is that something the teacher chooses ahead of time?

R: I try to work with the cooperating public schoolteachers, to identify issues that are local, that have seeds of social justice within them. These issues have to be related to our area, to the place.

D: Once you have your topic, then what happens?

R: The teachers and I plan the sequence. We start with an experience that gets the students involved and helps them to generate their own questions underneath the umbrella of the guiding question of the expedition. That's how it starts. We don't set the sub questions that the students will research. And that's really important. It has to be an inquiry question, a question that is compelling to the students. They devise a research plan and carry out that plan. And at the end, there must be a public presentation.

D: So, you plant many seeds with the original event, and then you develop questions, and finally you come to your inquiry question. And then you have to decide how you are going to find out about all this stuff?

R: Yes, because it's not enough to say one person will be my only source, because you absolutely must learn to find different sources, preferably conflicting sources, you have to make decisions about what to believe, what not to believe, and on what evidence, so it's not any more just a matter of personal belief. That's the level and the plane that you want to push for. The best expedition always has conflicting perspective on a specific question so you're always having to say, 'Oh wait a minute, if I'm looking at it from this way it's this, another way it's this. What am I going to do with that?'

The CARE teachers, as pre-service teachers are actually having to think ahead, be purposeful, be prepared with multiple questions that will animate and continue to motivate. They need to both be with the kids in the moment while also looking to the future so they can guide the expedition forward.

D: And there you are, as the teacher of the teachers of the kids...providing the structure and lattice work that will allow them to learn what they'll need in order to do it on their own, and to make sure they don't get sucked into something they can't escape.

R: Exactly, so I meet with them every week in their cooperative group, just the CARE teachers, and I'll say, 'Where are you going? Why are you going there? What pedagogical choices are you making? What do you see in two weeks? What might your question, or questions be? What do you want to see at the end of the term? Predict what you think what your kids will have learned and produced? How will you know if they know? How will you know that they've learned? What are you going to ask them to demonstrate? How are you going to assess? So, those kinds of questions move the CARE teachers back into the role of teacher.

And they do come to trust their kids. I want the CARE teachers to learn to trust themselves. Because they'll come to me and say, 'Is this ok, is this ok?' And I say, 'What do you think? What makes it ok to you?' They have to think for themselves,

It's like a three-dimensional-tick-tack-toe. You can't just walk in and make sense by going one step at a time, because there's a template upon a template upon a template, but the principles are very clear; the principles of curiosity, self awareness, critical thinking, mutual respect, and understanding something deeply. It is what I would consider democratic education.

D: It sounds like you are asking students to do what a more traditional educational approach asks them to do, to approach material as critical readers and thinkers. How is expeditionary learning different?

R: The character of depth, of making meaning, of purposeful work does make this distinct from a more traditional approach because in the traditional you're usually answering somebody else's questions. A service learning expedition is predicated on answering the kids' questions that emerge out of a compelling topic that is usually place based, and in the best case, it will be place based and will be concerned with social justice.

D: This book is about doing research. Can you talk about the research processes involved in these expeditions?

R: There's the content research, from the topic itself. There's research that the CARE students have to do, which requires them go back into any resources that they can find, not just for the content, but for the pedagogical content. It's the research that comes out of saying, 'Ok, if I'm going to teach about school finance, what are ways that I can approach this? Well, I can't know this unless I understand enough about school finance, and phantom revenue, let's say, to even ask the questions.' So it's metacognitive, they have to think about their thinking.

D: You're talking about both your students and their students.

R: Sure. Right now we have this ideology that is actually more than one hundred years old in the United States, that says the subject matter is paramount, it is the king; if you know the subject then you can teach. I violently disagree with that. You have to know the subject matter, but it is insufficient, it is not enough to be able to just go and teach. They need an experience so they can begin to say, 'Oh my god, yes.' Or, 'I don't know enough about phantom revenue... I did all this reading about phantom revenue and the kids know more than I do, what will I do with that?' The CARE students realize, from the inside, that they need to know more, that they and their students need to know more, and that drives them deeper into the research, into the process.

Colleen Ryan: Middle School Math Teacher

Colleen Ryan is a middle school math teacher in rural, upstate New York. She and a colleague embarked on a project helping their math students to explore the AuSable River, which runs through their community, and to link their in-school math curriculum to the real world around them. This project was the first "service learning" project that Colleen has done, and her first attempt at an extended, project-based learning unit. She talked about this first attempt at this place-based project and what she had learned from it.

C: My school district is located along the AuSable River, so it encompasses the AuSable River watershed and the point at which the AuSable empties into Lake Champlain. The watershed is a graphic presence for our kids. It's where they live, but they don't really know much about it. I had never tried place-based learning or service learning before, and didn't really know a lot about it. It was a very new experience for me, personally and professionally. It was a lot of fun and I learned quite a bit.

D: When you were thinking about doing this, what did you have in mind as you started on your path towards this unit? What did you hope was going to happen? What were your objectives?

C: I looked at what I was supposed to be doing according to the state of NY, first.

And I said, 'How can I make what I'm supposed to do fit in with this project?' One of the topics that I'm supposed to teach is recognizing the difference between linear and nonlinear graphs and relationships, and I thought it would be wonderful if they could collect data and somehow see those relationships. I also wanted them to make connections to other content areas. I hoped the students could go out and collect data and use that also to create arguments for why we need to change habits, why we need to improve the way we deal with water. My initial objective was to create a sense of urgency with the kids. They can be kind of passive, but they are at an age where it's easy to get them stirred up and passionate about something. I wanted to show them how precious a resource water is, and how little potable water there is in the world, and then help them to understand how much water they really do use in a day. I hoped this would create a sense of urgency, and help them to understand why we need good quality water, and then we could progress from there.

D: How did you work to create a sense of urgency?

C: One lesson involves taking a container holding 1000 milliliters of water, representing all of the water on earth, and then whittling it down to potable water, which I think was one drop. That model hit home, and of course it's math so we talked about percentages.

D: How did the kids react?

C: They were pretty surprised. I had some prompts for them for their journal reflections, and in their reflections after doing that activity there were some follow up questions that I asked to get them thinking about it. We compared the water resources we use in the Unites States to what people use in other places. And they began to realize how much water is required to do what we do. Even making one piece of paper takes a great deal of water, so that's why recycling is so important.

D: And we have a history here in NY State of rivers becoming incredibly fouled by paper mills.

C: There's the history of our community where there was a mill and factories along the river. They had a big cleanup in Cumberland Bay two years ago, because of PCBs. It scares me to think of how much swimming I did at that beach before the cleanup, when I was a kid. It was very toxic.

D: And so you helped the students to realize why the health of the river is important, and that they can't take that for granted. What came next?

C: Once we talked about how precious a resource water is, I had them measure their water use for a day, and then had them graph what that would look like over time. So they had the table of their water use, then a graph of their water use, and then we wrote an equation based on the graph, so it connected all those different ways of representing the same idea and data. It was through mathematics, but it really hit home with them so they could see how their water use compounds, even over a week's time. The students were seeing the impact of what they were doing. They were amazed at how much water a shower used. They came to realize how much water a fifteen- or twenty-minute shower wastes, and that really surprised them. And they took that home; they were talking about that with their families. It was nice having not only the kids get a sense of urgency, but to go home and talk about it. How often do you have dinner table math discussions?

D: You had a full array of learners involved in this project, from those who are typically successful in school to those who have struggled to keep up in their classes. What did you notice about the learning experience of your students?

C: I was impressed by their critical thinking, by the questions they would ask, and by their enthusiasm. Some of the "at risk" kids, it was good to see them more engaged in school and learning. Being surprised by some of the things they were hearing and learning. It made me wish I could do that all the time, because I think it reaches more kids when you are able to teach that way.

D: I know you didn't do everything you hoped to do this first time through. How do you hope to build on this year's experience?

C: One thing I want to work on is getting my team of teachers more involved. We meet every day, those of us who work with the same group of students, teaching math, social studies, science, and English. I'd like to direct more of our energy into doing more with that project at the end of the year. Help tie it in with the other areas.

One of my ultimate goals, which I did not get to, was to have the students create a persuasive argument, or presentation they can make to our school board, or to adults in the area, about water and water usage. The students would use their math learning and what they learned through their research to explain why we need to put in low-flow water meters, or filters, on our faucets at school because it would save this much money and this much electricity and this much water. It would be helping the environment.

D: There would be a real world, authentic consequence.

C: Authentic. Exactly. I think that would be very powerful. Hopefully I could get the English teacher to help me with that piece, because she uses a lot of technology, and I think it would be a great connection. Here's persuasion, that's English, and let's use the math to support the arguments.

D: What might be your next steps with the project?

C: In order to collect some of the data for one of the projects we wanted to work on was to have all of the kids take samples from different points along the river at the same time. We actually ordered water- testing kits, to take a look and see if there is anything that increases or decreases as the water flows through our district. We now have water-testing equipment. We haven't done that yet, but we'd like to do this next time.

D: Given that you've now done this place-based, service learning project once, and you have an appreciation, in all senses of the word, for what it means to be working in this way, next time, what will you do differently the next time? What will you take from the first round as you approach it a second time?

C: The biggest problem for me was the journaling. I had around eighty students and I was overwhelmed trying to read them all. I'm a math teacher, and not used to that. And I wanted to read all of their journals and respond to all of them. That was a lot of work for a math teacher.

D: For any teacher.

C: And I wasn't accustomed to that. I'll have to figure something else out, take random journals or something to make it manageable. But I loved reading the journals; that was my favorite part, but the most time consuming. We were able to write a grant for the watershed project to have them pay for the water-testing equipment so we have the stuff to be able to do that and see what happens. That's the biggest piece I want to include next time. Maybe eventually get to the presentation.

D: If someone were starting this for the first time, as you were last year, what advice might you give them?

C: Definitely find someone else to work with, a group of people.

D: Why?

C: It keeps you on the hook. You have many ideas and perspectives, and working with others can help you focus, and it just makes it a lot easier to work as a team towards a common goal. It was nice for Mike [the teacher she worked with on this project] and I to be able to work on this one project together. It really helped a lot.

D: This book is about research. What kind of research did the kids do? When you think about the process of research, what are you doing?

C: A lot of it was personal research. At first, it was looking at collecting their own data at home, and then what I'd hoped was having them maybe collect data along the river, making a mathematics and science connection. Maybe asking why, or looking at the social context of what was happening around the river and I was hoping they could get some of the historical/political issues. I mean it's very political, the use of the river. A common attitude around here is, 'I've been doing this all my life, why should I stop?' There are many economic issues related to water use. I was hoping to get that into the mix so it would involve interviewing local people, having them come in and speak so they could learn and ask questions of them about the watershed and get a more balanced view about what's going on in the backyard. That's what I hoped. That would lead to the persuasive speech at the end of the unit

D: That's an opportunity to teach interviewing skills, note taking skills, evaluating information, what you just heard and saw. This is a wonderful context in which to learn and practice those skills.

C: Absolutely. It's definitely a work in progress. I'll probably be very surprised where it ends up. I'm thinking one way now but the kids will take me in a whole different direction. I kind of left it open to where it could go.

CHAPTER SIX

Responding to the Invitation: Researching Hidden History

Students are not always prepared to respond to an invitation to choose a topic to research. Many have been trained away from following their interests, and such an open offer can be intimidating or overwhelming to inexperienced researchers. We can help our students to learn to identify and to act on their questions and interests by structuring research activities, and by giving them some clues and suggestions for where they might look when they are searching for possible topics. We can offer them the opportunity to look beyond and behind the news headlines and paragraph summaries, to locate history that is at once more personal and more complex and multi-faceted than what they find in their texts. I am calling this general category of potential research topics "hidden history," and much of it is easier to find than you or they might think.

Hidden history lives in places that you wouldn't think to look, you don't remember to look, you're not allowed to look, and also in places you do look but don't see. It is history that has helped to shape our towns and cities, our environment, and the ways that we live our lives, and its role is rarely or only grudgingly acknowledged. It is history that holds deep meaning, in its telling, in the ways that it is told, and at times in the fact of its not being told.

This history is hidden or inaccessible for many reasons. Some of them are intentional: governments, corporations, and individuals have worked hard to cover up history, to keep knowledge of events, deals, schemes, policies and actions from the awareness of the public, but that's not all of it. Some history is more lost than hidden, because those who know and/or care about the stories are no longer around or able to tell them, and there are fewer who know how to hear the history with understanding.

Stories are also hidden because times change in ways that leave behind what was once important, and even central to the lives and fortunes of a place and people. Those new to an area, to a neighborhood or to a situation often don't know what it was like before— don't know how to recognize clues and artifacts when they are looking right at them. It took me many months to realize that the large screened porches in houses all around Saranac Lake, N.Y. were artifacts of the town's history as a center for tuberculosis treatment and research. People who contracted tuberculosis in the tenements and factories in New York, Philadelphia, and other eastern cities would come to Saranac Lake to "take the cure" at the Trudeau Institute, and at sanitariums and cure cottages throughout the region. They would spend their days sitting on Adirondack chairs breathing the clear mountain air that was, for decades, the only curing strategy that offered the possibility of success. Once a medicinal cure was found in the 1950s, there was no longer a medical need for people to come to Saranac Lake. The town had to reinvent itself, and has struggled to do so in the decades since. The Trudeau Institute now researches cancer rather than tuberculosis, and many of the former cure cottages are now motels or vacation cabins. There is little mention of tuberculosis, as the town no longer wishes to be known as the "City of the Sick," as it was once.

And sometimes the history remains hidden because we have been taught to look through particular lenses that let some information through in particular ways and excludes any or all information that does not match the shape of the lens.

I've identified five major categories of hidden history, and offer them as possible directions for students exploring topics for research: history held in family stories and experiences; history held in the lives of people who have lived beneath or outside of society's radar; history held in place; history that has passed on with time, with movement, with change; and history that has been intentionally, and sometimes forcefully hidden by those with the means and perceived reasons to do so. There is clearly overlap across categories, though I will talk about them as if they are discrete.

Family Stories and Experiences

One of the most significant assumptions underlying this book is that content and process are most engaging if they matter to us, and for this reason, among others, family stories and experiences are excellent potential avenues for research. Our own lives and families do matter to us, and our students are immediately connected to what is happening in their (and our) classrooms if we are intentionally making links to their families, to their own lives. When I visited the classrooms of Seattle I saw students whose histories and cultures touch virtually every continent, who collectively speak more than 80 languages, and whose family stories reach back to much of not only the nation's history, but also the world's history. When we work through and with our students to encounter the world we are learning how to listen to each other, and to understand the role that point of view plays in understanding history. When we ask our students to explore their family's history, to learn about where their parents and grandparents lived and worked, how they came to where the family now lives, and what their lives were and are like we are telling the world's story and realizing that it is our own. The students are where they belong, at the center of the study and connected to each other, and they come to realize that this has been true throughout history; ordinary people living in a particular time and place become the historical figures who we read about, or who enact the history we read about in history books.

World War II was not simply the story of Eisenhower, Hitler, Churchill, Stalin, Hirohito, and Roosevelt, or even of the complex economic, political, social, and geographical factors that shaped policy: it was the story of millions of young men who spent years fighting and killing and dying for something they believed in, or because they were ordered to do so; of the families who watched them go, who sent them off with both pride and fear; of the women who worked at defense plants and in related industries, filling jobs that had long been denied them; and of African Americans who also found access to good-paying jobs in defense industries, in shipyards, and at other war-related job sites, and began to think of themselves differently in terms of what they could do and what they would settle for when the war ended. It is the story of soldiers of color who fought a war for freedom abroad only to return to second class citizenship at home; and it is the story of the many young men who refused to fight, either becoming conscientious objectors or going to jail for their beliefs. As long as we limit the story to what the leaders did, we keep history at a distance, and we remain outside of it. When we include those who served, like our fathers, uncles and grandfathers, and those who were affected at home, like our mothers, aunts, sisters and grandmothers, we are instantly invited inside, and those uninspiring paragraphs in our history texts are suddenly joined to the photos in our family albums. It makes all the difference.

It was a shock to read about the US-Vietnam War and the tumult and protest that accompanied it as a point in history as distant from the present as World War II had been when I was in high school. That war and era wasn't ancient history to me; it was my life, and now it was reduced to a couple of paragraphs in the class text. And they got it wrong!!!! I became immediately invested in adding my voice to the conversation, and so I became involved in making history, in joining history.

One year my middle school students and I were watching bits of a PBS series on the war in Vietnam. Our school's lead custodian came in to the classroom while we were watching, stared at the screen for a few minutes, and started to cry. He was from Vietnam and had lived through much of the war that destroyed many people he knew and the beautiful countryside in which he had lived; it was not just a television documentary for him. We invited him to talk about his experiences and thoughts regarding the war, and he brought us an understanding and perspective that we could not have gotten from our text. He "became" a real person for us, not simply one of the invisible ones who kept the school running.

Later I brought in a segment from a documentary on post-traumatic stress syndrome, a phenomenon that has touched many families in Washington State. As we watched, one of my students suddenly realized that she was living with a parent likely experiencing this trauma. Our study of the war in Vietnam had quickly moved from distant history to become personal and immediate.

I was able to talk about the demonstrations that I had been part of, and the anguish and tumult of the late 1960s and early 1970s as I, as an individual, and we as a nation struggled with that complex and troubling policy. As I shared my stories, and invited other family members and "elders" to share theirs, the text's two paragraph "coverage" of the war in Vietnam gave way to a very rich, complex, and personal look at a specific time and place in our history. What we talked about, read about, and learned mattered. It was a story that belonged to all of us, in all its messiness and complexity, and emotion.

There are several kinds of family stories that serve as vibrant and engaging entry points to the study of history. Here are a few of them:

Immigration/migration stories

How did our families come to be where we are today? Where did they come from, what was it like there and what did they do, why did they leave, how did they travel, where did they go, why did they go there, and how did they finally get to be where you are today? These stories are fascinating on their own, but even more so when connecting to the larger events going on in the state, nation, and world at the time. Students quickly learn that their isolated, unique family stories often coincide with mass movements due to job opportunities or the lack of jobs, to famine or natural disaster, to war, to political or religious oppression, or other factors. Many of our ancestors moved to cities at around the same time to work in factories, leaving farms or other rural work. Some might have come to the US from Ireland in the middle of the 19th century, during the "potato famine," which has deep political and colonial roots as well as fungal ones. Some of our students have ancestors who came to the country to work building the nation's rail system in the mid-to late 1800s, or came to a coastal city to work in shipyards, or in defense plants in the 1940s. Many of our students came to the states after wars or uproars that took place in their lifetimes. And the families of some students have been here all along, our nation's "first people," who have struggled to maintain their cultures, histories, and worldviews despite the intense changes brought to them by those others who arrived.

Work

Another fruitful avenue to explore is the story of the work that members of our families have done, in places they have moved from and in our current settings. When we move back through time we get a history of the technology, economy and society of those times and places in which our families lived. When we trace the work histories of our parents and grandparents, our uncles, aunts, cousins, and family friends, we get a picture of times and places beyond our current knowing, and they afford us a personal view and account of what once seemed beyond our interest. Frequently family members can tell stories about those times, those jobs, and the society that provided the context for their lives. Who were the big employers in their towns? What was the work like? Who was hired, and who was not hired, or restricted to certain kinds of work? What kinds of training and/or education were needed to get hired or to succeed at that work, and where did they get it? What were the relationships between employers and employees, between the companies and the towns? How was the town connected to the rest of the region and world through the products they produced? How was it similar or different in different parts of the world, or nation as we compare our family stories, and how do we understand that?

Housing, clothing, food, daily life

Learning about the construction of and nature of their dwellings, their clothes, their foods, and the way they spent their time will perhaps make them seem like they lived on the moon, to our students, but is the essence of history.

Some years back a senior citizen visited my US history class, and she brought her crank Victrola and some early records with her. She played the first one and the kids in the back asked her to turn up the volume. She opened the door to the cabinet; this was volume control. She told the students the story of her getting the Victrola, about the nights she and her friends would spend listening to the big bands of their day, and that she had no idea what most of her favorite singers looked like, since there was no television, and since she could not afford to attend concerts. And when she asked for a volunteer to wind the crank to play the next tune the students almost fell out of their chairs.

That somewhat light-hearted entry led into her account of her life during the Depression, and brought her and several students to tears as she helped them to understand, on a personal level what it meant to truly be without: without food, without heat, without hope. Students were able to share some of their own stories and experiences, reaching across generations to make connection with this guest who lived through what for them was distant history. This kind of experience allows our students to realize on a personal level that our stories and the choices we make today and tomorrow will be what students read about in their history books fifty years from now.

Finally, family stories can play a role in our investigations into other aspects of our search for hidden history. If we are investigating the history of buildings or structures, we may ask our family members if they remember anything like the factory or mill we are researching, and we may well find a family member who worked in one, or knew someone who did. If we are researching the connection between a disease such as tuberculosis and the impact it had on a particular time and location we may well find that someone in our family had the same illness, and perhaps had even gone through similar experiences as that which we are finding elsewhere. When I asked a friend about a glass- making company that was in operation near his home town in central Pennsylvania, he did some investigating and found that two of his family members had died from diseases they contracted through work related to that business. This is how it always is; when we start looking, the connections are there.

For those who can't research their families

We all have worked with students who either do not have access to family members, or whose family members are not able or willing to share information about their lives, or whose history has been taken from them. There are several possible ways to proceed, and I am sure that these are likely to be familiar to you. The students can research stories of people who are likely to have lived in the same places and times that their family members lived if that information is known. They can work with other students to find out what they can about the other student's family. The students pick a time or place that interests them, and have them follow a path that could have happened or that is of interest. You can help them to dig a bit to discover if there are family friends or more distant relatives with whom they can connect to gather information, or guidance about how they might take next steps. The Internet has made it more possible and affordable than it once was to make connection to those who live in other parts of the country or world.

As always, the key is to be sensitive and supportive to students, and to help them to move forward with their learning, but never at the expense of their well being. Family is as sensitive and primal an issue as we have, and you never want to embarrass or humiliate students by forcing them through a search that will cause them pain or discomfort. No assignment is more important than the students involved.

The Lives of the People

This category clearly overlaps with the previous section since our families are frequently those excluded because we are "ordinary" and at a distance from the center of power. Henry Kissinger is quoted by Howard Zinn in *A People's History of the United States* as saying that "History is the memory of states," and most would likely agree that this describes the way most of us were taught in schools. Students are required to learn the stories of leaders, be they political, military, royal, or economic, and the story of a nation or empire writ large. The revolution was led by a few good men. Abraham Lincoln and U.S. Grant won the Civil War, defeating Robert E Lee; Martin Luther King WAS the civil rights movement; Genghis Kahn was a bad dude, Alexander was great, and William the Conqueror won the Battle of Hastings in 1066. There is a vague awareness that theirs were not solo accomplishments, but there has been precious little written about, or attention given to the ordinary people who have actually lived the lives that are the facts of this nation, and all nations.

The history hidden in the lives of ordinary people not deemed worthy of noticing makes up a significant portion of the history of the United States, and the world. The founding fathers may get most of the historical ink, but it was really the founding mothers who held families, institutions and towns together, and the towns survived because of the efforts of nameless farmers, woodworkers, coopers, shopkeepers, blacksmiths and trades people who lived in them. Millions of enslaved Africans literally built the buildings, tended the fields that supplied the food and clothing of the young nation, and served that food to the wealthy and their children. Native American men, women, and children had to cope with or come to understand how to deal with the thousands upon thousands of European

Americans who showed up, uninvited, on their doorstep. Occasionally the inter-
actions were peaceful; more often they resulted in either death or forced reloca-
tion for those "first people," pushed out by those so-called founding fathers. The
Thanksgiving story most Americans have come to know, is a fictional European
American fairy tale. It is hardly the story told among those descendants of the
First People who were living in what is now the eastern United States in the
1600s.

Millions of men and women have shed blood, their own and others' through
our nation's hundreds of years of history. Hundreds of thousands of semi-
enslaved workers from China, from Ireland, from elsewhere were lured to the
US with promises of wealth and freedom, and driven from their homelands by
war, famine, oppression, colonization, and other tragedies. They built the rail-
roads and roads, and built the wagons, engines and autos that brought families
west. They became the backbone of the industries that brought the nation great
wealth and power, even as they themselves toiled in poverty and anonymity.

A more accurate and complete history of the United States would include
the stories of these so-called ordinary people, with an aim to understanding their
lives, their issues, and the ways in which their lives have been affected by decisions made by the rich and powerful. This more complete history would also
include the stories of those located even farther towards the fringes of "ordinary
society." Those making up these categories change from time to time, from place
to place, but they have usually been women, people of color, recent immigrants,
or those who were once recent immigrants, those who are out of work and perhaps out of homes, those who are struggling economically, and/or with their
health, and children. Their stories, their issues, their struggles are rarely recorded; they frequently do the work that is essential to a particular community
but deemed unworthy, or "menial" such as tending fields, doing laundry, collecting trash, waiting on tables, driving public transportation, fixing or building
roads, and other "unskilled" tasks. Many of our students come from families
who are, or once were among those living on the fringes, and it is crucial that our
students are able to find themselves in the story of their country. Otherwise, the
message is that their lives and the lives of their ancestors are really irrelevant to
the study of history, insignificant stories in light of the deeds and doings of the
"important" people. This is certainly not the message I want to send to my students, though there is plenty of evidence across the country that it is a message
received by way too many of our young people. How can we be surprised that so
many of our students are just saying no to what they rightly perceive to be a dis-

honest and dismissive telling of America's story, a story that places them outside of what matters.

Michael Grigsby's story of his "Uncle Brooks," living in mid-twentieth century Warren, Ohio, is an example of the way that our family stories and our local and national history are intertwined such that the study of one leads to the study of the other. Hiram Brooks was a caterer, in fact "the" caterer in Warren. Catering was one of the few careers open to an African American in mid-century Ohio, and Hiram Brooks was very successful. He catered events large and small and had an impeccable reputation for quality. He was also not allowed to dine with those he served, and was a mostly functional alcoholic who was respected for his professional skills but excluded socially because of his race.

Here are a few excerpts from Michael Grigsby's story about his Uncle Brooks, and life in Warren.

In 1963, as a result of my grandfather's involvement in the civil rights movement, our house was bombed because of some of his activities. He had been involved in getting young black men into apprenticeship programs like the electricians' union, the plumbers, those sorts of things, and often had to challenge the unions and companies to do so. He was successful, but it was resented. He frightened people.

Our house was bombed in February of 1963, by our next door neighbor. I saw him do it. And as a result, my grandfather and grandmother went to live, for about four months, with my grandfather's law partner, Mr. Breckinridge, and his family. My mother and I went to live with Uncle Brooks and Aunt Kitty, my godparents.

Uncle Brooks was a very successful caterer, and he was the only caterer, black or white in Warren, Ohio, so he got lots of business, from businesses, from engineering firms, from church groups...He was busy all the time, and he employed a lot of people, blacks and whites. Uncle Brooks had this huge, huge complex, a compound almost. He probably owned two square city blocks. His house was there, and then he had his garages and his warehouses. He had these large buildings full of cutlery, china, spices, and linens, and he had seven or eight station wagons and step vans where he would transport all this stuff, the food and the whole thing. He ran a very large, successful business, and this was a guy who had just graduated from high school in a small rural town in Virginia.

It was a business, it was a serious business. The logistics of that business are amazing. There's the acquiring of food, the preparation of the food, the acquiring of the people, the staff and insuring that they are trained. That was both ongoing and immediate; depending on the size of the event he would have to get his cooks in, and he cooked himself, and he had to get the food in.

He knew the folks and they knew him, and since business was constant.... I mean he was a whirlwind, a little, fat whirlwind, smoking cigars, and he wore penny loafers that he stuck the "counters" down in the back so they were like slippers. He was everywhere. He was cooking and talking with people and he was on the phone constantly, making sure everything was going right.

He was a pretty complex individual. He knew what he wanted and what he promised to give he gave. If he was contracted to cater a meal they got first class. I mean, it wasn't any of this cold chicken and limp green bean stuff. He knew how to shop. He focused on fresh vegetables so he had business interests, dealings with the Amish farmers in the region. Apparently he had interests with meat purveyors, butchers, that sort of thing. Everything he presented was always first class. He was famous for his standing rack of rib roasts. And if Brooks was catering, people looked forward to it, people talked about it.

But, as Michael tells the story, life was anything but simple for "Uncle Brooks."

He was a functioning alcoholic. Sometimes he'd get drunk and feel sorry for himself. When he'd get drunk and disappear, Aunt Kitty would send me after him and I always knew where he was. He would be sitting in his car overlooking one of the country clubs, in Warren, sitting up there dead drunk and crying about, "Good enough to feed them, but not good enough to socialize with them."

The racial and economic complexities of rust belt Warren, Ohio, were the story of much of America in the 1950s and 1960s, and they are all accessible through Michael Grigsby's family story. Our own family stories are no different in that they connect us to the times and places in which we have lived, which in turn existed within the larger context of the nation's stories.

History Held in Place

Place-based education is a growing field that is complex and complicated. It is really an integrated look at who we are and how we got that way, pulling together all the factors that link us to the land on which we live and the ways we live with it. It includes environmental and ecological study, but also includes anything that relates to the questions "How does living here affect the ways in which we live and view the world, and who we would be if we lived in some other place?" There is also a focus on how we can know more about the place in which we live so that we can make a difference there.

There are some obvious connections between place and "hidden history," including the ways in which clues for who we are and how we got that way reside in the work that we do, the ways that we live in the world, and the ways in which we relate to and with the world.

Building and Structures

The documentary film *The Uprising of '34* begins with a long, slow pan across the ruins of a red brick factory building in South Carolina. This once thriving textile factory stands forgotten, windows broken, fences rusted, machines long ago silenced by the company's move away from the town. It was the site of one of the most dramatic and extraordinary events in our country's labor history. Approximately 500,000 workers in cotton mills across the South went on strike in 1934. The National Guard was called in to protect the mills, and, in one South Carolina town seven strikers were murdered by their own townsmen serving in that guard. This strike is rarely featured in the study of United States history, and many of those living in the town where the murders occurred were ignorant of it until documentary film makers arrived to research the events of some sixty years before. As Kathy Lamb, the daughter of one of the strikers said about her father,

> I can't understand why my Dad didn't tell me. He could talk about the war and talk about people being blown to bits he couldn't talk about his neighbors beings killed. And it's like somebody trying to hide a dirty secret about their family, like they're ashamed of what happened to their families. They ought to be proud of 'em, they stood up when other people wouldn't.
>
> —*Kathy Lamb, p 6 of script.*

Many of those who knew of the strike and murders would not talk about it with their children, and those who came to town in the intervening decades had no clue that it had ever happened. Today many of the mills stand silent, abandoned; the work that once kept them at fever pitch is now done in China, or the Philippines, or Sri Lanka, and those who once worked there either moved on to other factories in other towns or found other work in town.

There is significant history in the buildings and structures of any place, of any environment. There is the obvious information conveyed by the kinds and size of land plots, dwellings and structures, the materials from which they are constructed, the slopes and angles of their roofs, the design and shape of their building footprints, and the length of time they are designed to last. These features tell us about the climate, the things that grow and thrive in a place, the ways that people interact with their environment, and with each other. But there are other stories told by the buildings and structures, more complex stories about who has lived in a place and how they have lived. Many of these stories are told most eloquently by those buildings that have been abandoned. Virtually every town or city in our age of new technologies, outsourcing, and corporate globalization features large, abandoned factories, often surrounded by chain-link fences, themselves rusted and compromised by time and weather. We walk, bike, bus, or drive past them on a daily basis, perhaps giving them a moment's notice but rarely two as we continue on to our destinations, which they no longer are.

They were once. These factories were the heartbeats of our towns and cities, served as the powerful magnets that attracted workers from farms and rural communities around the country to northern industrial cities, brought populations of people from around the world into a common work world, and determined the value and economic health of people's lives. The steel mills of Pittsburgh filled the town with fire and smoke, and provided the material needed to build the most prosperous nation in the world's history. Detroit, the motor city provided the cars that carried the population of the United States to the suburbs and across the country, and led to the development of the nation's highway systems, along with Eisenhower's defense department. Cotton mills across the South produced cloth and clothing worn around the world. Lumber mills shaped the fir, pine, oak, and maple that hard labor brought down from the forests of the Pacific Northwest, the Northeast, and the South. New England mills produced textiles and shoes, and changed the lives of thousands of young girls who stood shoulder to shoulder for eighty hours a week in the fetid environment of those cramped, infested work sites.

There is much to learn from these artifacts of an earlier time and technology, and a few simple questions can open the door to a deeper understanding of our towns and people. Here is a long list of the kinds of questions our students might ask:

What went on at the factory? What kind of work did they do?

What year was it built? Who owned it? Who built it? Had the work moved to this location from somewhere else or was this a new venture?

Who worked in the factory? Where did they come from? What had they been doing before this work?

What was it like to do the work? What was a typical work day? How were workers paid, and how much? How much did it cost to live? Were there options beyond the company store?

What was the relationship between the company and the town? What kind of influence did the company have with the politicians and other decision makers in the area?

How did the town change when the company came?

How did the workers relate to each other and to management?

What were relationships like between and among different ethnic and racial groups brought together in the work environment? How about between men and women? What was it like for the children of the workers?

Why did the company close the factory, and when?

Where did it move to, if it moved? Is the product still produced and sold today?

How was the town affected by the closing of the factory?

There are also buildings that are still standing and functioning but no longer occupied in the way that caused their being built in the first place. The Waltham Watch factory building stands at the end of Brown Street, in Waltham Mass, an immense building that once housed one of the preeminent watch making businesses in the world. The Waltham watch was one of the quality products of its time. It went out of business in 1957, and the factory building was refurbished and transformed into a home for smaller businesses, none of which have anything to do with watches. The story's much the same in cities and towns across the country.

Many who have come recently to neighborhoods or towns housing these buildings have no knowledge of the buildings' "former lives," and there is no reason why they would know it. And yet it is impossible to understand and appreciate the current day town of Waltham without acknowledging its history, its economic and social history in light of the watch factory and the changes it brought to that community.

We notice the new buildings built in support of new populations and new industry where we live today. The changes that the computer and software industry have brought to the Puget Sound region of Washington State were unimaginable in the 1970s, the time of the Boeing bust and the famous billboard, "Will the last person to leave Seattle please turn out the lights?" The arrival and development of the industry brought immense building growth to previously small towns like Redmond and Bellevue, and brought immense wealth and population to the area. We now take this phenomenal growth and change for granted, and act as if it is always been this way and always will be this way. But with Pittsburgh, the now steel-less steel city, and Detroit, the motor-less motor city as our guides, we can anticipate a point in the future when the focus of the Puget Sound region will be vastly different than it is now, and those of a future time will look back to those historical days of the latter twentieth century and early twenty-first with few clues beyond the abandoned or renovated and transformed buildings of the Microsoft Campus, and the densely populated cities on the east side of Lake Washington to guide them to an appreciation for what that time was like.

The Names of Things

Names can provide a doorway into the history of a time or a place. There is significant history residing in the names of streets, buildings, university and public school buildings, community centers, organizations, schools, and businesses. The names of streets reflect all kinds of change. Henry Yesler built a saw mill on the shores of Puget Sound shortly after European Americans arrived. Loggers would skid their logs down a steep road to Yesler's mill, and lumber from that mill was turned into the houses of the developing city of Seattle. The mill is long gone. That skid road, now known as Yesler Way, is evidence of what was a significant factor in Seattle's early story. Every city and town in the United States has streets named for people, for industry, for events that are significant to at least some of the people who live in the area, and who have the means to publicly honor and remember the name. Learning more about the naming of various streets can offer insight into local or regional history. Questions that might guide such an inquiry include the following:

For whom or what is this building/street/development/town named?

Who or what was this person, business, or organization? What was/is their relationship to the town? Why were/are they considered important and worth remembering with this street?

Who made the decision or proposal to name the street or building after them? What arguments or evidence did they provide to support this move?

Was there opposition to this naming? Were there reasons or arguments against the naming?

What does this tell us about what the values and history of the town?

How do the names of the streets or buildings reflect the history or changes a town has been through?

When I was growing up on rural Long Island, New York, there was a Meadowfarm Road and a Lake Drive in our neighborhood. Those street names remain, perhaps serving as a bit of a mystery to those living in the neighborhood today; there has not been a farm or lake there for close to fifty years. Both the farm and lake disappeared around the time that the Long Island Expressway was built and city dwellers moved to "the country." That lake and farm gave way to housing developments and young families buying homes on the GI Bill, families following corporations who moved to the relatively cheap locations of the former potato fields of Long Island. It came at a time when automobiles and an expanding highway system gave birth to a new, national phenomenon, the suburbs, and it marked a significant change in the way millions of people lived their lives.

Streets are often named after people, including those famous for national or international reasons, those who lived locally, as founders, significant employers, or people of importance to the local community. Occasionally the names of streets or housing developments are ironic nods to the past, or as advertising ploys such as when condominiums are entitled something like "Whispering Pines," the name referring to what once grew on site before it was clear cut to build the housing.

History Lost to Changing Times

It is time for dinner at the Huntington Terrace Senior Center and the residents shuffle, limp, wheel, or motor to their places. The youngest of them is nearing eighty, and they are living in a section of the facility reserved for those who are no longer able to live independently. Many are widows, some crippled, and some, like my mom are in an escalating stage of Alzheimer's, memories and the world around them becoming more vague and inaccessible on a nearly daily basis.

The conversations at these tables often center on the quality of the food, the perceived lack of quality in the service staff, recent medical incidents or accidents, and the exploits or challenges facing their children and grandchildren, who either do or do not visit.

Sometimes when I sit at tables with them an amazing thing happens. I am a relative, but also a relative outsider and an infrequent visitor, living as I do thousands of miles away. I have not yet heard their stories. When confronted with a new and interested audience, some residents seem to return from whatever suspended animation in which they have been living, and their stories emerge. Their talk is of fleeing the Russian Revolution in the back of a wagon, of traveling through China on business, running large corporations or large households, taking part in local or national politics, listening to Louis Armstrong on the radio, and living in the world as vibrant, active citizens throughout nearly the entire twentieth century. They remember the Great Depression, Roosevelt and the New Deal, the coming of electricity and "modern conveniences" such as refrigerators, supermarkets, television, automobiles, and highways. They fought in World War II and Korea or worked in factories while waiting nervously at home, remember

McCarthy's search for communists under every bed, saw Jackie Robinson put on a Brooklyn Dodgers uniform, and endured those turbulent sixties, as bewildered parents. Their stories have become hidden, unreachable, and, sadly close to being gone forever. Those with whom they live have either heard the stories already, have no interest in, or ability to engage with the stories of others, or have heard them and forgotten. The stories still alive and residing within those slow moving, quiet, shuffling residents in senior centers, or in our living rooms and "spare" bedrooms are also the stories of our own families, our towns, and the nation.

There is a great deal of history that is lost to the changes that come with time. Some of it is personal, as with my mother. Some is a lack of awareness of how who we are now comes from what happened then.

When we moved into the Central District of Seattle in the early 1980s it was still inhabited primarily by working class African Americans, many of them widows in their seventies, or eighties. The area had been redlined for years. The practice of redlining, now illegal, restricted where African Americans could live. Banks would draw a red circle on a map and only approve loans to African Americans seeking to buy houses within that circle. It left the city segregated, and, given the disparity in employment opportunities and wages, left the Central District in rough economic shape.

There have been massive changes over the past twenty-five plus years. Redlining was finally made illegal. Developers pushed through a change in zoning laws in our neighborhood that allowed multiple structures on the lots. Microsoft moved in across the lake and suddenly there were people coming to town with money and needing housing. The houses around us, even those newly built were cheaper than just about anywhere else in the city, and they were for sale as the widows passed on. Their children had houses of their own, or could not afford the rising property taxes they were now assessed, and were anxious to sell the family houses for as much money as they could. Interest rates came down as sale prices rose.

The neighborhood became whiter, was perceived by outsiders to be safer, and the larger community suddenly noticed how well situated we were geographically, close to Lake Washington, close to downtown Seattle, close to the University of Washington, close to a beautiful arboretum. We were suddenly a very desirable place to live.

Now the neighborhood is mostly white and middle class. The houses and condos are rehabbed, and we are surrounded by perpetual construction. There are several fancy restaurants nearby including a top of the line vegetarian restaurant occupying a building that used to house an extremely run-down laundromat and a storefront church whose small congregation had been comprised of elderly African Americans. There is no trace of what was here even one generation ago, and it does not necessarily occur to anyone moving in to ask about it since there are few clues to mark its passing. Occasionally someone who used to live on the block comes to visit, and they leave, shaking their heads about how white and foreign it has become. The children and grandchildren of those who once lived here have been moving south, pushed out of Seattle by rising prices into neighboring Renton, Skyway, Tukwila, Burien, and SeaTac. They cannot afford the taxes our newly appraised properties require, and it is no longer their home, their community.

This sequence has been lived out in communities across the nation. Change is a constant, an unavoidable fact of life, but it is important to understand why particular changes happen the way they do, and to understand that what they see now is not how it was, and may well not be how it remains. To look at our neighborhood as it is, is to miss the story of the African American community in Seattle, to miss the redlining and racism, subtle and obvious, and the struggles of class and community that have been part of the city's history. The recent subprime crisis may further reshape our neighborhood, or most certainly other neighborhoods around the nation. Those shifts are symptoms, artifacts of the history of our nation, played out, and as we learn about the changes going on around us, we are tapping into a deeper and broader story.

There are several approaches to learning about the history of a place, a neighborhood, a town over time.

Interview long time residents. Have them tell the story of the town as they perceive it. What was the town like when they came to it, and why did they or their family members move there? What was their experience in the beginning? What has changed over time? What is the same and what is different? How is the population different than it was, what jobs are available to people now, how do people spend their time?

Find local newspapers and other primary source documents from different decades or eras of the town's history and learn what you can from them. What was going on in the town, in the world? Who was in the news? What ads were featured, for what products? What jobs were advertised in help wanted? Were there clues about the roles of men, women, and children?

Focus on photographs depicting the main streets or buildings of the town, over a period of several decades. How have the main streets changed over time? What buildings have come, what have gone? What businesses have come and gone? Who do you see on the streets? What are they wearing, what are they doing?

School yearbooks and newspapers might offer some information about what life was like in the town through its history. Local history museums, university collections, and historical societies are often wonderful repositories of historical data and artifacts.

Finally, family members can likely add to your understanding of how the town has changed over time. Invite long time residents of the community to share their stories, photos, and histories with students in your classroom.

History That Is Intentionally Hidden

The final category of hidden history deals with history has been intentionally hidden by governments, by religious institutions, by business titans, by political leaders, by various institutions and individuals with the means to do so and with something to hide or to sell. Many of us grew up believing that the Pilgrims and Natives sat down together at the first Thanksgiving, that a band of heroic Texans defended the Alamo against murderous Mexicans, that European American settlers brought civilization and bounty to the plains and west by defeating the savage Indians, and that America has stood as the leader of the forces of good in the world, with God and John Wayne on our side.

The problem is that these stories are myths, lies or half truths that come to us through our history texts and curriculum, our media, political rhetoric, and even our advertising, and as a result, we do not know who we are, and have little understanding of who we are in relation to others. As we try to understand the wars in Iraq and Afghanistan, or the financial crisis that "no one could have predicted," we are blocked by our miseducation, by the fairy tales we have been told over the years about our goodness as a nation, about our heroes, the rich and powerful operating on Wall Street, and on the role of the government as the servant of the people. The point isn't to label the United States as a good or bad country; it is neither. We are a nation that acts in an incredibly complex environment, as do all nations, and we serve our nation best if we guide our students to appreciate the dynamics in which we live and to learn how to accurately assess the situations in which we find ourselves. That often begins with looking again at the history we have been mis-taught, with the intention of investigating the more complete nature of our history, in hopes of learning how we arrived at this point in history.

When Howard Zinn wrote *A People's History of the United States*, he ushered in what has come to be called revisionist history. Professor Zinn took a new look at U.S. history, and his agenda was to tell our nation's history while including as many relevant voices and points of view as possible. Adding previously excluded voices and viewpoints changed how we understood our story, and it was not always comfortable. Many of the stories he tells are stories that do not present the US or its ruling elite in an admirable light, and they are stories that, in many cases, have intentionally been kept from the general public for that reason. Professor Zinn's accounts of corporate crime, land grabs, sweetheart deals between government and the moneyed and powerful, and of moves made by political and social leaders that were governed by greed rather than by a desire to form "a more perfect union" move his readers to rethink what they knew, or thought they knew about the nature of the nation, and to question other stories we have been told about the men and women who blazed the trails to our present day. That is what revision means, "To look again."

Examples of this sort of hidden history range from the well-known Columbus story, where the full nature of his interaction with the Taino was unknown to the larger community for nearly 500 years, to the stories of the monopolies created by the robber barons of the late 1800s, who were lauded as captains of industry by an adoring press and by many textbooks, to the role of the US military in protecting the economic rights of United Fruit and others in Central and South Americas, and the ways in which discriminatory practices continue to land African Americans and other people of color into US prisons at alarmingly disproportionate rates.

The United States is hardly unique in attempting to shape the history that is told and taught. All nations have their secrets, the stories they wish to keep quiet, and the image they wish to present to the world. Those images are part of what separate us from each other and keep us from working together for the benefit of all. They keep us at war, by demonizing the other as we pump up our own virtues, and they keep us ignorant of our own stories. The more we can help our students to look beyond the simplistic and incomplete paragraphs in our textbooks, and to approach the history presented to us through our media with a skeptical and critical eye, the closer they will come to a true appreciation of who we are and how we came to be here.

Hidden history, then, comes in many forms, shapes, and sizes and shares one essential element in common; there are stories that we don't know, about how we have come to be who we are, about who we are, and about our place in the world. We cannot heal or change elements of our society and world that we don't like if we don't understand their root causes and the emotional, physical, psychological, and emotional hurt that has come along with them. We can't expect to make change quickly if those changes require undoing centuries of societal and institutional racism and class-based oppression. And those working for change must understand that the change they want will be actively resisted by those in power, by those with wealth if they perceive that those changes will be at their expense. That learning is embedded, so to speak, in the stories that always lie just behind the headlines, just under the surface, the stories of the people who have endured, have persisted, have labored to support themselves, their families, and their communities in "ordinary" ways.

CHAPTER SEVEN

Bringing Inquiry Research into Your Classroom

I have made the claim throughout this book that if we want our students to become responsible citizens and life-long learners, then we have to organize our classrooms and design our curriculum with those intentions in mind. We know that good teaching has to begin by meeting the students where they are, rather than where we want them to be, and our students typically have little experience in a student-centered, inquiry-based classroom when they come to us. We have to provide scaffolding, as Steve Goldenberg labeled it, so that our students can develop the skills and dispositions that will enable them to become skilled and effective researchers. There are steps we can take, lessons and units we can offer that will facilitate this growth. I will provide some examples of those steps and lessons in this chapter, beginning with small, introductory, skill-building exercises, and moving to extended expeditions, as examples of what is possible. Some of the exercises come from other educators, and I've indicated this where appropriate. Some of the exercises have been written about in other books or articles, and in those cases I present a brief summary of those lessons and then refer the reader to the original publications for a fuller presentation of the material.

Car Talk

Many of the education students with whom I work become overwhelmed as they begin to appreciate the complexity of, and the possibilities in, teaching through student-centered inquiry research projects. They love the projects themselves and are excited by the idea of organizing their classrooms to engage in active, in-depth learning experiences. but they get nervous at the prospect of actually planning and managing these complex, extended investigations. Suddenly reading the chapter and answering the questions at the end does not sound all that bad to them. It is at this point that, with a nod to Click and Clack, the Tappet Brothers, we have the "car talk."

Learning to teach is very similar to learning to drive a car. We tend not to think about the act of teaching (or driving) when we are not the teacher (or driver) and frequently arrive at our destination unsure of how we got there.

Many things change when we first sit behind the wheel of a car. Even before we've turned the key, many of us feel nervous as we survey the many mirrors, dials, and pedals "staring" back at us. Though we are impatient to get on the road, the prospect can also be intimidating. Our first trips are typically made on side roads with little traffic. We practice accelerating up to 15 or 20 mph and eventually learn to operate the vehicle without causing extensive damage to ourselves or our white-knuckled passengers. We gradually move through a learning curve to the point where we are taking our place on the road, comfortably traveling at the speed limit with growing confidence and skill. It takes time, support, and practice.

The same is true for those learning to become teachers. Few of us are ready for the "freeway," that is, teaching through extended projects, using a range of challenging material that takes students well beyond the textbook. We properly begin on side streets, leaning on the assigned textbooks, materials, and the plans of others, and by taking very small steps in the direction of in-depth research. Most of those teachers we admire started this way during their first years of teaching. We may be impatient to take on more rewarding and involving projects, but we are being responsible to ourselves and our students when we choose to go only as fast as we are ready to handle. We tell young drivers not to outdrive their headlights, to make sure they are not going so fast that they can't respond to what might be ahead. The same is true for teachers. We should travel guilt-free at a pace that we can manage and introduce changes as we and our students gain the skills and confidence to handle them successfully.

Remember the Lessons Learned

In Chapter Two I shared the major themes that surfaced from my interviews addressing the question of what made for effective inquiry research projects. Those themes apply to the work that we do in the classroom, and it serves us well to remember them as we approach the task of designing experiences for our students. To recap briefly:

* The most valuable research tasks are of interest or relevance to the students, and if the topics are not of their own choosing, the teacher best serves her students by making strong connections between the topic and the lives of the

students. There is little point in carrying out the work if it means nothing to the kids.

- Research takes time, and while we don't always know what will come up, we can allow for that time in our plans.
- Research frequently requires the researcher to move beyond the boundaries of any one subject or discipline in order to "follow the thread."
- Listening may well be the most important of the research skills.
- The most effective research experiences result in an authentic, meaningful consequence, for the researcher and hopefully for others.
- There is no one best way to communicate research findings to the intended audience. Students are best served if they are encouraged to consider what they want to say, to whom they want to say it, what impact they hope to have, and their resources, and then decide the most effective means of doing so.
- Finally, the process of finding out about the world is an extremely rewarding and liberating experience, and the more we encourage and support our students to become practiced and effective in their research skills, the more likely it is that they will carry these skills and dispositions through the rest of their lives.

Process or Content before Process and Content

I have had most success in introducing students to new material when I have them learn or practice either content or skills, but not both at once. If they are learning or practicing a particular process or skill, I keep the content easy for them so they can focus on learning that process or skill. They are far more likely to learn the technique if they practice on less-challenging, high-interest passages and articles. They can then apply their newly mastered skills to more challenging texts.

If students are learning new content, I don't ask them to also learn new processes at the same time, as it might be overwhelming for some. They are more able to focus on the new content if they are using familiar and mastered processes. Once they become familiar with content and process, there is time to challenge them to put both together in new and synthesizing ways that call forth higher-level thinking skills and behaviors.

I find it most effective to introduce new skills, to allow the students to practice them enough to get the basic idea, and then to offer them the opportunity to use those skills in a more authentic context, in service to a larger goal. Once they learn to read nonfiction for meaning, for example, I have them read a piece of nonfiction as a piece of a larger project that offers a desirable payoff. They will then use the new skill, receive the payoff—such as learning about something they truly care about—and experience the satisfaction of having done the work effectively.

An Ethnographic Approach

Bringing an ethnographic approach to gathering information can play an important role in the outcome of research. Ethnographers attempt to understand what they are researching from the context and point of view of those they are researching. Ideally, if we are studying a community, we observe that community on its own terms over a period of time. We get to know the stories and systems of the community by observing them in action, by having informants who are knowledgeable and who tell their stories in their own way, while we, as researchers, withhold judgment throughout the process. We are learning a people's story from them, through what they say and do as they live their lives, and refraining from defining them from our point of view as outsiders.

This approach, of essentially moving into a community for an extended period of time, is unrealistic for most of us, but we can take away some important insights from the approach. As researchers, we can withhold our judgments and put aside our attitudes as we investigate our topic. We can approach our interviews, readings, and other data-gathering in a manner that allows and encourages those with whom we speak to tell their own stories in their own way. Our work as interviewers and as researchers is to find out what we can, to come as close to the truth as we can, wherever that might lead us. That implies being open to what we find and approaching our task in a way that elicits as much information and insight as possible.

We bring the same approach to all the sources we encounter as we engage in our research. We first attempt to understand what the source is telling us and to appreciate the evidence and reasoning behind what they are saying, while withholding judgment so that we hear/read what they have to say without the contamination of our own opinions and attitudes. This attempt to really listen is rarely modeled in public media and requires both modeling and practice in the classroom. It is well worth the time and attention we give it, as it is fundamental to the research projects we offer to our students.

The Basics

There are several basic skills or building blocks that together form the foundation for carrying out successful research projects. In Chapter Four I outlined the steps required to navigate the research process, starting with the ability to form and pursue questions and continuing through to the successful communication of the results of the research to our intended audience. In this section I focus on some foundational skills required to actually gather and process the information we have set out to find. These skills include reading for meaning from a variety of sources, listening to others, interviewing, and "reading" visual information, such as a photograph or documentary. I provide strategies for developing each of these skills in this section of the chapter.

Reading for Meaning

Much of what we know about the world comes to us through text. If our students are to become skilled researchers, they need to learn to read critically, to challenge and question any and all texts rather than automatically accept the author's information, evidence, and conclusions as written. Reading critically and analytically can be taught, and it should be taught in small steps. Begin with relatively simple, clear articles that are easy to read while the students learn and practice analyzing them. The first attempts can be done together in class and completed within an hour if the articles are short enough.

Two-Column Note Taking

Researchers have to be careful to separate what their sources say from their own (the researchers') reactions, thoughts, and ideas. Two-column note taking is a technique that can assist in keeping this separation clear.

The basic notion of this is very simple. Readers divide a piece of paper down the middle the long way, or "hot dog-style," as they say in elementary school. The left side is for text, and the right side is for comments/reactions/associations/connections/ideas. The researcher writes down the page number and any ideas that he thinks are important. He need not copy a whole paragraph or page; a phrase, paraphrase, or brief quote will do, and he keeps all this in the left, or text column. I emphasize to students that whatever is written down in the text column comes from the author of the article or text; there is no reader interpretation or reaction on the left side of the page.

If the reader has a comment to make ("what a great idea"; "that can't be true"; "that reminds me of a reading from last week"; "I could do this in my third-period class"), that goes on the right side of the paper, clearly on the comments/reaction side. The intention here is to be clear about what the text says and to separate that from the reader's own reactions, insights, and ideas. It sounds simple, and it is, but many of my students have found it helpful and have made use of the technique in contexts outside of my classroom. They learn to actually read the text and to understand what the author is saying before jumping in with both feet with their own opinions and reactions.

Dr. Jean Ann Hunt, a colleague at Plattsburgh State University, has her students add a third column, in which they note their new understanding of the topic or issue. This pushes them to move beyond recording and reacting, to processing and synthesizing the material.

Analyzing Current Events Texts

I usually begin an introduction to the analysis of text by working with current events. I want students to become more aware of their world. More importantly, I want students to become clear about the value of reading critically and the limits of relying on any one piece of text for the whole story before we analyze and confront Columbus, the Alamo, and other celebrated events from U.S. history that can generate strong feelings and reactions as students come to find that they have been mis-educated about their history. The students will be able to apply what they have learned from their work with current events to any other reading they do.

Begin by introducing the entire class to the process of analyzing and evaluating current events articles. Choose an article dealing with a current issue that is most likely to be of interest to your students, introduce them to the topic that the article deals with, and ask them to write down their initial thoughts/reactions/attitudes about the topic. What do they know, or think they know, and what questions do they have? Have a brief discussion about their responses, and then ask them to read the article and to respond to all or some of the following questions.

What is the title of the article? Who wrote it? What was the date it appeared, and where did it appear?

What does the author say in the article? What points does he or she make about the topic?

What evidence or reasoning does the author provide to support his or her conclusions?

Is there evidence of any particular bias or slant to the coverage?

Are all relevant voices included?

Are the terms used to describe varying sides involved in the situation of relatively neutral value, or do they provide evidence of allegiance or animus toward one side or the other?

Are the selected quotes "fair and balanced"?

What questions are you left with after reading the article?

Who would you like to hear from?

Where might you go to find more information?

How does what you read agree with or challenge your initial assumptions about the topic?

What do you know now, and how do you feel about the topic or issue?

After the students have had time to respond individually, have them work in small groups to compare their responses, and then process the exercise as a whole group. As you process with the group, you have the opportunity to assess their efforts and can determine whether to offer continued practice of this technique or whether the group is ready to move on to more complex work. Since the success of research projects depends so heavily on students reading for meaning, it is worth taking the time to make sure students master the necessary skills. In my experience, practicing only once is rarely enough for most students. Provide a range of articles or readings representing a range of complexity so that all students are encountering appropriately challenging materials on which to practice.

When the class is ready to move to the next step, introduce another article on the same topic, but from a different point of view. Have students repeat the process with this second article, and then have a discussion about what they now know, and how they might proceed. Some discussion questions might include the following: Which article has presented the issue most accurately, most honestly? How can we tell? What should we believe? How do we make sense of the two articles together? What are our next steps?

Add a third or fourth point of view if desired, though the second article should make the point that no one article or point of view carries the complete, accurate, and unbiased truth. This is a good time for a discussion of what historians or researchers do when they encounter differing accounts or interpretations of the same event or issue. Brainstorm with the students as to how they might move forward or approach this seemingly contradictory material. Explore the relevance of evidence, the preponderance of evidence, the role of bias and point of view, and how that affects how we see the world. Ask them to consider what we now know, what questions we still have, and where we might go next.

A Current Events Assignment

After practicing with the entire class in the manner described above, have your students carry out their own investigations of a current issue of interest to them. I typically have them work in groups of three or four, with each group deciding on an issue or topic to investigate. Part of the charge is to make sure that the articles that students select as a group represent a range of points of view related to the topic or issue in question so that they are representing as wide a range of relevant viewpoints as possible. Each student is responsible for analyzing one article related to his or her group's chosen topic. Once each student has analyzed his/her article the group members come together to combine and organize their information and to decide what to share with their classmates.

Students are unlikely to be familiar with a wide range of sources and are frequently unaware of what the term "political spectrum" means, so I take the time to spell it out and then provide a starter set of sources for them. They are certainly not limited to the sites on the list that follows.

Sources from the progressive end of the spectrum include Democracy Now (www.democracynow.org), common dreams (www.commondreams.org), AlterNet (www.alternet.org), *The Progressive* (www.theprogressive.org), *The Nation* (www.thenation.org), the Rouge Forum (www.pipeline.com/~rgibson/rouge_forum/), Truth Dig (www.truthdig.com), Znet (www.zmag.org), and Counterpunch (www.counterpunch.org). More moderate sources include *Time* and *Newsweek*, the *New York Times* (www.nytimes.com), the news pages of the *Wall Street Journal* (www.wsj.com) (their editorials are very conservative), the *Christian Science Monitor* (www.csmonitor.com), and many daily papers across the country. The more conservative sources include the *National Review* (www.nationalreview.com), the *American Spectator* (www.spectator.org), *Forbes* (www.forbes.com), the *Weekly Standard* (www.weeklystandard.com), the editorial pages of the *Wall Street Journal* (www.wsj.com), and some daily papers. You would also want to include news sources from other countries. There are a couple of websites that make this task easier than it might seem, as they collect news from around the world. Two of them are www.dailyearth.com and http://newslink.com. the *Economist* (www.economist.com) is based in Europe and comes at its material from a relatively conservative, economics-centered viewpoint. *the International Herald Tribune* combines resources of *the New York Times* and *Washington Post* and an overseas eye for a slightly different perspective (www.iht.com). Neighborhood journals and papers from various local communities may or may not have a perspective to share on national and international events. Google news (www.news.google.com) is a good place to begin a search for material, since it includes articles from around the country related to particular topics. The site doesn't tend to include sources too far out of the mainstream, so it's not enough just to work with its collection of stories.

Schedule the assignment so that there are no more than one or two groups reporting on current events each week. The exercise is presented in more detail in Chapter Five of *History in the Present Tense* (Heinemann, 2003).

Analyzing Texts for Bias

Many students overlook the author's point of view when encountering a text, and so I now take the time to teach them to analyze texts for author bias. We consider a range of texts, from children's storybooks to class textbooks, using a structured checklist or guide, such as the one developed by the Council on Interracial Books for Children, to help us in our assessments. I want students to consider the role that an author's point of view may play in how she presents material, including what she decides to include or omit, how she frames and describes events and issues that are included, whose voices she chooses to include and how she chooses to include them, and what messages she communicates through her story or text. Recognizing author bias or a particular allegiance to a particular point of view provides a context that allows students to accurately appreciate what they are reading.

Start this process by working together as a class to analyze a picture book or children's book that makes the process clear. Work through each category on the Council on Interracial Books for Children's "10 Quick Ways to Analyze Children's Books for Racism and Sexism" guide (http://www.osi.hu/iep/Workshops/anti_bias/ten_ways.htm), first in small groups, and then as a whole class. Once the students are clear about the process, have them work in groups of two or three to analyze books from the school library or the classroom library. I begin with children's books, including picture books, focusing on materials that they or their students will likely be reading, and then move on to textual materials.

This exercise can be done in stages, and the sessions for doing this can be carried out in less than an hour. When students have come to recognize that anything written has a point of view, they will begin to incorporate that awareness into their approach to reading and, presumably, to the sources they encounter as they carry out their research. I make clear that the students need not disregard or discard a book or article because there is evidence of bias; there may still be much of value in the text. An awareness of bias or a particular allegiance or animus can help them to accurately read and process what is there and to notice what—or who—is missing.

Listening

The researchers with whom I spoke all identified listening as the most important skill for a researcher to master. The researcher must listen first to herself, then listen to the range of sources she encounters as she engages in the research process. We make a mistake as teachers if we assume that our students automatically know how to listen, or to listen critically. Listening is a skill, and it can be taught and practiced. I introduce some in-class exercises for developing listening skills in the next section, and follow that with some suggestions for conducting interviews.

Dyads

Dyads is an exercise in listening and speaking. Students work in pairs, with each partner taking a turn speaking on a topic for two minutes without interruption or comment from his or her partner. Ask the students to talk about a controversial topic they've been studying in class, or choose a topic that will generate interest and energy for the students. The first student talks for two minutes. His or her partner says nothing, perhaps nodding or making other encouraging gestures to keep the speaker going. If the speaker falls silent or seems stuck, the listener can prompt the speaker with a leading question ("tell me more about..."), but this should be done only if absolutely necessary, and as efficiently as possible. Then, after two minutes, the two switch roles; the former listener becomes the speaker for two minutes on the same topic. The structure keeps the "listener" listening, rather than waiting for his or her turn to speak, and insures the speaker that she is being listened to for the full two minutes.

I add a paraphrase extension to this exercise, asking each listener to sum up briefly, in his or her own words, what the speaker has said, checking that they have heard correctly. This does not add much time and helps students to tune up their listening skills. It also confirms for each speaker that they have been heard correctly and models the process of checking comprehension, an essential task when interviewing or when gathering information via listening. I close by giving the students an additional one- to two-minute opportunity to share how it was to talk and how it was to listen within the framework of this exercise.

It is a surprisingly powerful experience for many speakers to be fully listened to for two full minutes, without interruption and without competing for airtime. This exercise helps students to feel comfortable speaking, helps develop their listening skills, and builds trust and connection in the room.

Triads and Quads

This next listening exercise builds on the dyads experience and comes from Jan Maher. Students work in groups of three or four, and as in the dyads exercise, each group member has a specific role. One person is the speaker, one is the scribe, and one or two are encouragers. The speaker talks for two or three minutes on a topic of interest. The scribe takes notes while the encourager(s) support the speaker to keep going, as the listener did in the dyad exercise. When the speaker has finished, the scribe reads back the notes and the speaker either corrects them or approves and signs off on them, indicating that they are accurate. Then the process is repeated with group members switching roles until each member has had an opportunity to take on each role. The students then process the experience briefly as a group, and then talk together as a whole class about what they have noticed and learned.

Listening to a Speaker

Another basic exercise is to give brief lectures, lasting no more than ten minutes, during which the students take notes. The lectures should be on relevant course content, but one of the objectives of the exercise is to have the students practice listening critically and accurately to the information presented in a lecture format. I give the students a brief list of questions to answer, such as:

What was the main topic of the talk?

What were the major points made?

What evidence or reasoning was presented to support the major points?

Did I, as the speaker, seem to be biased, or aligned to a particular point of view? Why or why not?

What questions do you have about the topic now?

The students respond to the questions once I've finished the brief talk and then compare notes with each other in small groups. We follow with a whole-class discussion. We talk about the major points, and the students discuss how they knew what to write down. We note areas of disagreement, where students heard different things, and refer to the text to see what I actually said. At times I video-tape the talk so we can notice body language and other cues and clues that might help them to track the talk.

We practice this more than once. During other lectures I ask the students to write down whatever seems important, or whatever they notice, without any guiding questions, and we repeat the same procedure of comparing in pairs or small groups, and then as a whole class. Some of these lectures are neutral in tone and presentation; others are more intentionally slanted or biased, giving students the opportunity to compare and contrast.

Interviewing

Once the students have been introduced to and have practiced listening to and with each other, they are ready to learn how to prepare for and to conduct inter-views. While skilled interviewers make the process look effortless, successful interviews are the result of solid preparation, research, and attention to detail. Like most things, it's a lot harder than it appears, and students who assume they can simply sit down and interview someone are often surprised by how much is involved.

Analyzing the Work of Others

One way to introduce the interviewing process is to observe and then analyze the work of expert interviewers. The first person who comes to mind is Studs Terkel, the legendary broadcaster from Chicago who wrote several books based on his interviews with a wide cross-section of Americans, and who interviewed an incredible range of people on his radio program over several decades. Other well-known interviewers include Bill Moyers (of *Bill Moyers Journal*), Teri Gross (*Fresh Air*), Tavis Smiley (*The Tavis Smiley Show*), and Amy Goodman (*Democracy Now*).

Have your students watch or listen to a complete interview, or a segment if the interview is a long one. Play the interviews twice, the first time so that the students can get a sense of the overall conversation, and the second time so they can concentrate on details. Have them respond to the following questions:

What was the topic under consideration?
What do you think the interviewer most wanted to know?

What kinds of questions did the interviewer ask that produced the most interesting information?

What did he or she do either to encourage or discourage (shut down) the interviewee?

Do you think the interviewer was fair to the interviewee? Why or why not?

Would you have wanted to be the person being interviewed?

What have you learned from how they conducted the interview? What is something you might try when you interview someone?

I also hand out chapters or selections from some of Studs Terkel's oral history work. Mr. Terkel often published his books without many—or any—of his questions included. I ask the students to think through what questions he might have asked to generate the responses he got, and we compare and analyze the questions we imagine he asked.

Interview Practice in Partners

Interviewing someone you don't know can feel a bit risky, especially the first time out, and this is true whether the interview is carried out in person or over the telephone. Practicing in a safe environment is important. I find it useful to have students practice interviewing each other before they are scheduled to interview someone out in the world. There are several reasons for this. One is that it helps the students to develop relevant and focused interview questions and then to test those questions in a safe and supportive environment. It helps students to understand how much time an interview can take and to recognize the kinds of questions that generate the most informative answers. It demands of the students that they learn enough about the topic so that when it is their turn to be interviewed they have something to say in response to the questions. It also gives students a better understanding of what it is like to be interviewed. which will help them to gain both compassion and insight into the experience, and will contribute to their growth as interviewers.

Group Interviews

A next step in practicing interviewing is to invite guests from outside to come into the classroom to be interviewed by the class. When my class was studying immigration, we asked a number of the school's instructional assistants, many of whom were relatively recent immigrants, if we could interview them about their experiences. We developed a list of questions based on what we wanted to know, decided what order to ask them in, and then actually conducted the interviews. We videotaped the interviews (with permission) and were able to watch them later in order to analyze how they went and how they could have been improved. Practicing in this structured, whole-group arrangement paves the way for students to go out to interview sources.

Moving Out of the Classroom to Conduct Interviews

Finally, there is no real substitute for actually conducting interviews. There are several things to keep in mind when considering whether to conduct an interview. Historian Lorraine McConaghy has prepared a handout on conducting a successful oral history interview, and I am including several of the suggestions she makes.

Choose to interview someone because that is the best—or only—way to get the information you need. You are asking them to donate their time, and you don't want to ask that of them unless you can't get what you need in other ways.

Set up the interview date and time as soon as you can. People's calendars fill up quickly and you want to make sure they are available when you need them. Ask if it's okay to call them a day or two before the scheduled interview to make sure that everything is still good to go.

Prepare as thoroughly as you can. Do background research on the topic and on your interviewee's relationship to the topic so that you become clear about what questions to ask. You will also have the best chance of fully understanding their responses if you have done your background reading.

Develop a list of interview questions. These should contain as many open-ended questions as possible. Open-ended questions are questions that offer your subject as much room as possible to choose how to respond. "Can you tell me what it was like in the factory?" is an open-ended question, since your subject can choose what to talk about and how to talk about it. There's nothing limiting about the question.

Avoid closed-ended questions, or make sure there are only a few in your interview. These questions are called closed-ended because they don't lead anywhere. "What year did the factory open?" is a closed-ended question because once your subject has answered "1927," there's nowhere else to go. You could get the same information in a much more open-ended way by asking "Can you talk about the opening of the factory?"

Once the interview has begun, your most important task is to encourage your informant to talk on the topic, to share what stories he or she has to tell.

Ask your question and then listen carefully. A good interview is one in which the subject does most of the talking. You might want to pick up on something the interviewee has said, to ask him or her to expand on or to explain something, and you might need to gently bring them back to the topic you are researching if they wander in other directions.

If you intend to record the interview, ask permission when you first set up the appointment. Practice with your equipment so you know how it works. Make sure you have extra tapes, batteries, and whatever other equipment you might need. Write up a permission slip and have the interviewee sign it at the time of the interview, so you don't have to chase them down later should you want to include part of their interview in your product. Be specific about what permission you are seeking, so that the interviewee is clear how his or her words may be used, and where.

Once the interview is complete, transcribe it as soon as possible. This can help if words are garbled and gives you the chance to hear what was said a second time. This will assist you in determining if you got the information you were hoping to get, if you missed a question you should have asked, or if there was something your interviewee said that surprised you and that has led you to more questions. You do have the option of contacting your subject again and asking if he or she would mind responding to one more question, or would be willing to clarify something that is not clear to you after listening to the playback. This does not require another interview session but could be a brief phone conversation or e-mail exchange. Be sensitive to your subject's time, and follow this course as efficiently as possible.

I usually have students work in pairs and practice how they are going to share asking questions, taking notes, and keeping track of how the interview is going before actually conducting it. I never send them out alone to interview someone, no matter what their age, so most of our interviews take place by phone or at the school. The logistics of sending students out are generally too complicated to be worth the trouble and the potential risk.

Analyzing Photographs

When I was young, we often heard the phrase "Seeing is believing," and were encouraged to trust what we saw with our own eyes. That is no longer the case. Back in the 1990s I remember watching a young woman having her picture taken at a booth at a fair, standing alone in front of a neutral backdrop. When the picture was developed, there she was, standing next to Bill Clinton and Al Gore, and the three of them were apparently very good friends. And this was before Photoshop. Gone are the days when an attorney could blithely present a photograph that proved or disproved the innocence of a client.

In addition, the notion that a photograph doesn't lie presumed that there was no bias or point of view connected to it; what we saw in the photograph were simply the facts. We do well to help our students to appreciate that a photographer's "voice" is as much a part of what we know and take away from a photograph as is the voice of a writer.

Researchers and historians bring an analytical approach to working with photographs, and part of our responsibility is to help our students learn how to analyze photographs as part of their skill development as researchers. This can be done very efficiently and, as always, has greatest effect when practiced over time.

Place a photograph on a screen so that all students can see it. Have each student respond individually to a set of questions about the photograph, and then compare responses with one or more classmates before sharing as a whole class. The students will learn that they see things their classmates don't, and vice versa, and that we each bring unique insights, experiences, and information to what we view.

Here are some basic questions to bring to analyzing a photograph. Add or substitute other questions, and encourage students to add their own questions if desired.

How do you feel when you look at the photo?
What do you see in the picture? (not what it means, but simply what is there)
What does the photograph seem to be about?
Where is your eye drawn? What seems to be the central point in the photograph?
Where was the photographer standing in relation to what was photographed?
How might the scene have looked if he or she were standing elsewhere?
What was happening just beyond the frame of the photograph?
What point of view/attitude does the photographer seem to have about the photograph? What point is he or she trying to make?
How might another photographer have portrayed the event or topic differently?
What meaning do you take from the photograph? What is your current understanding of the event or issue?

This can be taken a step further by offering a range of photographs of the same event or on the same topic but expressing different points of view, similar to what we did with text. We want our students to recognize that a photographer brings her attitudes, experiences, and point of view to what she photographs, as do we when we view her work. As the students become more skilled and comfortable with the process of reading photographs, we can increase the complexity of the photographs, the content being depicted, or the clarity of the images/statements.

An example of a more complex research task would involve gathering photographs of the same scene over several decades. For example, bring in photographs taken 5 or 10 years apart showing the same section of downtown over a 50-year span, or photos documenting changes to an industrial area. Students then have the opportunity to notice what seems to have changed over time, and to research the stories behind those changes. They might also speculate about the changes that are likely to come in the next 50 years, imagining what photographs might reveal to students and researchers of the future.

Photographs are easier and easier to find, given our current capabilities. Local libraries, newspaper archives, university collections, history museums, and historical societies are good sources for photographs. So are the town's senior citizens, including relatives of members of the class or school community, who might have photographs as well. School yearbooks or archives might contain relevant photographs, as might the archives of long-standing local businesses or organizations. The Internet offers photographic search possibilities we could not have imagined even a few years ago, and the Library of Congress is still an amazing source for photographs.

Putting the Cameras in the Hands of the Student Researchers

The best learning almost always comes through students engaging in the process of creating media and then analyzing their own work with the tools they have practiced in class. An effective step you can take in helping students to learn about reading photographs is to have them take their own photos to create their own statements about aspects of their lives, their families, or about issues that matter to them. They can bring in photos to share with their classmates, and the students can practice analyzing their own photographs in the same manner as described above.

Working with Multiple Points of View

The world is rarely simple, though it often appears that way in textbook presentations of our history. The strategies in this next section are designed to help students search for and incorporate different points of view in their research, as they strive to fully understand and communicate an issue. We begin with an extension of the photography work described in the previous section.

Photo Documentaries: A Step Beyond

We can help our students move further along this pathway of photo analysis by having them create their own photo documentaries of an issue or topic of concern or interest to them. The students research a topic and then share what they have learned through a series of photographs that they take, arrange, and caption. Introduce the process of photo documentaries by displaying work done by professionals, discussing with the students the ways in which the photographers have used their photos to tell their story, and then encourage the students to go forth, guided by some basic questions such as these:

What is your topic?

Why do you care about the topic? Why does it matter to you?

What are your assumptions about the topic as you start out?

What are your questions about the topic as you start out?

What sources of information might help you to pursue those questions? Whose voices should be included in this research?

What seems most important to communicate? How might you do this with photographs?

What point of view are you bringing to your presentation?

How might captions help to communicate your research?

What audience is most appropriate for your photo documentary? What impact do you hope to have on them?

Students might choose to create a photo documentary that covers a local issue, like the safety of a particular intersection or crosswalk, the unequal attention given to parks at various places in the city, or perhaps an issue particular to their school, such as the crowded hallways, the unhygienic bathrooms, or the harried lives of students trying to get from one class to another in three minutes. They might also document a local landmark or "institution," be it a park, barbershop/hair salon, grocery, sports field, or artwork. I make sure that students clear their intended topics with me before they begin their research, and that they have clear timelines and checkpoints along the way so that I can review progress and help to problem-solve, if necessary.

I have four major objectives for this assignment: I want students to carry out research into an issue that has local relevance and interest; to learn to identify and to include relevant, and contrasting voices; to learn about the process of putting together a photo documentary; and to gain practice and skill at presenting research findings to an authentic audience, validating the work they have done.

Documentary Films, Videos, and DVDs

This same process can also be brought to documentary films and videos. Documentaries are frequently presented at schools as if they are value neutral, though we know better. Our students must come to recognize that they must evaluate the information they are taking from documentary films in the same way that they evaluate information from other sources.

All documentary filmmakers have a reason for creating their work: a story they want to tell, an audience they want to reach, and an agenda they want to support. They carry out research as thoroughly as possible, shoot the film informed by that research, and then compose and construct the finished product. They cut and edit, deciding which frames to keep or omit and the order in which to place them. They add music, or use a particular fade or transition. They might switch the order in which they present people they interviewed, and they might decide they need to add another voice. When they are done they will have created a coherent intentional work that comments on whatever topic they have chosen, and it is anything but value neutral. It represents the vision, skill, creativity, and intention of the maker.

We can help students to recognize this in several ways. One of the simplest is to show powerful documentaries in class, stopping every few minutes to notice with the students the choices the filmmakers have made. I ask them to respond to questions such as these, which help deconstruct the documentary process:

Who or what is the subject of the documentary?
Who is telling the story? From whose point of view are we seeing?
What is their point of view? How are they presenting it, and what evidence are they providing?
Does the supporting evidence seem adequate? Do you trust it? How might you verify or challenge what is being said in the film?
What other points of view might be relevant, and are they given voice in the film?

Whose voices and points of view have been excluded, overlooked, or not included?

What questions do you now have about the person or issue?

Who is funding the film? Are the sources of funding for the film connected to
  the people or issues addressed in the film?

What bias or prior knowledge did you bring to the film?

When was the documentary made, and why was it made?

How does this align with what you have previously encountered about the topic?

What do you think about the topic now? What questions do you have? Where
  might you go to find out more?

It would be ideal to work with students to create a documentary about a particular topic relevant to them and/or to the community. When students create media,
they have to learn about it and then make use of it; once they do that they will
never watch passively again. Asking them to carry out research and then to make
a digital story or a video documentary presenting what they have found to an
authentic audience teaches them about documentaries the way nothing else
could.

Analyzing Conflicting Historical Documents

Once the students have become savvy about the role that point of view plays in
shaping the reporting of events and are clear that no one source has all the answers, we can bring this awareness to accounts of historical events, including
class textbooks and other basic sources of information.

Take two essays or short pieces devoted to the same topic but expressing
very different accounts or understandings of the event or topic. For example, you
might place a section from virtually any U.S. history text side by side with a section from Howard Zinn's *A People's History of the United States*, James
Loewen's *Lies My Teacher Told Me*, or Ron Takaki's *A Different Mirror*. The
students analyze each article or passage on its own, using guiding questions such
as the ones they practiced with above, but then they face the additional challenge
of making meaning of the texts in a larger context. What do we do, as researchers or historians, if each text seems internally consistent, if the authors have supported their claims with relevant evidence, and if they seem to be presenting the
information in a relatively unbiased manner, and yet they come to very different
conclusions? Both can't be completely true or accurate, since their attitudes and
conclusions about the topics are so radically different. This exercise, at the very
least, presents students with irrefutable evidence that one source on a topic is

never enough to guarantee that we are getting the full story. I often stop at this point, content to have that question raised, and knowing that we will work with it later in the term.

A Step Further

We could go further still in asking how we might, as readers, address the contradictions. How can we come as close as possible to whatever "the truth" is? Whose voices have been included and whose voices left out? Where is the preponderance of evidence supporting what each and other versions say about the topic? How might we research further to establish a sense of trust in one piece of writing or the other? This would clearly extend the duration of the assignment and lead to a more in-depth exploration of both the topic and the research process, but it's only possible if there is time available.

RAFTS

RAFTS is an approach writers and writing teachers employ to help improve focus and to bring depth and sharpness to virtually any writing project. I was first introduced to RAFTS by Kim Norton and Holly Stein at the Puget Sound Writing Project in the mid-1990s and found that it changed not only my writing, but my teaching. RAFTS provides a structure to bring together critical thinking, creativity, and content in a manner that fosters a new approach and a deeper understanding of the topic. I've used the approach extensively as a writer and as a teacher of writing, and have also found it relevant and useful while structuring research assignments for my students.

RAFTS is an acronym, with each letter standing for an aspect of a project that the writer or researcher needs to consider.

R stands for role (Who am I as the writer? What is the context in which I am writing?)

A for audience (To whom am I writing this? To whom do I most want to direct this work?)

F for format (What kind of writing is this? Is it a speech, trial summation, inaugural address, song lyric or poem, advertising copy, letter to a friend, op-ed piece, retirement speech?)

T for topic (What is this writing about?)

S for strong verb (What am I trying to do with this writing? What do I want my intended audience to experience as a consequence of reading what I've written? What do I want them to do as a result of my writing?)

It is the writer's challenge to clearly define or account for each of those letters, and the consequence of doing so is sharper, more effective writing. When the writer knows why she is writing, and to whom, she is able to bring more energy and personal presence to the work than if she is simply writing to fulfill an assignment, with little at stake besides a grade.

The same dynamics hold true when creating research assignments for students. The best assignments offer students a structure that provides them with a clear focus for their work. When we structure an assignment that makes clear what their purpose is, and who their audience is, they are better able to organize and evaluate the information they have gathered, and better able to prepare their communication about the research they have done, informed by their assigned purpose.

Let's say that students are studying water-quality issues and the impact that various forms of pollution are having on the waterways of the region and on all of the things that live in these waterways. The teacher could assign a traditional research paper, with students to present what they have learned in a "just-the-facts" kind of way. The RAFTS approach offers students a more creative context in which to communicate learning and knowledge. One example would be to ask students to write a letter, as a salmon, to the governor of the state, requesting (demanding, begging) that the state clean up the rivers in which she and her offspring swim. The students would have to gather and make use of the same factual information, demonstrating the same learning in this RAFTS assignment, but there would be the additional opportunity to offer a creative, effective set of arguments that bring an emotional component to the conversation. Jan Maher created side-by-side examples of a straight-ahead, encyclopedic report and a RAFTS-style plea from a salmon mother to illustrate the differences for her students. Notice that while both require students to learn and communicate the same factual information, the quality and nature of the writing is significantly different.

Here's the "just-the-facts" version:

Salmon live in the sea most of the time, but when it is time for them to reproduce, they swim to freshwater streams or ponds. Once the female has laid eggs and the male has fertilized them (called spawning) most of the salmon die.

Eight salmon and related species spawn in the Stillaguamish River: Chinook, Coho, chum, pink, and sockeye salmon, and steelhead, sea-run cutthroat, and bull trout.

There used to be lots of old-growth trees that washed into the river during winter floods in the mountains. The clumps of logs and roots made good areas for young salmon (called fry) to hide and find food before they went out to sea. Now there is mostly mud and grass. That has made it very hard for the salmon to survive long enough to get to the ocean.

When they come back as mature fish to spawn, salmon don't eat, but they still need places to hide from predators such as bears and eagles.

The changes that people have made to the near shore by cutting down the trees that used to fall naturally into the river have caused Chinook salmon to be endangered.

This version is organized through a RAFTS structure:

Dear Governor,

Have you ever tried to get back to your house after a hard day's work while bears and eagles are trying to kill you and eat you for their dinner? Worse yet, have you ever had to drive through air that is so bad that you think you are going to choke?

That's what it's like for me. For me, the water is like air. You see, I'm a Chinook salmon. This time of year I'm supposed to be finding my way back to the stream where I was born. Let me tell you, it hasn't been easy!

Oh, I know where I'm supposed to go. But since I swam downstream into the ocean things have changed, and not for the better. First of all, there used to be trees by the river most of the way. That's why I got out to sea in the first place. I was one of the lucky ones who didn't end up as somebody else's dinner. I would swim right next to the shore, hidden in the tangled roots of the trees. Also, the water was just the right temperature because the trees made shade.

Now the trees have been cut down and there's just mud and grass. It's way too hot, and my friends and I are easy pickings for the bears and eagles. So I'm writing to ask you a favor. I'm not writing for myself. I know I'll be dead by the end of the season. But I'm writing for my unborn children. Next season, when they swim out to sea, they need cool water. They need places to hide and places to eat along the way. They need clean water so they don't choke to death.

So I'm begging you please to think of the salmon and do something to clean up our river. Please make sure humans stop dumping poisons into the water. If they want to dump something, tell them to dump trees so we have shade and hiding spots again.

It may seem like a small deal to you, but to us salmon, it's a matter of life and death.

Thank you very much, Governor, for listening to my story. And remember, you could go down in history as the governor who saved the Chinook salmon from extinction!

Sincerely,
Gwendolyn Chinook

In this example, the Role is that of a salmon mother; the Audience is the governor of the state; the Format is a letter; the Topic has to do with water quality, or cleaning up rivers; and the Strong verb is to convince the governor to take action to clean up the river. The students have fun taking on their personas in order to write as their characters, and they write more focused and passionate pieces when they are writing to the governor than they write when they are simply writing to me to complete an assignment. Several of the longer projects included in this chapter are presented in a RAFTS format, in that the students are provided with a role and context in which to carry out their research and to communicate their findings, and something they are trying to accomplish by completing the task.

Stories from Multiple Points of View

We tend to associate stories with the voice and perspective of the teller. We assume that the narrator, whether inside or outside the story, knows all relevant information and is telling the story truthfully and accurately. We assume this whether we are hearing a fairy tale or reading a historical account, and only question their truthfulness or accuracy when something jars us into doing so. Once we begin to question, we begin to notice who is speaking and who is not, whose voices and points of view are included and whose are not. As Howard Zinn noted in his interview, as he studied the "Columbus" story he came to notice that the voices of the Native Americans were absent, and that led him to "discover" the writings of the Spanish priest Bartolomé Las Casas, which enabled Zinn to offer a more complete account of the encounters of Columbus and the Taino.

Researchers have to remember to include all relevant voices, to make sure that they are not allowing one to dominate or to remain missing. There are some simple exercises we can bring to the classroom to help students to appreciate this.

Working with Fairy Tales

The task here is simple. Take a fairy tale such as "Little Red Riding Hood," and lay out the basic elements of the plot so that all are working with the same basic version of the story. In Red's case, the plot points are familiar: Little Red lives with her mother in the woods; they get a call from Granny, who is sick on the other side of the woods; Mom sends Red with a basket of goodies and warns her to stay on the path; Red meets the Wolf; Red goes off the path to pick flowers for Granny, at the Wolf's suggestion; the Wolf speeds to Granny's while Red is picking those flowers; the Wolf ties up Granny and throws her in the closet; Red comes in, finds "Granny" in bed, and goes through the sequence about her big ears, eyes, nose, and teeth; the Wolf jumps out of bed and chases Red around the room; the Woodcutter hears the commotion and charges through the door, either killing the Wolf or chasing the Wolf off. The story ends with all living happily ever after, except perhaps the Wolf.

Then we talk about the point of view of the story. The storyteller is an omniscient narrator, a person who knows the whole story and is presumably outside of it. When it comes to the narration of the Red Riding Hood story, it is clear that, while the narrator may be omniscient, her sympathies are with Little Red, and we are hearing the story from that frame of reference. How does that alignment affect the telling of the story and our understanding of what truly happened on that day in the woods? We can ask our students to help us to answer that question by creating and staging a brief play.

Creating the Play

We start with a question. How would the other characters in the Red Riding Hood story tell it, assuming they too knew everything that happened, and to whom would they tell what they know? How would Granny tell the story, and to whom? What would the Wolf's version sound like, or that of Red herself? How would she tell the story of what happened to her? Divide the class into groups of approximately five and ask each group to tell the story of Red Riding Hood from the point of view of one of the major characters. I take the time to divide the groups by preference ("Who would like to present the story from the Wolf's point of view?"), though another option is to simply assign each group a character to represent (group one tells the story from Granny's point of view, group two from the Wolf's point of view, etc.). The groups are charged with deciding on the story that their character would tell, and then acting that story out for the rest of the class. They need not worry about props or accents or acting skills, because this really isn't an acting exercise; the focus is on sharing the various stories.

The class brainstorms the list of characters who might have a point of view of the story. The list usually includes Little Red, Mom, Granny, the Wolf, and the Woodcutter. We assume that all of the characters know all of the events of the story, and that they will tell the story truthfully, *from their point of view as they understand it.*

Each group acts out the story and must follow the basic events of the story. Red must be heading for Granny's house, she must meet the Wolf on the road, and they must converge on Granny's house at the end. What happens at each of those points is what we come to learn from the multiple points of view as each group acts out the formerly familiar tale.

We then see all of the presentations, noting how they either line up or contradict each other. We are reminded that no one point of view, no one person, tells the whole story.

The exercise can easily be seen in the context of the RAFTS structure by asking the students to make some decisions corresponding to the RAFTS categories.

R: From whose point of view are they telling the story (The Wolf? Little Red? The Woodcutter?)

A: To whom are they telling the story? To whom might Red tell her story? A judge or jury? One of her friends? Her dad, with whom she spends every other weekend? A reporter sent to cover the events that took place that day?

F: What is the format? The group could stage their tale as a trial, an interview, a police investigation, a conversation between friends or family members, Mom remembering an event from her past, to the delight of her grandchildren ("It all started 50 years ago, when I was still living with Little Red, your mother, at the edge of the woods…"). One group of university students began their skit by having Red text message her saga with three of her friends. Her first text was, "OMG, Im so bstd…."

T: The topic is the Red Riding Hood story

S: The strong verb depends on the context you've created. The Wolf might have been trying to convince a jury that she was only doing what wolves do, and as the forest shrunk around her and her cubs, she had few options for food.

Granny might be telling a story to entertain and educate her grandchildren on the need to follow instructions and to be careful. A news reporter might be telling the story in a way that will sell papers, or keep viewers watching the six o'clock news.

This exercise easily transfers to looking either at current events or history. As we look at famous events in U.S. history, the same basic questions apply: What do we know about the event, and how do we know it? Who else might have a point of view, or knowledge of the events? How do they tell the story and how might we access their accounts? How does that affect what we know? Why have we not heard their versions before, and what difference does that make? How might we tell familiar stories from our history in ways that give voice to those from whom we have heard little or nothing? What might the Native Americans say about that first contact with Columbus? How would they tell the story? How might women talk about the Revolutionary War or the politics of the nation before they were allowed to vote? How might the Vietnamese talk about the war they fought with the United States, and what would citizens of Iraq or Afghanistan say about the wars taking place on their soil? How might those living in Alaska, including birds or fish, talk of the Exxon Valdez oil spill? We don't generally hear those voices, and when we do it shocks us, reminds us that our history is not simply the history of the powerful. Judith Helfand's film *The Uprising of '34*, which deals with textile strikes across the South during that year, transforms one spare line in a history textbook into a much fuller orchestration. The film highlights the voices of "ordinary citizens," including mill workers, family members, and African Americans involved in the strike. If students are given the research task of presenting familiar stories with the addition of as many relevant voices and points of view as possible, they will be creating a more balanced, more honest history of our country.

History of the Class

The History of the Class is another in-class exercise that helps students to understand the role that point of view and power play in determining what we do or do not know about history, and about what is currently going on in our world. It is an exercise that can be done easily within a class period and requires very little preparation. I've described it in detail in *History in the Present Tense* (Heinemann, 2003) and will present only a brief version of the lesson here.

Hand each student a blank piece of paper. These should stay anonymous. Ask each student to tell the story of an event that we have all experienced, whether in class, in the community, or in the world. I often ask students to tell the story of our U.S. history class, assuming we are several weeks into the term. Give them eight to ten minutes to tell their story, recognizing with them that they may have to leave something out. They may not consult a syllabus or notes; this is what they remember and what they choose to tell. They may use any format or style they choose, and when they ask how they should do it, I tell them to do what makes most sense. Collect the stories and put them to the side for the moment. Let the students know you will be coming back to them in a few minutes.

Then ask the class what might happen in the world over the course of the next 230 years or so. I choose that number since that is the same distance as we are from 1776, a point I return to later in the lesson. The students will usually start with disasters, such as plagues, war, or global warming, and I make sure there are positives as well, such as cures for diseases, world peace, and freedom from fossil fuels. When someone says something like global warming, ask for a specific thing we would see if that were to happen, such as flooding along the coasts, or disappearing ice caps.

Once the board is fairly full, pick up the student-written stories and start dropping them on the floor, one or a few at time, linking each to something on the board, narrating as you drop. These were lost when the seas flooded the West Coast. This one was used as packing material when a ship left earth to colonize the moon. These were deemed politically untenable. These were used to start a fire in a woodstove when the wood ran out, and so on. Drop stories until there is only one left. Announce that this is the official, surviving history of the event that you have all experienced. Since no one from that shared experience is still alive, future scholars will only know what is on this one piece of paper.

Read the story two times, so that students really hear what is in it. Ask if the author missed anything. Also, notice what facts, what opinions, what information is included. What would we know and not know? What questions do we have about the event described? How might we pursue our questions?

Then pick up another story from the floor, announcing that one of the colonizing space ships has returned, or the story was found in a bottle floating off the newly formed coastline of Nevada. Read it and compare/contrast it with the first story. Is it about the same topic? What clues do we have about that? What facts does it contain, and what opinions, and how do these compare or contrast with those in the first story?

What questions do we have after hearing the two (or three, if you read a third) stories? How would we pursue questions we had if we wanted to go back in time and determine what the true story was? How do we resolve or make sense of discrepancies between the stories? What do we do as historians when stories disagree? What kinds of evidence or data do we need in order to have faith in something?

Ask the students how they felt when you started dropping the stories. Some might say they were relieved once they realized that the story carried the entire weight of the history of the event, but most are frustrated and angry that the stories that they worked to write are simply discarded.

Now shift the focus of the discussion to our own society's stories. Whose stories are regularly "dropped" to the floor? Whose stories do we hear? Are the stories of some segments of the population discarded so that we rarely, if ever, hear from them? Why is that? Whose stories survive, and why is that?

How does it change things to hear more than one story about something? When we hear only one story, what do we gain and what do we lose? How does it change things when we hear more than one account of something?

How might we bring this to our study of history? What lessons from this exercise apply to our study of U.S. history? What happened 233 years ago? The Declaration of Independence was written, the colonies were declaring their independence from Great Britain, Native Americans were being pushed off their lands, many African Americans were still enslaved, and women could not vote or own land. What do we know of that time, and how do we know it? Whose accounts do we hear? Whose voices do we not hear? How might it change things if we could hear those voices?

You might bring in an account from an ordinary citizen living during the Revolutionary War era that offers a very different picture of the time, such as selections from *Voices of a People's History of the United States*, by Howard Zinn and Anthony Arnove (Seven Stories Press, 2004). How do the voices of ordinary citizens compare and contrast with the history we have been fed throughout our schooling? How do those voices change our understanding of those times and events? What questions do they raise, and what do we do as students of history?

Longer-Term Projects and Units

Learning is strongest when, following an introduction to new learning and an opportunity to practice it, it can be put to use in service to an authentic, meaningful task. It's all well and good to learn to hammer a nail, plane a board, or wire a light, but the learning becomes real when put to use building a house, barn, or other structure. Then the discreet skills and exercises come together in an authentic manner, and the builder truly integrates those prior experiences.

The lessons and units that follow offer students complex and interesting invitations to research that will require them to make use of the skills they have been developing and practicing through exercises such as those described at the beginning of this chapter. Now when they are analyzing a piece of writing or a photograph, or conducting an interview, they are doing so in order to carry out a multistep research quest.

The lessons and units are of varying complexity and difficulty and have been designed for a range of contexts and grade levels. They are, of course, only examples of the kind of research tasks that we can bring into our classrooms.

Product Research Project

The product research project is an example of an extended research project that involves students personally while building up and making use of skills and content knowledge. It provides a context to integrate learning across the social studies spectrum. I have described this assignment in detail in Chapter Four of *History in the Present Tense* (Heinemann, 2003) and so will provide only the general outline here.

The Assignment

Given our increasing concern over the state of the environment, over the ways in which people and resources are exploited, we are beginning to pay more attention to the "true cost" of the choices we make. This project is designed to help us gain a more complete understanding of the impact that the manufacturing of the goods that we use has on the environment, on workers, on the cities and towns in which the factories and businesses are located, and may help us to assess the value we get from the products versus the true cost of manufacturing them.

Working in groups of four or five, find out as much as you can about a product that is produced outside of the United States and brought into the country for sale in our area. There are guiding questions provided that will lead you to investigate the impact that the making of the product has on the environment, on the lives of the workers, and on the society in general. You will be prompted to understand the economics of the operation and the ways in which the business has changed the places in which they exist.

Your group will make a fifteen- to twenty-minute presentation to the class, sharing what you have discovered. You will decide what to communicate and how best to do it. You might use diagrams and charts, design poster boards, create theater skits, offer demonstrations, play music, or engage in interactive conversation (with each other or with your "audience"). Your task is to help us to understand what you have learned and to know why it is important. Help us think about whether your product does more good than harm, or at least help us to understand the true cost of producing it. Is this a product we should continue to sell in our stores, or would you recommend that we stop selling it, due to the true cost of manufacturing it?

We are not playing "gotcha" with this assignment. Your goal is not to find the dirt on corporations; your goal is to understand what it takes and what it costs to actually get goods manufactured and to market.

You must include a map showing where your product is made, and how it gets to consumers in your town or region. Your group must also include a briefly annotated resource page that shows your research trail. Where did you go for your information, what was useful, and what, briefly, did you find at those sites and sources?

Here are some guiding questions to get you started. You do not have to answer all of them, and you may find that you concentrate on only a few of them in your presentation. Please substitute your own questions if they are more appropriate to your topic, but please check with me first.

Ecology and Environmental

1. Where is your product made?
2. Approximately how long has it been produced there?
3. Where was it produced before that?
4. What materials are used in producing your product? Where do they come from and how are they gathered?
5. What is the geography of the place in which the product is made?

Social and Societal

6. Who gathers/grows/ manufactures the materials used to make the product?
7. What is involved in that process? Who is involved in that process? What are the working conditions like for the workers? What are they paid? How does that compare to what they were doing before and what others are making in the local area?

8. Same questions for the manufacture/production of your product. Who manufactures and/or assembles the product? Describe the working conditions, living conditions, pay rates, and health of those who make the product.

9. How have the lives of people been changed by this manufacturing operation? What might the workers have done before the arrival of the factory? How has the town or city or family been changed by the coming of the company?

Connections to the Rest of the World

**10. How does your product get to the United States, and then to stores in your area?

11. What does it cost to buy your product in a local store? How much does it cost to produce? How much do they spend on advertising, other expenses? How much profit do they make?

12. Who makes decisions about the production of the product? Sizes, shapes, colors, how many, pricing, etc.?

13. Who uses the product? How do they find out about it?

14. Where was your product produced fifty years ago?

15. Where might it be produced fifty years from now?

** This is often a difficult question for groups to answer. I encourage groups to try and find out and, if they are unsuccessful after a good-faith effort, to let it go and put their time into other questions. We talk as a group about why it might be difficult to determine how the products are transported and why companies might not want to make that information available, and then move on to other questions and considerations.

- -

Farm to Table

This is very similar to the Product Research assignment just described but focuses on how the food we eat gets to our tables from where it is produced. It is a question we rarely consider. Food, for many of us, magically appears when it is supposed to. At home that means that our families have provided the food, and while we may grumble about certain offerings, we rarely question where it comes from, though at some point we realize it "comes" from a store. At school we tend to head for the cafeteria without considering how the food got there, or why the particular food being served is the food being served. Conducting research about the food in our lives catches students' attention the way few topics can, and it is a topic than can easily reach across disciplines, into history, science and nutrition, economics, colonialism, world systems, globalization, ecology, community gardens, and more.

It is not unusual for elementary students to be taken on farm-to-table tours, especially when they are in the earliest grades. They typically begin by going to a farm and seeing what grows there, and then following the pathway from the farm to the store and then to home. It's a revelation for many, especially those living in cities where little or nothing grows, and of course not all food comes to us from nearby farms. Learning about how food gets to us is a valuable activity with young children but is rarely carried out as a research project, since it tends to be entirely teacher directed; the young students simply come along for the ride. It becomes quite a revelation for older students when they are offered the opportunity to carry out the research themselves, especially about foods they like or foods that they are served in the school cafeteria. Researching the "manufacturing" of these foods takes students into the relationship of work, climate, and environment, into the work lives of those who are essentially toiling on plantations, into the economic structures that have shaped the world food markets, highlights the changing agricultural scene in this country, and emphasizes the global economy and connections that affect everyone on the planet. For example, it is two degrees below zero as I write this, and there are bananas and a mango downstairs. How does this happen, and what does it mean, for we who buy the food, for those who "own' and sell the food, and for those who tend the crops and harvest them?

Students approach this research task as they approached the product assignment described in the previous section. They work in small groups to find out as much as they can about how a favorite food grows, how it's tended and harvested, how it's prepared for sale, and how it gets to the stores or stands where it is sold. Students might consider five general areas to research: geography/climate; the workers who grow and harvest the food; the preparation and transport of the food; the sales aspect of the process, including the pricing; and the relationship between those who own the business and the people who work for them. Students find out as much as they can about each area and share what they find with the rest of the class through a presentation. Requiring students to present their findings to their classmates offers them the opportunity of learning from each other and also gives the class the opportunity to compare and contrast the information from each group's research. What do all the stories have in common? In what ways are there differences? What can we learn about how our food arrives on our tables, and about the lives of those who make it happen?

Another possible angle to this assignment is to focus on the manufacturing/production of the food that is served in the school cafeteria. School lunch is always a topic that elicits eye rolls, groans, and worse, but it is a staple of our lives from our first days at elementary school through our last days in high school. Interestingly enough, we know little or nothing about the food we eat in the cafeteria. We don't know where it comes from, who grows it, how it's grown, how it's harvested, how it arrives at the school, what it costs to produce and process, who makes all the decisions along the way, and how much they make by providing food to schools. Students could launch a research effort focused on school lunch programs for their individual school or for their district.

Researching school lunches can be politically sensitive, and I feel compelled to offer a word of caution. There may be people involved in the school lunch process who are uncomfortable with students or anyone asking about that process. District officials may not want students to question the school lunch program and may try to discourage the inquiry. Each school and district is different, and it is beneficial to scope out the scene before involving your students in what might be a problematic situation. Resistance from school officials should not necessarily stop the project. The information should be public, since the schools are public institutions, and some administrative resistance may make the assignment even more compelling to students, but it is wise to know what we are getting ourselves and our students into before taking the plunge.

Questions that students might pose and pursue related to the lunches include:

What company or companies provide(s) the lunches?
Where do their food sources come from, and why from there?
Who owns the land where the food is grown?
Who plants, tends, and harvests the various items that are sold in the school?
What are their lives like? Under what conditions do they work? How much are they paid? Are there health risks or issues associated with their work?
How does the food get from the growing sites to the school?
How much does the process cost to complete, and how much do the lunches cost?
Who makes the profit?

You will have to decide as a class what, if anything, to do with the information you have found. The student research may suggest topics for further research, and students could take that on, either as an assignment or on their own. There may be aspects of the food cycle that raise concerns, and students may want to follow up with questions of those who are involved in the process, or to communicate with others in the community. It's also very possible that the presentations and following discussion/reflection bring the project to a close, and you move on to whatever is next.

An Extended Research Project Integrating Several Disciplines

Deep Space 3000

This exercise is lightly adapted from the Deep Space 3000 lesson that comes from the book *Engaging Students through Global Issues*, published by the organization Facing the Future. See page 217 in the Appendix to see a description of the organization, or go to their website, www.facingthefuture.org, for more information.

The basic setup is as follows:

The earth is "sick," and life cannot continue until it has healed itself; it is estimated that this will take around 3,000 years. NASA (or some imaginary agency) is planning to send groups into space in order to save a maximum number of lives and to make it possible to re-establish life on earth 3,000 years in the future, when it is safe to re-inhabit. We can assume that the technology exists to build spacecrafts capable of making the voyage, and we need not worry about gathering the materials, the money to pay for it, or the means to propel the ships into space.

Our task is to design the systems inside of the spacecraft so that they can support life for 3,000 years or more. The environment must be self sustaining; nothing can come into the ship and nothing can leave it, including waste materials.

NASA has sent out an RFP (Request for Proposals) for individuals or groups who will create the systems that will sustain the traveling population for 3,000 years.

Design teams must account for developing the means to provide the following:

Air
Food
Water
Waste
Decision Making/Government
Health

Recreation

Other (anything else that you deem to be important to include)

Groups will prepare their presentations and make them to representatives of the NASA board (me and their classmates) on _____. Decisions will be made based on the following criteria:

Did you provide designs for sustainable systems in each category?

Did your designs reflect accurate scientific and social principles?

Can your sustainable systems support or interact with each other?

Are all group members able to answer questions from the board members?

Have you included relevant course material in your presentation?

Have you provided for a diverse traveling population, with attention to those who have a range of needs and requirements?

Deep Space 3000 can be carried out over one or two days, with students pooling their existing knowledge and problem-solving skills to respond to the design question posed by the prompt, but the exercise can also launch an extensive unit of study of sustainability, of the intersection of various cycles and systems that must function in a coherent manner if we are to sustain life on our planet. Students could identify what it is they need to learn in order to knowledgeably and effectively respond to the launching prompt, and this could form the outline for weeks of research and study.

The date for presentations is set well in advance, so that groups must establish and carry out a research schedule that has them ready to go on that date. As groups present their design to the NASA committee, they should be ready to respond to questions. Depending on your available time and objectives, you can offer groups additional times to amend their designs in response to their experience in front of the "committee."

Dig Deep

Dig Deep is a multi-week unit that I developed with Tom Ikeda and Patricia Kiyono of the Densho Project in Seattle. Densho is an organization that had as its original mission the collecting of stories from Japanese Americans who had been incarcerated during World War II. Few Japanese Americans had shared their stories of incarceration with anyone, and they were becoming elderly; their stories were being lost. Once the U.S. government formally apologized for the incarceration, many elders were willing to start sharing those stories. Densho now has hundreds of hours of videotaped interviews about their experiences during

World War II, and also has extensive resources and artifacts about the camps. Densho has added a focus on social justice in the present and future to its mission and has been creating curriculum designed to support students to become critical thinkers and responsible citizens who work for peace and justice. Tom Ikeda and his colleagues at Densho are committed to doing what they can to prevent what happened to Japanese Americans during World War II from happening to anyone else, ever again.

The Dig Deep unit focuses on supporting students to develop research skills and a critical approach to the media. There is also a focus on people and organizations that have worked for peace and justice. We wanted students to know that it is possible to make a difference and wanted them to become familiar with people and organizations that had done so. The unit is designed to be taught near the end of the school year, and we make the assumption that students have already learned much of what is required to respond to the prompt, or that their teachers will teach the necessary skills and content within the context of the unit, which lengthens the time the unit will take.

The research assignment that follows is the culminating project for the Dig Deep unit and requires that students make use of what they have learned about research, the media, and the actions that individuals and groups have taken to work for peace and justice to respond to the prompt. Note that the assignment is presented in the form of a RAFTS assignment.

The Culminating Project

A publisher is compiling a book on social movements and efforts toward peace and justice. Your classmates and I represent an editorial board that is making decisions about which individuals, groups, or movements should be included in the book. Your task is to work in small groups to research various individuals, groups, or movements that have worked toward social justice and/or bringing peace to the world. Your group will then make a recommendation to the board about whether the person, group, or organization you have researched should or should not be included in this book. Your recommendation should be based on the actions your nominee has taken to work for peace and/or social justice. You must include the following information in your nomination packet and presentation:

The name of the person, group, or organization you have researched. Include the approximate years of their work, and the geographical area in which they worked.

With what issue(s) is your nominee most associated?

Please provide an overview of the essential elements of the issue(s) and provide a historical overview and context for the issue(s).

What actions did your nominee take?

What forces, people, or circumstances opposed their efforts?

In what ways did their efforts bring about more justice, or move the world closer to peace?

Are there any who might oppose the inclusion of your person, group, or organization in the book? If so, who and for what reasons?

What is your final recommendation, and why?

In order to successfully carry out this assignment, you must:

- Identify and analyze between five and ten written sources spanning a range of points of view about the topic.
- Include information from at least one primary source.
- Include an image of at least one visual source, such as a photograph, drawing, architectural plan, or reproduction of a work of art.
- Include a bibliography of sources used in this research project.

Your paper and/or oral presentation should respond to some or all of the following questions:

- Why is this issue important?
- What did you know about it before you began your research?
- What is the historical context for this issue? How long has it been going on, and who has been involved and affected by it?
- Who has benefited from the unjust situation you researched, and who has suffered?
- Whose voices have been heard regarding the issue? Whose voices and points of view have been minimized or shut out? How has this affected what we know about the topic?
- What is the current state of the situation? What efforts are being made to prevent change?
- What efforts are being made to make change?
- Which of the efforts for change have been successful and why?

Possible topics include, but are not limited to:

- Native Americans rights
- Enslaved Africans and abolitionists fighting the institution of slavery

- Union organizers and laborers seeking to improve working conditions in factories, mines, fields, and other worksites
- Women working for equal rights, voting rights, equal pay, access to management and electoral positions, recognition of the work they do in the home
- Students and adults standing up to instances of censorship
- Peace movements through the twentieth and twenty-first centuries
- Justice movements through the twentieth and twenty-first centuries
- Challengers to discrimination in any area, toward any people
- Supporters of small farmers struggling to survive the growth of agribusiness
- Individuals addressing disparities in population health, health care, insurance
- Efforts to end child labor
- Work on behalf of the elderly
- Detainees, past and current
- Environmental work for toxic waste cleanups, oil spills, or other
- Health and safety advocates challenging toxic toys, unhealthy prepared foods, car manufacturers
- Concerns over war; for example, in Mexico, Vietnam, Iraq, against Native Americans
- Others you think should be considered

The Product

Each group will make a ten-minute presentation to the board, guided by the questions outlined above. Your task is to organize your presentation so that we on the board are clear about your recommendation and the reasons for it. Your reasons must be based on the actual data you have found through your research efforts.

In addition, each individual is to write a five- to ten-page paper on the individual or organization you have chosen, communicating what you have found. You may share information with your group members, so that by preparing your group presentation you will also be supporting the individual papers that each member will write. The papers are due on the same day as the presentations are made.

Specific Examples of Extended Units in Particular Classrooms

The preceding research assignments are examples of units and extended lessons that I and others have used in classrooms over the years. While these assignments have been implemented many times over, they are general descriptions rather than specific examples from particular classrooms during particular years. The examples that follow are specific examples, taken from the experiences of specific teachers and classrooms. They come from classrooms ranging from fourth grade through university, and are presented with a minimum of commentary.

Expeditionary Learning

Libby Sinclair taught for many years in a school in which every classroom embarked on an expedition for the year. Teachers at the school were aware of what other teachers were doing and shared support and resources along the way. The school in which Libby taught had very few African American students, and Libby often chose to investigate topics that would increase her students' knowledge of and appreciation of diversity, and of African American experiences and history. Her expedition on the Negro Baseball Leagues is a strong example of this work. (She spoke in detail about this expedition in her interview in Chapter Five.)

An Expedition on the Negro Leagues from Libby Sinclair, in a Fourth/Fifth-Grade Classroom

Libby Sinclair carried out an expedition with her fourth/fifth-grade class focused on the Negro Baseball Leagues. She chose the Negro Leagues as the subject of the class expedition based on an awareness of what her students were required to learn, including skills, content, and dispositions, an awareness of what interested her students, the immediacy of the current situation in Seattle (which had at the time an exciting baseball team, a new, state-of-the-art stadium, and the All-Star game), and what she wanted her students to experience, explore, and learn. Libby organized her work around the required skills and content in reading, writing, math, U.S. history, geography, and art. Two essential questions guided the work they did all year:

Baseball: How did a game that didn't exist in this country in 1800 become our "national pastime" by 1900?

The Negro Leagues: What were they? Why did they exist? Who were some of the players and what were they known for? What happened to them and why?

The expedition was woven throughout the school year, with Libby and class focusing on different aspects at different times. Some weeks they hardly engaged with the expedition, while other weeks they spent much of their time focused on the Negro League topic.

Here is a summary of the various components of Sinclair's unit.

Research

The backbone of this months-long expedition was research. Students began by learning about the history of African Americans and then moved into research on the Negro Leagues. They spent weeks reading biographies of Negro League players and came to appreciate the relationship of Negro League baseball to the major league system we have now. The students learned how to carry out the research process and how to communicate what they learned to others via an array of media. Sinclair would teach basic research skills, and then the students would engage in tasks related to their unit that caused them to practice and apply the skills they had just learned. The unit was modular in that many of the pieces could have stood alone and together created an extraordinary "whole" that guided the students through many of their learning requirements and brought them to extraordinary knowledge about a significant aspect of U.S. history.

History

Libby Sinclair started out by asking her students what they knew about African American history, and it proved to be very little. She decided she could not really teach about the Negro Leagues unless the students knew more of the context in which they developed and existed, so she spent time helping students learn more about the history of African Americans in the country. She read novels to them that carried some aspects of the African American experience. They read materials from various history texts, journals, and other sources, and watched films and video such as the "Shadow Ball" episode from Ken Burns's series on baseball. They focused on the constitutional rights of African Americans, noting that the Negro Leagues basically paralleled the period from *Plessy v. Ferguson* (1896) to *Brown v. Board of Education* (1954), and studied the experience of African Americans in Seattle, where their school is located. The students learned historical content and approached their research as historians as they began to learn the context in which the Negro Leagues existed. They then read deeply into the lives of players in the Negro Leagues. Each student researched the life of a particular Negro League player and created a brief book about his or her research subject.

Geography

Sinclair taught the five themes of geography in connection with the baseball unit. She addressed the themes in the following manner.

Location: Students had to identify all 50 U.S. states and then locate various states or cities relevant to the study they were conducting. They located the cities that fielded Negro League teams, the cities or towns in which the players they were learning about were born or lived, barnstorming cites, and the routes the players took to travel from one town to the next.

Place: The students researched the various towns and cities where games were played, including the racial tensions and discrimination associated with many of the towns. They learned what it was like to actually be at a game, interviewing people who had attended Negro League games, studying pictures and text associated with the various stadiums and the experience. They studied the ways in which cities and towns were changed by the spread of baseball.

Movement: The class was able to trace the spread of baseball across the country and to connect the movement of the game with the movement of populations of African Americans and others during the same period of time. They researched who the players were, where they came from, where they played, and how that changed over time. They took their study up to the late 1950s, when two major league teams moved to California from New York, so that baseball spanned the entire country, and continued to trace the movement through the 1970s, when baseball arrived in Seattle, in the Pacific Northwest.

Regions: As the rural populations moved toward cities, the cities in turn expanded and became industrial, social, artistic, and economic centers for whole sections of the country. These regions were often defined by geographic features, but formed an identity around those economic and social elements. Baseball teams brought people together from across the various regions, and the Negro League teams were very important to African Americans in and around those growing population centers.

Human-environmental Interaction: When teams moved into new locations, they had to decide on a land-use policy, which included clearing land to build stadiums, parking lots, improved roads to handle additional traffic, and so on. They either used materials from the local area to build the new parks or brought it in from elsewhere. These steps changed the environment. They also brought populations into the area that changed each place in unique ways. And, of course, the specter of racism had an impact on where they played, where they moved, and how they were received when they arrived in a town. As players came through towns on a regular basis, both the players and the towns were changed forever.

Social Action: Libby and her students also engaged in social action as part of their expedition. She believes strongly that there should be an action component to any expedition and includes such a component in any unit she designs. During the Negro Leagues expedition, her students carried out two major actions.

The class raised several hundred dollars for the Negro League Museum through the sale of tee shirts that the students designed. These shirts featured the names of the Negro League teams, and one design featured several of pitcher Satchel Paige's most famous quotes. The students created the shirts, carried out the sales, did the accounting, and sent the check to the museum.

Their second action arose from a discovery the class made while engaged in their research. The class discovered that a history of African Americans in the United States did not mention the Negro Leagues, and they were distressed by this omission. The students pulled together their learning concerning African American history, the history of the Negro Leagues, and the research they had done on the experiences of individual players and on towns and regions, and wrote persuasive letters advocating for inclusion of the Negro Leagues in the next edition of the history. They did not receive responses from the author, and communication from the publisher made them understand that he was ill. Despite their lack of success in this mission, they were engaged in social action. They identified something that was wrong and took steps to address it, which hopefully will encourage them to take action again in the future.

> *Libby Sinclair's work with her fourth/fifth grade students is one of two units on the Negro Leagues included in this chapter. While she did take her students to meet with Gary Thomsen's high school class to learn about the work they were doing related to the Negro Leagues, their projects were not connected, and they focused on different aspects of the Negro League experience. Gary Thomsen talks about the research his students conducted on the Negro Leagues in his interview in Chapter Five. He and a second group of students carried out a follow-up project hosting the Negro League traveling exhibit several years later; that project is described later in this chapter.*

An Extended Research Project in Middle School

Wendy Ewbank (Chapter Five) and her seventh-grade students carried out this problem-based learning project during the 2007–2008 school year. Ewbank provides a rationale and context for the assignment, lays out the parameters and steps students are to take, and defines the form the final presentations will take. This project may seem overwhelming for seventh-graders, but remember that they have engaged in smaller, building-block projects throughout the year leading up to this, and are given time, support, suggestions, and guidance toward strategies and resources as they engage with their work. The students work on the assignment over several weeks, and Wendy introduces various skills and content, provides resources in the form of articles, websites, ideas about how to search for various topics, and structured assignments that require students to stay close to a realistic timeline as they engage in their work. There are frequent check-ins along the way, so the students are receiving plenty of support, even as they are forging their own path toward responding to the problem. Wendy believes that with sufficient support, structure, guidance, and space, our students rise to our expectations.

The Nature of CONFLICT Today

By Wendy Ewbank
7th Grade Faculty, Seattle Girls' School

Background

The nature of conflict changed over the course of the 20th and early 21st centuries.

- **10%** of the casualties in World War I were civilians (non military)
- **50%** of all casualties were civilians in WWII
- **Today over 90%** of casualties are civilians, the vast majority being women and children. They are not simply "collateral damage" but are often targeted.

Also, **most conflicts today are civil wars** *within* not *between* countries.

Finally, the majority of conflicts today are about *identity*, so who you are (or are perceived to be or *choose* to be) determines victim status. Examples of identities in conflict are the Hutu/Tutsi in Rwanda (1990s), Serbs, Croats, and Muslims in the former Yugoslavia (1980s), and Sunni, Kurds, and Shiites in Iraq (in conflict right now).

Your Assignment

Using the research-based criteria attached, you will conduct research in groups of 3 to 4 simulating teams working for the **United Nations Department of Political Affairs**. This is the UN branch that directs peace-building missions.

After completing your analysis (using the "useful websites" section), you will attempt to **persuade the class, in a 10-minute presentation, which countries require intervention**, in the form of peace-keeping missions, Security Council resolutions, humanitarian observers, mediation, etc. The class will then have 5 minutes to ask questions.

Your presentation will be assessed on: depth of content knowledge, application of the criteria that predicts conflict, use of multiple sources of information, consideration of various stakeholders, and relevant supporting evidence to advance your conclusions.

Suggested regions to look at:

- Central Africa (focus on the Democratic Republic of the Congo, Rwanda, Burundi)
- West Africa (focus on Nigeria, Sierra Leone, Uganda, Liberia, Guinea, Senegal, Ivory Coast)
- East Africa (focus on Sudan, Ethiopia, Somalia, Kenya, Eritrea, Djibouti)
- Southern Africa (focus on Zimbabwe, South Africa, Mozambique)
- Middle East (include Israel, Palestinian Territories, Jordan, Syria, Iran, Iraq, Lebanon, Kuwait)
- Latin America (Nicaragua, El Salvador, Panama, Cuba, Haiti, Colombia, Peru, Bolivia, Argentina, Brazil, Chile)
- East and SE Asia (focus on Indonesia, Vietnam, Thailand, North Korea, China)
- South Asia (to include India, Pakistan, Nepal, Burma)

You should consider some of the following issues:

- Whether more than one of the criteria that predict conflict can be applied to a country or region
- History of any current conflicts or others from the recent past
- Role of outside countries, observers, or other entities
- Multiple perspectives of people living with the given conflict. (Most conflicts cannot be reduced to two perspectives. What are the other perspectives?)

Other thoughts:

Can democratization be a cause of conflict? Democracy may introduce more competition and exacerbate a tendency to be violent. For example, elections create winners and losers (as in Iraq); in a society that is not a mature democracy the "losers" may take up arms to ensure their survival if they perceive the elected government to be a threat. In fact, the *worst way to test for a democracy may be the presence of elections.*

A more telling indicator is a peaceful transition of power (as in South Africa).

Some conflicts have to do with **background conditions** in a country, which are inherited and impossible to change, versus **root causes** of conflicts, which are things that *can* be changed.

Examples of background conditions:

- access to resources
- historical conflicts
- bad neighbors

Examples of root causes:

- social, political, or economic institutions
- leaders
- government or societal practices

Between 2005 and 2050, **just 8 countries are expected to contribute to half of the world's population increase:** India, Nigeria, Pakistan, the Democratic Republic of Congo, Ethiopia, USA, Bangladesh, and China. Are any of these countries at risk for conflict?

You should also suggest potential solutions.

Interventions that have been shown to reduce conflict:

- Increasing secondary school enrollment
- Reforming school curriculum to create the desired informed citizenry
- Empowering women, who—especially during conflicts—are the backbone of society. They maintain the food supply, are mothers/teachers, and can manage resources effectively (including during the reconstruction phase that follows a conflict). Microlending to women entrepreneurs has proven highly successful in many developing countries.
- Reversing cycles of environmental degradation by regulating fishing, hunting, soil erosion, water use

- Addressing and attempting to reverse climate change that destabilizes communities
- Strengthening the ability of local industries and government officials to diversify their incomes and become less dependent on cash crops
- Strengthening civic participation by empowering regional nonprofit organizations, homegrown businesses

The Legends Project:
The Negro Leagues Traveling Museum Exhibit at Sealth High School

Gary Thomsen (Chapter Five) and his "sports marketing and events" students researched Negro League baseball, with an emphasis on the barnstorming that Negro League players did through Canada during the 1999—2000 school year. They carried out research on the players, the towns and cities in which they barnstormed, and actually took a trip of their own, retracing the steps of those early barnstormers to draw attention to the Negro League museum. Gary talks about that project, which they called the "Legends of the Road," in his interview in Chapter Five. A later group of students built on the Legends Project to create a significant research project of their own. They did the research, created the proposal, raised the funds, and dealt with the logistics that allowed them to bring the traveling exhibit from the Negro Leagues Baseball Museum to Seattle, the first time the traveling exhibit had been brought to the West Coast by anyone. The students worked with the school, school district, and city to house the exhibit and to create community-based projects and learning opportunities focused on the topics of race and social justice. The students created learning experiences for other students throughout the district (elementary through high school), organized and produced a twelve-lecture/discussion series on topics related to race and social justice that was free and open to the public, and created opportunities for Sealth students to work with younger students in the community. They also organized or took part in several events related to Black History Month taking place all over Seattle.

I asked Gary Thomsen to talk about the project, focusing on what the students had to research, what they had to learn, and what they did, and am sharing a description of this project via that conversation.

Negro Leagues Museum Exhibit

G: Since this project had a completely new set of kids than the bike trip of 2000 [see Gary Thomsen's interview in Chapter Five], we had to start with the basics, which included: What were the Negro Leagues, who were the principal players, the importance the Leagues played in American society, especially African American society, and the timeline of their existence. The one advantage this group of kids enjoyed was that they had access to all of the research that was done by the group in 2000. They still had to read through available books on the subject, as well as talk with former players to become thoroughly familiar with the subject. This was especially important because the exhibit was open from 9 AM until 9 PM, Monday through Saturday, and the kids rotated through as docents, with at least two present at all times. Since each of the "tours" lasted half an hour, they had to be very knowledgeable about the history of the various Leagues and the eighty-plus players featured in the exhibit. They also had to research how one goes about staging a museum exhibit. Temperature and humidity control, sunlight aversion, lighting requirements, and security were all written into the contract and had to be satisfied. We also decided early on to sell Negro Leagues merchandise, which required research into space allocation, pricing, inventorying, staffing, security, and of course advertising. Each of these had to be thoroughly researched and thought through given the value of the exhibit itself.

I think their biggest challenge was creating a floor plan. Since the school had just been remodeled, the principal wanted some sort of event to get people into the building, which given the conventional wisdom of education meant a barbecue with cheerleaders and the pep band. Needless to say, hosting a major exhibit took him by surprise, but he warmed to the idea right away and so we had to figure out how to put the exhibit in our library, which was the only location that satisfied the various contractual obligations. The challenge was how to create an appealing yet functional space, approximating what you'd find in a museum, in a high school library. At the end of the day the kids came up with a very creative design that fit seamlessly into the surroundings and provided a quality viewing experience.

D: I assume you targeted local business for funding.... Did the kids put the funding proposals together, and did they approach the corporations?

G: Our primary funding came from a grant the kids wrote, which covered about 70 percent of the expenses. The remaining monies came from sponsorships. We spent nearly three weeks learning about sponsorship packages and how to write a sponsorship proposal. I thought we would have a tough go of it getting sponsorships. What I didn't figure on was how enthusiastic the community was in having the exhibit come out. The kids secured the remaining amount of money in their first two presentations and were actually kind of upset they couldn't keep on selling. Given their success, they were starting to see themselves as fledgling "Trumps," as one kid referred to their newfound sales ability.

D: What role did the kids play in the seminar series?

G: They actually came up with the idea of having panels comprised of folks from different sectors (media, education, government, community, religious, etc.) to discuss Race and Social Justice issues from their perspective. Once they identified the sectors, the students began researching who, from that particular group, should be on the panel. And then, of course, they had to talk with each one and get a commitment out of them. In the end, these kids experienced the same thing as the sponsorship group; everyone they talked with wanted to be on a panel.

Once the seminars were scheduled, the kids created and oversaw the publicity and promotion of the series, which included print and radio ads along with posters and flyers. Given that seating for the seminars was limited, 100 seats for each seminar, the kids also had to monitor RSVPs and prepare topic packages for each of the attendees. Finally, we had three kids who rotated as moderators, which required a great deal of research into not only the topic, but also the panel members.

D: What work did they do with students in other schools? Did they work with elementary or middle school students, or communicate with them in some way?

G: First of all they created an information sheet on the exhibit, which included curriculum tie-in opportunities, art and photo contests, and tour options. Once these were done they contacted each school's principal to get a contact in that school with whom they could follow up. Given there were over 100 public schools in Seattle, this took the better part of a month for them to get through the list. In the end we had over 70 schools participate in one way or another, with over 50 schools visiting the exhibit. In the eight West Seattle schools that included curriculum on the Negro Leagues, the kids visited each school and gave historical overviews on the Negro Leagues along with a presentation on the exhibit itself.

D: What do you think they came away with from the experience?

G: Certainly organizational and communication skills. Time management, budgeting, dealing with inventory, research, and no doubt a healthy understanding of event production. Of the 22 kids who were involved in the project, I think each of them acquired a tremendous appreciation for the Negro Leagues players and the history of black baseball in general. And of course they also felt a great sense of pride and accomplishment. They not only brought the touring exhibit to the West Coast for the first time, but the exhibit drew over 9,000 people, which was the largest number of people to view the exhibit in that time frame.

Newspapers and Newscasts in High School

One structure for organizing and structuring research is to create newspapers or newscasts from a particular time and place, or that deal with a particular event. I worked with my U.S. history students to create a Revolutionary War-era newspaper as we covered that particular course content, and have had students create papers "covering" the Vietnam War and the Great Depression. I know of a high school language arts teacher who created a paper from Shakespeare's England and another whose students created a paper from the midst of the Harlem Renaissance. It's a straightforward process that works for virtually any time, place, war, or issue. I have written about it before (*Living History in the Classroom*, 1993), so I will introduce the idea only briefly here, making reference to the work done by my high school students in a U.S. history class in creating *The Revolutionary Rag*.

I began by teaching the structure and content of a daily newspaper, because many of my students were unfamiliar with it. We spent time looking at newspapers to become familiar with what's inside. We read and analyzed articles from the daily Seattle papers and from t*he New York Times*, and then wrote straight news stories, editorials, feature articles, interviews, opinion pieces, entertainment reviews, classified ads, and weather reports, using content from our lives, from the school, and from our imaginations. We learned to analyze editorial cartoons and created our own, and reported on sports events, school plays and concerts, and community meetings.

Once the students became familiar with the basic construct of a newspaper, we began to create our Revolutionary-era paper. As the editor of the paper, I created a list of stories that needed to be covered, which came from my list of required topics. Students added relevant stories that interested them, choosing, for example, to research the weapons used by both sides during the war, and choosing to interview Ben Franklin and George Washington. The students also decided to include the Declaration of Independence on the front page of our paper, just as it was on the front page of Ben Franklin's paper in July 1776, and next to it we ran ads asking for help in returning runaway slaves, as did Franklin's paper. The irony of that juxtaposition was not lost on the students, and they insisted that it be a part of our paper.

The students worked alone or in pairs to research and then write their stories. I required them to consult with a minimum of three sources, reflecting a range of points of view or understanding. We then put the paper together, which went home to families and also served as a study guide for our unit-ending test.

Parallel Papers

I have added a step in recent years to the newspaper assignment by dividing the class in half and having each half create a paper representing different orientations or points of view. During the Revolutionary War era, for example, half the students work on creating a paper from the colonists' point of view, while the other half create a *London Times*, reporting on the events from the British point of view. We make sure, in both cases, to include the voices of women, enslaved Africans, and various Native American tribes. I don't worry about actually comparing the structure of foreign papers for this assignment. My objectives are more focused on learning the historical content of the particular era, with emphasis on the various points of view of the time and on learning about the structure and content of a paper in the United States, which the students are more likely to encounter.

Newscasts

When creating a newscast rather than a newspaper, additional steps are in order. Students observe newscasts to analyze the kinds of stories that are featured on a nightly basis, to recognize the difference between reporting and editorializing, and to appreciate what media critics mean when they say "if it bleeds it leads," which is another way of saying that television is a visual medium, and stories get on the air if they have good visuals. Television plays to emotions much more than to thought, and so newscasts prefer dramatic scenes—aerial shots of forest fires, car chases, and cute kittens being rescued from trees.

Once the basics have been mastered, I present the list of required stories to be covered, and students can add their own interests to the list, as is true for the newspaper. They then research and assemble their newscast. They make decisions about the visuals and graphics they will use as part of presenting their stories. They also create commercials (after we study how commercials work) and they decide on guest experts to interview (with students acting as the experts), and whatever else they decide will serve the newscast. My job as teacher/director is to make sure that the most important course content is covered by the reporters to our satisfaction, and to support students as they put their new learning to use.

There is a wide range of technology available from high school to high school, so there has to be flexibility in terms of recording the broadcast. I usually bring in a video camera and record in the classroom, but I have at times been able to work with local colleges to bring my students to their studios so that their production students can film the newscast. There's definitely a boost in energy and excitement when we have recorded in a "real" studio.

Readers' Theater in High School

Readers' theater offers both excitement and structure to student researchers. Students research a topic of interest and create a play based on the research they have done. Jan Maher has written a book about creating and implementing readers' theater in the classroom, *Most Dangerous Women* (Heinemann, 2006) and talked about the process and about a specific readers' theater piece she helped students to create following the WTO demonstrations in Seattle in 1999.

D: What is readers' theater?

J: It's theater that's intended to be read rather than memorized. Documentary readers' theater is a way of presenting information that you've researched to an audience. You can emphasize high points or key points of a body of research that's done on a particular topic by using character voices, documents, songs, poems, and any and all texts that relate.

D: What is the advantage of doing readers' theater rather than full theater?

J: The advantage of doing readers' theater is, among other things, the very low-tech requirements. All you need is a circle of chairs. The focus is on the ideas and the words, on the drama within the particular segment or piece or monologue. It's not about one character confronting another. It's more about confronting the topic through character voices.

D: You and the students at Cleveland High School researched the WTO, and particularly the events surrounding the WTO meeting in Seattle in 1999. How did you choose that specific topic, and what makes for a good topic for readers' theater?

J: There are a number of ways to choose a topic, and they range from the most student-centered to the most teacher-centered. In the case of the WTO project it was kind of a happy marriage of both of those things at the same time. The classroom teacher saw the WTO demonstration in Seattle as a perfect opportunity to bring together language arts, drama, and social studies, and the students themselves were extremely interested, for a number of reasons. Some of the students were participating in the demonstrations themselves. Several of them had teachers who they knew were participating in the demonstrations. One or more of them had family members who were in law enforcement and were involved in the demonstrations from the standpoint of public safety. Some of them were involved because they either had to take off from jobs that were affected by the demonstrations, or they had to try and move through the protestors to get to work. And they were all watching their televisions at night, watching what was happening in their home city, literally happening on their doorstep.

D: Is there a particular set of characteristics that makes a topic better or worse for readers' theater?

J: There has to be controversy of some kind. Otherwise it's polemic rather than theater. Theater is about exploring multiple points of view. There's got to be some kind of play of ideas. The ideas are the players, not the characters.

D: Once you have decided on a topic, how do you proceed?

J: The first step is always a version of the old K-W-L chart; what do we know or think we know, what do we want to know, what are our questions? Who might be able to help us to find answers? What are our local resources, and where else might we look? The teacher's role in this process is to help the students to realize the full scope of the possibilities there. In the case of the WTO project, our primary sources were participants in the event. In another topic there might be more book research. We brainstormed the points of view that we were interested in discovering or finding out about. The students wanted to know what it was like from the point of view of somebody who was attending the WTO ministerial meeting as a delegate, from the standpoint of somebody who was protesting in the streets, and what it was like from the police standpoint. They also wondered what it was like for the organizers who invited the whole thing there. That led us to many of the classroom interviews we did. We had quite a few people who had been involved in the protest in one way or another who were happy to come into the classroom and talk about it, which made our data a bit one-sided. We had a lot of people like that, so we had to say, what's going to balance this out? It proved difficult to get a police point of view because there were many lawsuits ongoing at the time and there was a gag order on the police; they couldn't talk to us. The police did provide us with a huge packet of information that included official police policy, and information on how they prepared for the event. Their point of view, expressed through those information

packets, was more generic than we would have liked, and there was less opportunity to ask direct questions since we couldn't talk to them until the trials were
resolved.

D: It's one of the realities of doing actual research. It doesn't always unfold
as you design it.

J: Because the kids felt strongly that they wanted that point of view included
in the play they were creating, the material that the police provided did give us a
way to create a theoretical policeman's voice. That was sort of a creative writing
exercise drawn from the actual police department material.

D: So you gather information and you can't use everything the kids have
found, since there's so much information, so what's the process for working with
the material that's been gathered?

J: The teacher and the students collaborate to identify the kinds of things
they want in the final piece. In this case they wanted a variety of contrasting
voices and experiences, and some factual information about what the WTO was.
Then we had to edit this massive amount of material we'd gathered. We used the
process that is described in both *History in the Present Tense* (Heinemann,
2003), and *Most Dangerous Women* (Heinemann, 2006) of having printouts of
the full texts of the interviews, and having the students work in teams of two to
three to read through an assigned chunk of text, highlighting what they thought
were the most important thoughts, lines, and sentiments. What might be a five-
page interview would produce five or six paragraphs that would really be the
crux of it.

All of the material that was identified as being the really key ideas would
then be arranged into a rough draft, according to the outline that had been determined by class discussion. Then it becomes a process of reading through that
really rough draft to identify holes or missing pieces of the story, to listen for
voices or points of view that are too dominating and that need to be turned down
a bit. You might find that there are still questions that are unanswered, and you
might have to locate additional headlines, or statistics, or perhaps even to conduct an additional interview. Your goal at this point is to do whatever you need
to do to accurately tell your story.

Now you have all the information laid out, you have a great deal of factual
material arranged sequentially, but it may not yet be very interesting theater. It
might need something with a little more pizzazz. You start looking for some of
those things that might bring a bit more theatricality to what you have gathered.
Sometimes it could be slides or video. It could be music, especially music asso-

ciated with a particular time period. In the WTO piece we added a few impro-
vised scenes based around confrontation and conflict that we used to link various
sections of the text, and we included chants that the protestors were chanting in
the streets, woven through and around the texts to make it a more theatrical and
energetic play.

D: And then?

J: Then you rehearse it and perform it. You do some very basic things in re-
hearsal that sound very simple but are crucial to making the play work. You
have students practice projecting their voices so they can be heard in the back
row. They learn to keep their scripts from in front of their faces so the audience
can see them. They practice picking up on cues from each other so they are
ready when it's their turn to read a line. Those little things make a difference in
the flow and energy of the performance and pay huge dividends in a piece actually working for an audience.

D: What do you think the kids got from this particular readers' theater experience, dealing with the WTO?

J: In this particular case they got a sense that they were really participating
in history. They were there on the front lines of something that was historical
and important, and because they were paying a kind of attention to it that was
structured and scholarly, they were able to understand these events on a much
deeper level than most of the people around them, including the adults.

D: They presented to adults?

J: They presented to fellow students and adults. They performed for other
classes in the building, and they performed for the general public.

See *Most Dangerous Women* (Heinemann, 2006) for a more detailed description of the Readers' Theater process.

"A Day in the Life" Project at the University Level

We want our students to understand that other people's lives are both similar and
different from our own, and that there are many factors that feed into the ways in
which we live. We also want our students to learn how to learn about others and
to appreciate others on their own terms. This next assignment contributes to that
learning and offers the classroom learning community a means by which to
compare and contrast the lives of people from around the world and to gain an
insight into the reasons for those similarities and differences. The storytelling
also offers our students a way to make personal the consequences of the decisions of governments and leaders as they come to understand the impact of those

decisions on "ordinary" men, women, and children trying simply to live their lives.

I use this assignment in my university methods classes but have used variations with middle and high school classes. The examples included below come from one of my spring 2009 social studies methods classes at Plattsburgh State University.

The Assignment

Your assignment is to create an ordinary person living in a particular location, and to tell the story of an ordinary day in your character's life. What would they do during the day? What would they see, hear, smell, touch, taste? Who might they spend time with and what would that be like? What are their daily chores or responsibilities? What matters to them? What are the people around them doing? How do they interact with the world around them and how are they affected by it?

Note that it is not a tale of superhero behavior, and it should not contain fantastical images or mythical beasts. You are creating a realistic historical fiction; the items your character sees should be what one might really see in the location you've chosen. The people they meet in your story should be people they really would be likely to meet on their daily rounds. Your objective is to try and communicate about a distant place in story form. Remember that it is better to show us than to tell us. Don't tell us it's hot; have your character stop for a drink, take some water from the village well, and wet a handkerchief that he ties around his neck.

You are most likely to find success if you ground the story part in the senses, noting what people might see, hear, touch, smell, and taste as they move through their day. In order to know what to write you need to gather quite a bit of information. Remember that when we read *The Day of Ahmed's Secret* (a children's picture book that follows a young Egyptian boy through his day in Cairo), we made a list of what the authors and illustrator needed to know in order to write the story. That list included climate, architecture, clothing, gender roles, family traditions and roles, religion, racial and ethnic composition of the city, history, geography within and outside of the city, modes of transportation, flora and fauna, food, the lives of children, educational experiences and literacy rates, family and societal economics, social structures and institutions, basic rhythms and sounds of the city, and the Arabic language. You may not choose to include such a long list of details, but consider what is important to communicate so that we have a strong sense of this place.

After you decide on a place in which you will situate your story, you will need to formulate a research plan for gathering the information you require. We will work together as a class to brainstorm some sources that are likely to be productive, and I will read several stories that will model what these days can communicate, from locations around the world.

Have fun with the assignment. Don't worry about including every possible tale; help us to know what it might feel like to live in a large coastal town in mainland China, or in a mountain village in Nepal, or in Mexico City on an ordinary day.

Here are excerpts from two stories written by students in my social studies methods classes, the first "told" by a young boy in Sri Lanka, the second by a young boy in Uganda.

I wake up in the morning to the smell of hoppers being cooked up. School begins at 7:45 so my sister and I eat and are out the door by 7:15. It is the first day of February and there is a cool breeze coming off the Gulf of Mannar. It feels well below 15 degrees Celsius so both Neja and I grab a windbreaker for the walk. I would rather have it be chilly than a monsoon, but there is no worry of a monsoon until around May....

We arrive home around 6 pm. My sister and I decide to take a walk down by the water and mother said to be back home by 8. The coast is only a kilometer away from our house so we take this walk quite often. We stroll into Viharama-hadevil Park where we see others playing Frisbee. Neja drops off a book a the library and we walk past an art museum, the Colombo National Museum, by the American Embassy, cut through the train station, and we are there.

By 6:30 the beach crowds have almost all left and both Neja and I run around barefoot in the sand and collect whatever the tide brings in. I stop to watch a man who was fishing at the beach bring in a fish. It looked like a jack but he tossed it back before I got a good look at it.....

—Matt Rogers

It is 6:30 am. I just woke up from drips of water hitting my face. I look around the small shack made of sun baked, mud bricks, covered by the tin roof that is leaking from the pouring rain outside. I look around our one room house and see from wall to wall and realize it's time to get up for school. My father and uncle have already left for work. I walk to the bathroom, which is an outhouse, down a path that we share with many other families and the relatives that live with us. Together there are seven people in our hut, which is not a lot compared to other families around us in Uganda.

My father is a hard worker. He works as a night watchman for a well off family from 7 in the evening to 7 in the morning. He is often very tired but comes home, sleeps for only a few hours before he goes into town to try and make more money for our family. My sister is twelve years old and doesn't go to school because she's a girl and is expected to take care of the house, cook, and clean. The reason I am able to go to school is because I was the first born boy and my father was working extra hours in town, which allowed just enough to pay for my education....

—Megan Coolbaugh

I offer this assignment early in a unit of study. I share several picture books that effectively convey the essence, or an essence of a place, and we talk in some detail about the elements involved. We study how authors help us to know about a particular place by reading evocative passages from different genres and practice communicating places from our own lives. We practice telling an ordinary day in our own lives, breaking our own days into two-hour blocs and describing what we do during each segment. We also study a particular place related to our required content and create a story in small groups, communicating about that common site.

Some students choose to tell their stories as picture books, others as comic books. Most write short stories. The choice is theirs, as long as they are meeting the criteria of the assignment.

A Problem-Based Learning Assignment in Teacher Education

Here is an example of a term-long research project that Dr. Tina Dawson and I assigned to our teacher education students at Antioch University. We organized this problem-based learning assignment so that the students would have to explore/consider/research what we wanted them to learn/consider throughout the course.

This is a large project. We presented the assignment at the beginning of the term and designed our course so that the students would have learned what they needed in order to respond to the problem by the end of the term.

PBL Unit on an Educational Plan for a Classroom

Focus on Addressing Student Learning

The "Problem":

You are a first-year teacher in grade ___ (your group decides). Your team is establishing its goals and plans for the year. Your plan will include and not be limited to the following:

  Team goals—What do you want to accomplish with your students next year?

  Team philosophy—What do you believe about how children learn?

  Learning theories that serve as the bases for how you approach the teaching process

  Types of curricula that are most appropriate

  Teaching strategies you will use

  Most appropriate role for education within the society

Therefore a description of the classroom situation should include:

Mission statement

  Community setting (including who the families are)

  Size of the class, range of ages, grades, diversity, learner characteristics

Curriculum Framework

  Content bases (upon what is what you teach based?)

  Structure and organization of classes

  Instructional approaches

  Family involvement

  Other foci?

Assessment plans

Each group will prepare a twenty- to thirty-minute presentation in which they will share their plans. The oral presentation should be accompanied by a written report. Each individual will create a summary reflection about the experience and the products created. Remember: A vision for learning will never be a terminal product. It will require continuous changes and improvements. It will often not be possible to gain unanimous agreement and disagreement along the way.

Objectives:

As a result of participating in this PBL, participants will:

1. articulate a vision for learning that takes into consideration conditions in the present day
2. use available databases
3. make an effective presentation to a critical peer group
4. demonstrate strategies for effective participation in group decision making
5. reflect on teaching and its effects on student growth and learning
6. describe and apply theories of human development and learning
7. plan instruction based on knowledge of the content area, the community, and curriculum goals
8. recognize effective instructional strategies for students at all levels of academic abilities and talents
9. recognize a variety of instructional strategies for developing critical thinking, problem solving, and performance skills
10. understand formal and informal assessment strategies for evaluating and ensuring the continuous intellectual, social, and physical development of the learners
11. apply research and experience-based principles of effective practice for encouraging the intellectual, social, and personal development of students

Guiding questions to consider as your group addresses the problem (also refer to other questions in the syllabus):

1. What would an observer see and hear in our classroom in which students were actively engaged and achieving to high levels in a challenging curriculum? Consider:
    a. The tasks and activities in which students would be engaged.
    b. How teachers would assess student learning and performance.
    c. What teachers would be doing.
    d. What materials and resources students and teachers would be using.
2. How is your vision aligned to and/or supportive of other visions of high student achievement, curriculum frameworks, assessments, special needs requirements, and mandates? How have you taken into account the Multi-Ethnic Think Tank (METT) paper, the state standards, and other state documents? What are the responsibilities of educators related to an ongoing focus on issues of social justice?

3. How can teaching and learning across disciplines be made more efficient and effective? How have you addressed the arts? Health and fitness issues? Other areas that you deem important, such as environmental education, as an example?

4. What instructional approaches have you seen with what student populations? How has this informed your work? How will you provide and support a challenging curriculum through engaging instructional practices (e.g., collaborative learning, problem-based learning, problem solving, critical thinking, constructivist classrooms, project-based learning, direct instruction, and so on)?

5. How will you create your class's accountability and assessment system? How will the students know how they are doing? How will you communicate with others about this?

6. How will you create positive home-school-community collaborations? What is the nature of the influences of the larger community on processes within schools? What is the nature of the influences on school outcomes? What constituencies interact with the schools? What perspectives do we need to examine? What processes can we use to tap these perspectives?

7. What have been and what are the impacts and the uses of technology, including access issues and media literacy? How are you addressing these?

8. How and why have you made these choices? What theories, practices, observations, and beliefs guided you?

Presentation assessment guidelines:

-   Public speaking (preparation and delivery)
-   Evidence for solution (use of data; reliable sources of information)
-   Group participation (each member participates and can answer questions)
-   Quality of materials (handouts for class and other materials used or created)

Final portfolio elements from this experience include:

-   The proposed solution accompanied by explanations and supporting information
-   Assessment of group processes; assessment of own work and reflection on how you maximized your own learning and the learning of others in the group
-   Assessment of the problem and activities: suggestions for next time

APPENDIX A

Resources

Resources and support materials are essential for those of us who want to teach through student-centered, inquiry research projects, and it's especially true for new teachers who are just beginning to build their own personal libraries. School districts tend to buy expensive textbooks that provide teachers with a page-by-page walk along the surface of history, but that offer little to those who wish to engage in actual research. We know we are not likely to find useful materials within the school's supply closets, and there is less and less money available to support the purchase of outside materials, so we face a real challenge.

Fortunately there are numerous organizations that produce materials geared toward supporting research in the classroom, so that teachers do not have to re-invent the wheel, as the saying goes, and there is incredible information available online. I've included a starter set of resources below.

Printed Material on the Research Process

Chiseri-Slater, Elizabeth, & Sunstein, Bonnie (2005). *What works?: A practical guide to teacher research*. Portsmouth, NH: Heinemann.

Dana, Nancy, & Yendol-Silva, Dianae (2003). *The reflective educator's guide to classroom research: Learning to teach and teaching to learn through practitioner inquiry*. Thousand Oaks, California: Corwin Press.

Falk, Beverly, & Blumenreich, Megan (2005). *The power of questions: A guide to teacher and student research*. Portsmouth, NH: Heinemann.

Hendricks, Cher C. (2008). *Improving schools through action research: A comprehensive guide for educators* (2nd ed.). [AU: city and publisher?]Boston: Allyn and Bacon.

Merriam, Sharan (1997). *Qualitative research and case study applications in education*. Rev. and expanded from *Case study research in education*. San Francisco: Jossey-Bass.

Sagor, Richard (1993). *How to conduct collaborative action research*. Alexandria, VA: ASCD.

Torp, Linda, & Sage, Sara (2002). *Problems as possibilities: Problem-based learning for K–16 education* (2nd ed.). Alexandria, VA: ASCD.

Material Found on the Web

Alternet: (www.alternet.org). Alternet is a progressive digest of news stories from a progressive point of view. Their stories originate from news services, blogs, and media from around the country and the world.

Blackpast.org: (www.blackpast.org). This 3,000-page reference center is dedicated to providing information to the general public on African American history in the United States and on the history of the more than one billion people of African ancestry around the world. It includes an online encyclopedia of hundreds of famous and lesser-known figures in African American history, global African history, and specifically the history of African Americans in the West. There are links to a wide range of sites and sources. All of the information provided by this site is free and accessible to the public.

Choices Program: (http://www.choices.edu/). The Choices program has operated out of Brown University since the early 1980s. The program provides indepth curriculum on a range of historical and current topics. They also offer workshops and professional development opportunities, resource materials, and other support.

The Civil Rights Project/Proyecto Derechos Civiles at UCLA: (www.civilrightsproject.ucla.edu). This website is focused on keeping the Civil Rights movement current and active. They offer articles, resources, workshops, and support for anyone interested in civil rights issues. This project used to be housed at Harvard University.

Coalition of Essential Schools: (www.essentialschools.org).This is an organization that has worked with student-centered research projects for years. They have emphasized capstone (graduation)-type projects, with students demonstrating learning through an extended research effort on a topic of their choice, which culminates in a public presentation. CES offers many resources at (http://www.essentialschools.org/pub/ces_docs/resources/resources.html).

Common Dreams: (www.commondreams.org). Another progressive news digest, featuring articles, stories, and blogs from across the progressive spectrum.

Democracy Now: (**www.democracynow.org**). *Democracy Now* is a radio news program that is now simulcast; the program reaches over 700 stations around the country. It is a source of in-depth reporting from a progressive point of view, covering stories that are not treated in the mainstream press, or most certainly not to the depth to which they are covered here. Their website offers transcripts of their daily broadcasts and extensive resource material for teachers and students looking to move beyond the headline news. Amy Goodman's extended interviews are with people who are rarely invited to the nightly news programs, and offer viewpoints rarely heard in the mainstream media.

Densho: (**www.densho.org**). Densho began as a project to gather stories from Japanese Americans who had been incarcerated in camps during World War II. Because many of those senior Japanese Americans had never talked about their experiences in the camps, their stories were in danger of being lost. Thus the Densho project was organized to gather those stories. They conducted video-taped interviews and now have hundreds of them, as well as an extraordinary collection of artifacts and materials connected to the incarceration. More recently, Densho has broadened its focus to look at current issues of social justice, with a particular focus on discrimination, especially the targeting of groups based on race, religion, ethnicity, or class. They offer a wide range of resources connected to the internment and also curriculum units focusing on the Constitution, immigration, and the research process.

Expeditionary Learning/Outward Bound. (**www.elschools.org**).This site presents the basic tenets of expeditionary learning and connects to resources and ideas for educators who wish to carry out their own expeditions.

Facing the Future: (**www.facingthefuture.org**). Facing the Future is a nonprofit organization whose mission is to educate and motivate today's students to be responsible stewards of tomorrow's world. Facing the Future develops and delivers standards-based, hands-on lessons, student textbooks, curriculum units, and professional development opportunities for educators that promote critical thinking on global issues, sustainability, and positive solutions. Facing the Future curriculum is used across multiple subject areas by teachers and students in K–12, undergraduate, and graduate classes in all 50 states and over 85 countries.

Fairness and Accuracy in Reporting: (**www.fair.org**). FAIR describes itself as a media watchdog organization. Their focus is on challenging media bias and fighting censorship. They provide information, articles, and resources about media-related issues, with particular attention to what does or does not make it on the air, or into print.

Fair Test: (**www.fairtest.org**). Fair Test is an organization that "advances quality education and equal opportunity by promoting fair, open, valid and educationally beneficial evaluations of students, teachers and schools. Fair Test also works to end the misuses and flaws of testing practices that impede those goals. We place special emphasis on eliminating the racial, class, gender, and cultural barriers to equal opportunity posed by standardized tests, and preventing their damage to the quality of education." The organization is a repository of information about testing and assessment practices around the country. It hosts a very active website, produces a newsletter, and provide resources for those interested in researching testing and assessment issues, with strong resources related to No Child Left Behind.

Free Press: (**www.freepress.net**). Free Press is an organization dedicated to freeing the media and restoring democracy, to use their words. To quote from their website, Free Press "is a national, nonpartisan organization working to reform the media. Through education, organizing and advocacy, we promote diverse and independent media ownership, strong public media, and universal access to communications. Free Press was launched in late 2002 by media scholar Robert W. McChesney, journalist John Nichols and Josh Silver, our executive director. They host a yearly conference on the media, publish books, articles, columns, and curricula, offer workshops, videos and DVDs, and give talks aimed at educating the public about the current state of the media, with the aim of creating/inspiring the public to collective action."

Gapminder: (**www.gapminder.com**). This website offers a series of maps showing the relationships between various factors in a society in a series of interactive maps. These maps "move," showing the relationship between demographic, economic, and social factors over time. It is a very strong tool for helping students to investigate the interconnectedness of factors around the world, and it makes clear the difference between the haves and have-nots around the world, especially in terms of life expectancy, infant mortality, and education.

Google Earth: (**http://earth.google.com**). This site offers a look at the earth from disturbingly effective satellite imagery and offers a wide range of tools connected with our ability to spy from the sky. The capabilities of this site keep developing, and they offer an extraordinary range of information.

Library of Congress (http://rs6.loc.gov). The Library of Congress is the nation's library. They offer extraordinary resources to the researcher, including primary source documents, photographs, journals, videotapes, and articles dealing with the nation's history. It is both overwhelming in its scope and extraordinary in what it offers. This same address takes you to the National Archives.

The Living Room Candidate: **(http://www.livingroomcandidate.org)**. This site traces political advertising on television since its beginnings in 1952. Students have the opportunity to compare and contrast the ways in which the campaigning process has changed over time, and makes clear the link between politics, advertising, and campaign finance.

National Council for the Social Studies: **(www.ncss.org)**. This is a national organization of social studies educators that holds yearly conferences (in November), offers workshops and publications on social studies-related topics. NCSS published a bulletin in 1994, *Expectations of Excellence*, that presents a conceptual approach to teaching social studies, which leads to a deeper and more meaningful experience than does the strict textbook/chapter questions approach. Their ten themes are still relevant and useful today, and their "consumer reports"-type breakdown of social studies skills (in *Expectations of Excellence*) is also useful as a guide in planning K–12 curriculum. NCSS offers reviews of children's literature published each year, organized by topic and social studies strand, and that list of notable books is a good source of material. Each state has a more local organization of social studies educators, and there is information at the national website that can lead you to your state organization.

National Geographic: **(www.nationalgeographic.org)**. Most everyone is familiar with the magazine/journal that has been published for decades. The NG website offers extraordinary resources for teachers, including a range of map-creating materials, in-depth resources for researchers, lesson plan ideas, and connections to other websites. An invaluable resource.

National History Day: **(http://www.nationalhistoryday.org)**. This organization organizes a "competition" each year that invites students to carry out research, working individually or in groups. Many history teachers incorporate National History Day into their teaching plans for the year. NHD publishes guides, examples of past projects, and offers support to teachers interested in using its materials.

Oyate: **(http://www.oyate.org/aboutus.html)**. The Oyate website offers materials that present history from a range of Native American perspectives. Their work provides students the opportunity to approach U.S. history from perspectives beyond the traditional versions offered in textbooks and helps them to understand "our" history more fully. There are resource guides, critiques of more traditional texts, and a list of books, articles, and other materials for those seeking to include more voices and perspectives in their study.

Population Reference Bureau: (**www.prb.org**). This site offers both U.S. Census information and data from around the world. The bureau describes what they do on their website as follows: "PRB informs people from around the world and in the United States about issues related to population, health, and the environment. To do this, we transform technical data and research into accurate, easy-to-understand information." This site can support research efforts through population data sheets; they have data broken down by continent, region, and country.

Problem-based learning clearinghouse: (**https://chico.nss.udel.edu/Pbl**). This site is for educators. You have to register, but it is free and they offer a number of different problems and articles, with teaching ideas and supporting material. It is hosted by the University of Delaware.

PBLI: (**http://www.pbli.org**). This website is dedicated to supporting those who are interested in problem-based learning. To quote the website: "The PBLI is a group of teachers and researchers involved in PBL and active in faculty educational development (see faculty). They are able to provide education, consultation and support to teachers and organizations in any discipline, profession, training program or educational level (kindergarten through infinity) either involved in PBL or interested in adopting PBL into their teaching or training programs.... Although located in a medical school the PBLI represents a platform for PBL interests, both inside and outside of medicine." Includes excellent materials that are useful to teachers.

Rethinking Schools: (**www.rethinkingschools.org**). Rethinking Schools offers a range of curricular materials written by teachers for teachers. Rethinking Schools is a national organization based in Milwaukee and primarily focusing on working with students in urban populations, but the materials are relevant and effective for anyone teaching anywhere. The publications focus on teaching for justice. RS materials are creative, well researched, and very accessible. The target audience includes teachers, community members, and others who work with children in schools and who are looking for both theory and practical suggestions for how to put that theory to use. Visit their website to access past journal articles and their list of publications.

Rouge Forum: (**http://www.richgibson.com/rouge_forum**). The Rouge Forum website, maintained by co-founder Rich Gibson, provides extraordinary resources that provide context, radical analysis, teaching approaches, and research/reading citations that offer teachers a progressive analysis of the current world situation. The Rouge Forum also publishes a newsletter, provides weekly updates filled with resources and articles, and sponsors a yearly conference. The Forum, to quote from its website, "is a group of educators, students, and parents seeking a democratic society. We are concerned about questions like these: How can we teach against racism, national chauvinism and sexism in an increasingly authoritarian and undemocratic society? How can we gain enough real power to keep our ideals and still teach—or learn? Whose interests shall school serve in a society that is ever more unequal? We are both research and action oriented. We want to learn about equality, democracy and social justice as we simultaneously struggle to bring into practice our present understanding of what that is. We seek to build a caring inclusive community which understands that an injury to one is an injury to all."

Southern Poverty Law Center: (**www.splcenter.org**). This organization has been working to track and defeat hate groups and movements around the country since 1971. Morris Dees and his colleagues have worked through the courts, through *Teaching Tolerance*, their journal, and through workshops and talks to stand up to a wide variety of hate groups. They feature a hatemap, tracking hate groups around the country, have a hateblog, with information about actions by and related to these groups, and have information about their own actions.

SPICE: (**www.spice.stanford.edu**). From the website: "Since 1976 the Stanford Program on International and Cross-Cultural Education (SPICE) has supported efforts to internationalize elementary and secondary school curricula by linking the research and teaching at Stanford University to the schools through the production of high-quality curriculum materials on international and cross-cultural topics.... SPICE has produced over 100 supplementary curriculum units on Africa, Asia and the Pacific, Europe, Latin America, the global environment, and international political economy. SPICE draws upon the diverse faculty and programmatic interests of Stanford University to link knowledge, inquiry, and practice in exemplary curriculum materials."

Brief Biographical Sketches of the Consultants

Howard Zinn is a historian, author, speaker, and an active figure in the social justice/antiwar movement. He is professor emeritus from Boston University. Professor Zinn's book, *A People's History of the United States* was a turning point in the teaching of US History, and his work as a historian has inspired others to take a critical look at the history we have been taught. Howard Zinn, in his words, "Started out from a kind of general philosophical question that is, What are the points of view that are omitted in any traditional telling of history?" and has consistently included those voices that have been suppressed, or marginalized in the traditional textbooks. He has written dozens of books, hundreds of articles, and still maintains regular columns in a number of journals. Please go to www.howardzinn.org to see more about this extraordinary teacher, author, and activist.

Roger Shimomura is a painter and performance artist who has created art addressing issues of racism, oppression, and injustice for decades. Mr. Shimomura was incarcerated, along with more than one hundred and twenty thousand other Japanese Americans during World War II, and has created two series of paintings dedicated to telling that story. The paintings, based on journal entries made by his grandmother, who was also incarcerated, have been shown around the world, have won awards, and, more importantly, tell an important and troubling story that still has resonance today. Mr. Shimomura recently retired as a professor of art at Kansas University, where he had taught for thirty five years. You can see Mr. Shimomura's work at his website, www.rshim.com, or at the Greg Kucera gallery website, www.gregkucera.com/shimomura.htm.

Don Fels is an artist who has created a dizzying array of work, mostly focused on trade, and on the flow of goods, ideas, and culture. He has (re) created a Malaysian street scene in order to explore the impact of the rubber and tin trade in Malaysia; constructed a giant plywood "tree house" containing and exploring various artifacts and aspects of the life and death of "the plywood era" in American life; built a series of viewers along a Seattle waterfront that show both a current view of the shoreline and an accompanying vision of what the same scene looked like in 1851, when European Americans first arrived; created a 5/8-sized wooden fishing vessel, raised thirty feet in the air, as part of a public art installation telling the story of the destruction of the Duwamish River, in south Seattle; and most recently, a series of billboard/paintings, in Bollywood style, exploring the arrival of world trade via Vasco daGama's landing in southern India in search of pepper, his era's black gold. Fels has exhibited his art around the world, and had seven different exhibits opening in the fall of 2008. He was also a classroom teacher for fifteen years, working in NYC public schools, and later, in a small private school outside of Seattle. You can see descriptions of his work at his website, www.artisthinker.com, and see examples of his paintings at davidsongalleries.com/artists/fels/fels.php .

Georgia Heard is an award-winning poet who has written several books on teaching poetry to young children, and has published volumes of her own work. She offers dozens of workshops and speeches to teachers and to writers every year, and has done extensive work as a visiting artist in schools around the country. Georgia helps her students to approach poetry as researchers, looking into their worlds and themselves, in depth, to find and to communicate authentically, and meaningfully. Georgia's website is www.georgiaheard.com, and there are links there to her books and a schedule of her appearances around the country at that site.

Jan Maher is a writer and educator who published her first novel, *Heaven, Indiana*, in 2000, and who is in the midst of completing a second, *Earth As It Is*. Dr. Maher has also written and produced plays, poetry, and short stories, and has been an educator/artist in residence for decades, working with students as a writer in residence, a theater director, and teacher. She was outreach poet for the state of Vermont, and is currently an adjunct faculty member at Plattsburgh State University, teaching writing, and the teaching of writing to students in the teacher education program. Please contact Jan through Dog Hollow Press (www.doghollow.com) for more information about her work.

Judith Helfand is a documentary film maker based in New York City. Judith studied with the legendary documentary film maker George Stoney, and worked with him to create *The Uprising of '34*, a documentary film about the textile strikes that took place across the south during that year. Judith has also written, produced and directed *A Healthy Baby Girl*, a documentary dealing with malfeasance in the pharmaceutical industry, which resulted in her own cancer; *Blue Vinyl*, a documentary dealing with malfeasance in the vinyl industry, which has created cancer in thousands of workers and the creation of toxic materials currently littering the earth, and *Everything's Cool*, a 2007 film dealing with global warming. Ms Helfand currently teaches film making at NYU. Please find her website at www.judithhelfand.com for more information about her work.

Lorraine McConaghy is the staff historian at the Museum of History and Industry in Seattle. Dr. McConaghy has taught at the university level and served as historian at the museum for many years, and is currently in the midst of research on a book about the navy ship the *Decatur*, which arrived in Seattle in the 1850s. She has been active at teaching research skills to community members interested in learning more about their own neighborhoods in a program called Nearby History, and has offered workshops and presentations to educators interested in bringing local history into their classrooms. Lorraine can be reached at the museum: lorraine.mcconaghy@seattlehistory.org.

I also spoke with a number of educators who offer their students an extensive introduction to and experience with research in their classrooms.

Steve Goldenberg teaches five- and six- year olds at a small private school near Seattle. He has taught there for nearly thirty years and is a master at organizing his classroom so that his students have the opportunity to explore their own interests and curiosities, while taking part in a highly interactive learning community. Steve consistently builds time into his school day so that students can "do something important," an approach that has served as a goal and model for my teaching since I began my work. I'm still not there, but Steve's work remains a personal beacon.

Libby Sinclair teaches fourth/fifth grade in Seattle. She has carried out the expeditionary learning process for many years, leading students to explore topics in depth over several months. Her explorations have included investigating the Harlem Renaissance, opera, the natural world, and the history of the Negro Leagues.

Wendy Ewbank teaches middle school in Seattle, after years of teaching in the Edmonds, Washington, public schools. Ms Ewbank is an award-winning social studies teacher, a former president of the Washington State Council for Social Studies, and a former Washington State "teacher of the year" in global education. Wendy is a passionate and indefatigable learner, and her curiosity and excitement communicate to her students.

Gary Thomsen is a high school "sports marketing and events" teacher at a Seattle public high school. He is a teaching legend in Seattle, working with a student population that is very diverse racially, ethnically, and economically. He comes out of the business world, and brings his project-based experience to his work in the classroom. His students consistently engage in complex projects that teach them required skills, offer service to the community, and take them out into the world. You can visit a website dedicated to one of Gary's most recent classroom projects, focused on environmental concerns, at www.inconvenientride.com. Gary and his classes worked to remove invasive species in a nearby neighborhood park, and then and planted a thousand trees. They also worked with elementary classrooms on environmental awareness and took a bike ride across country to make connection with cities interested in following a more environmentally aware agenda. The story of that effort is on that website.

Rosalie Romano is an assistant professor at Western Washington University, in Bellingham, Washington. Dr. Romano spent many years as the director of the CARE program at Ohio University, creating and supervising the semester-long, in-depth expeditions carried out by education students in Ohio public schools. Dr. Romano has been involved with teacher education for decades, working at both the public school and university levels, and has written about teacher education for Peter Lang publishing. Her books with Peter Lang include *Forging an Educative Community* (2000) and *Hungry Minds in Hard Times* (2002), written with Catherine Glascock.

Ted Wright has been involved with education for decades, with a particular focus on serving the Native American community. Dr. Wright has been involved in a ground-breaking project in southeast Alaska, creating and teaching a place- and cultural- based curriculum designed to help Tlingit young people to become reconnected to their cultural and locally based roots and history. Ted is also working with educators around the country to help them to work with their students, to ground them in their own cultures and locations.

Colleen Ryan is a middle school math teacher in rural, upstate New York. Colleen and a teaching partner engaged their students in an investigation of water usage in their community. This was an opportunity for them to connect the math their students were learning in the classroom with the river that runs through their community, and with the environmental issues that continue to challenge the residents of their town and region. This was Colleen's first attempt at an extended, place-based project, and she shared what she and her students learned from the experience.

Michael Grigsby teaches at Edmonds Community College, north of Seattle, after years of working as a director of training for King County, in Washington State. Michael is also a former high school social studies teacher. He took on a family research project that is closely analogous to what we might ask our students to do; he researched the story of his godfather, Hiram Brooks, who was a caterer in Warren, Ohio, the town in which Michael grew up. Mr. Brooks, an African American working in one of the few professions open to him, created a very successful business, but was excluded from any social acceptance because of his race. Michael's personal search linked quickly to the larger social, economic, and political issues of the time, and models the ways in which researching personal stories provide a connection to national and even international content.

INDEX